Film Remakes, Adaptations and Fan Productions

Film Remakes, Adaptations and Fan Productions

Remake | Remodel

Edited by

Kathleen Loock
Georg-August University of Göttingen, Germany

and

Constantine Verevis
Senior Lecturer, Monash University, Australia

First published 2012 by
PALGRAVE MACMILLAN

Palgrave Macmillan in the UK is an imprint of Macmillan Publishers Limited, registered in England, company number 785998, of Houndmills, Basingstoke, Hampshire RG21 6XS.

Palgrave Macmillan in the US is a division of St Martin's Press LLC, 175 Fifth Avenue, New York, NY 10010.

Palgrave Macmillan is the global academic imprint of the above companies and has companies and representatives throughout the world.

Palgrave® and Macmillan® are registered trademarks in the United States, the United Kingdom, Europe and other countries

ISBN: 978–1–137–26334–6

This book is printed on paper suitable for recycling and made from fully managed and sustained forest sources. Logging, pulping and manufacturing processes are expected to conform to the environmental regulations of the country of origin.

A catalogue record for this book is available from the British Library.

A catalog record for this book is available from the Library of Congress.

10 9 8 7 6 5 4 3 2 1
21 20 19 18 17 16 15 14 13 12

Printed and bound in Great Britain by
CPI Antony Rowe, Chippenham and Eastbourne

For Hans-Joachim, Doris, and Ilka Loock
—KL

For George, Angela, and Erin, and in loving memory of
Paul Verevis (2 Jan. 1980–23 Jan. 2012)
—CV

Contents

vii

Illustrations

Acknowledgements

The editors would like to thank the following people for their relevant assistance, uplifting encouragement and inspiring conversations that stimulated the production of this book: Álvaro Ceballos Viro, Frank Kelleter, Julie Palmer, Claire Perkins, Diana Rosenhagen, Dorothea Schuller, Daniel Stein, and Deane Williams. We are grateful for the generous financial support of the US Consulate General Hamburg and the University of Göttingen for the 2010 Remake | Remodel conference from which this book emerged. A warm thanks to Gina Ziebell, Moritz Emmelmann, and Mario Rewers for their indispensable help at various stages of that conference. Thank you also to the American Studies Division of the English Department at the University of Göttingen for furnishing the book with images. At Palgrave Macmillan, thanks to Felicity Plester and Catherine Mitchell for their support and assistance throughout the project. Finally, a special word of thanks to our contributors: it has been a genuine pleasure to work with each one of you.

Contributors

Sonja Georgi is Lecturer in American Studies at the Johannes Gutenberg-University Mainz, Germany. She received her Master's degree in American Studies, Applied Linguistics and Economics from the University of Siegen and has recently published her dissertation titled Bodies and/as Technology: Counter-Discourses on Ethnicity and Globalization in the Works of Alejandro Morales, Larissa Lai and Nalo Hopkinson (2011). Her fields of interest include science fiction, ethnic studies, Native American and African American Literature. She has co-edited the essay collection *Of Body Snatchers and Cyberpunks: Student Essays on American Science Fiction Film* (with Kathleen Loock, 2011).

Lili Hartwig studied Media Culture at the University of Hamburg, Germany and graduated in 2010 with her Master's thesis "Niemals in Ihrem Kino: Zur transformativen Aneignung von Filmtrailern im Zeitalter der Convergence Culture." She has worked in the organization and programming of the International Short Film Festival Hamburg and other film and video events. She has also curated film programs about video remix and transformative works.

Frank Kelleter is Chair of American Studies at the University of Göttingen, Germany. He is the author of three books and has also co-edited *American Studies as Media Studies* (with Daniel Stein, 2008) and *Melodrama! The Mode of Excess from Early America to Hollywood* (with Ruth Mayer, 2007). He is the initiator and director of the Göttingen-based research group "Popular Seriality: Aesthetics and Practice," funded by the German Research Foundation (DFG), and is currently editing an essay collection on serial narratives.

Kathleen Loock is a member of the American Studies Program at the University of Göttingen, Germany, where she is writing her PhD thesis on the ethnicization of Christopher Columbus in the late nineteenth- and early twentieth-century United States. She is currently working as administrator of the Göttingen-based research group "Popular Seriality: Aesthetics and Practice," funded by the German Research Foundation (DFG). She has co-edited the essay collection *Of Body Snatchers and Cyberpunks: Student Essays on American Science Fiction Film* (with Sonja Georgi, 2011).

Sibylle Machat has been working at the University of Flensburg, Germany, since 2006, where she is a lecturer in the "Culture-Language-Media" MA program, a Danish–German cooperation project. She holds a Magistra Artium from the University of Mannheim and a Master of Arts from the University of London and submitted her PhD thesis in January 2012.

Amy Martin graduated in 2007 from the University of St Andrews with an MA in English before going on to complete an M.Phil. at Trinity College Dublin in Popular Literature, graduating with a Distinction. She has recently been awarded a doctoral studentship at Queen Margaret University, Edinburgh, and will be researching the rise of the anti-hero in mid-twentieth-century film adaptations.

Birte Otten is a member of the American Studies Program at the University of Göttingen, Germany. She completed her studies at the University of Göttingen and the University of California, Santa Cruz, with an MA in English, Political Science and Social Psychology, and is currently working on a dissertation which investigates the historical imagination in American alternate histories.

Robin Anne Reid is Professor of English at the Department of Literature & Languages at Texas A&M University-Commerce. She has published critical theory introductions to Arthur C. Clarke (1997) and Ray Bradbury (2000), and is the editor of the recently released and first *Encyclopedia on Women in Science Fiction and Fantasy* (2008). She is currently working with faculty in psychology, sociology and linguistics on developing an interdisciplinary grant to be submitted to the National Science Foundation on the "Intersectional Internet," and is planning a lesbian werewolf fantasy novel.

Kathryn Schweishelm is a doctoral candidate in the Graduate School of North American Studies at Freie Universität Berlin, Germany, where she is writing her dissertation on the evolution of cosmetic surgery's representation within popular culture. Her earlier studies were completed at McGill University and Ryerson and York Universities (Canada). She is also a contributing editor at *Worn Fashion Journal*.

Stephanie Sommerfeld is a member of the American Studies Program at the University of Göttingen, Germany. She completed her studies at the University of Göttingen and the University of California, Santa Barbara, with a degree in German, French and English/American

Studies and is currently working on her PhD thesis, which investigates transfigurations of the sublime in Poe and beyond.

Daniel Stein is a member of the American Studies Program at the University of Göttingen, Germany, where he recently received his PhD. His publications include the co-edited essay collections *American Studies as Media Studies* (with Frank Kelleter, 2008) and *Comics: Zur Geschichte und Theorie eines populärkulturellen Mediums* (with Stephan Ditschke and Katerina Kroucheva, 2009) as well as a monograph on Louis Armstrong's autobiographical writings (2012). He is currently working on the history of American superhero comics as a member of the Göttingen-based research group "Popular Seriality: Aesthetics and Practice," funded by the German Research Foundation (DFG).

Constantine Verevis is Senior Lecturer in Film and Television Studies at Monash University, Melbourne, Australia. He is author of *Film Remakes* (2006) and co-editor of *Second Takes: Critical Approaches to the Film Sequel* (2010), *After Taste: Cultural Value and the Moving Image* (2012), and *Film Trilogies: New Critical Approaches* (2012). He is presently completing the co-authored *Australian Film Theory and Criticism Vol 1: Critical Positions* (2012).

Introduction: Remake | Remodel

Kathleen Loock and Constantine Verevis

Given that this collection of essays—"Remake | Remodel"—takes its title from the opening track of a retro-album, *Roxy Music* (1972) by Roxy Music, it seems appropriate to begin with music writer Simon Reynolds' recent book, *Retromania: Pop Culture's Addiction to Its Own Past.* "Instead of being the threshold of the future," writes Reynolds, "the first ten years of the twenty-first century turned out to be the 'Re' Decade. The 2000s were dominated by the 're-' prefix: *re*vivals, *re*issues, *re*makes, *re*-enactments" (xi). Across the book, Reynolds mainly takes an interest in a "retro-consciousness" prevalent in contemporary popular music— band reformations and reunion tours, album reissues and revivals, cover versions and mash-ups—but he notes that the current "malaise is not restricted to pop music. ... Look at the Hollywood mania for remaking blockbuster movies from a couple of decades earlier. ... When they're not revamping proven box-office successes of the past, the movie industry is adapting much-loved 'iconic' TV series for the big screen" (xv). And Reynolds does not stop there. In addition to these "visibly fevered zones of retro-mania," he discerns other areas of cultural *re*-production: retro fashion, retro toys, retro games, retro food, retro candy ... even retro porn (xvii–xviii). Although the evidence suggests that "the 2000s' most commercially prominent trends involved recycling" (xix), Reynolds is quick to point out that "*Retromania* is not a straightforward denunciation of retro as a manifestation of cultural regression or decadence" and that research into the book revealed "the extent to which retro-related issues have been a *long-running preoccupation*" (xxi–xxii, emphasis added).

At least a quarter-century before Reynolds undertook his account of "retromania," *Village Voice* film critic J. Hoberman had looked back over a "momentous" decade of American filmmaking, the period 1975–85, to similarly discern a "mania" for recycling—a penchant for revision and

1

revival in the form of remakes, sequels, and series—which he describes as the cultural condition of "sequelitis" (38). Although Hoberman's comment belies the fact that cinema has repeated and replayed its own narratives and genres from its very beginnings, his description of the phenomenon as a *malady* is consistent with a certain critical discourse that routinely seeks to establish a distinction between production and *re*-production and condemn serial film (and televisual) work for its commercial orientation and automatic self-cannibalization. A recent article in the *New York Times* appears to subscribe to this position, declaring: "In the sausage factory of moviemaking the remake is an age-old temptation. For love or money (but usually money) studios have tapped old stories for different times, fresh stars and ambitious directors, streamlining conceits and translating foreign languages. Fans of the originals usually cry desecration" (Rapold 10). Commenting on television "reboots," Melbourne's *Age* newspaper similarly observes:

> They say in television there are no new ideas. And they're right. But there are an awful lot of old ideas dusted off and remade. Many of them awfully.... For television networks, remakes are an attractive idea—rather than invest in a risky new show, it is safer to sink their money into a TV series that comes with a built-in business plan and an audience already familiar with the idea. (Idato 12)

While newspaper and trade publications continue to condemn remakes for their commercial imperatives, the last decade has seen the appearance of a number of works that contest the idea that the remake is a debased copy of some superior original, seeking instead to understand the practice of remaking as one of several industrial and cultural activities of repetition (and variation) which range from quotation and allusion, adaptation and parody, to the process-like nature of genre and serial filmmaking. These recent publications include: Andrew Horton and Stuart Y. McDougal's edited collection *Play It Again, Sam: Retakes on Remakes* (1998); Lucy Mazdon's *Encore Hollywood: Remaking French Cinema* (2000); Jennifer Forrest and Leonard R. Koos's edition *Dead Ringers: The Remake in Theory and Practice* (2002); and Constantine Verevis' *Film Remakes* (2006).[1] Even more recently, this endeavor to situate various forms of cinematic and televisual *re*-production within a wider context of cultural translation and rewriting has been extended to other serial forms. These surveys include an analysis of sequels in Carolyn Jess-Cooke's *Film Sequels: Theory and Practice from Hollywood to Bollywood* (2009) and Jess-Cooke and Verevis' anthology *Second*

Takes: Critical Approaches to the Film Sequel (2010); series in Forrest's edition *The Legend Returns and Dies Harder Another Day: Essays on Film Series* (2008); and trilogies in Claire Perkins and Verevis' edited collection *Film Trilogies: New Critical Approaches* (2012).

The present volume of essays seeks to engage with and extend these accounts of processes of cultural reproduction—remaking and remodeling—to attend to a variety of forms of adaptation and cross-cultural translation in film, television, and new media.[2] While there has been ample discussion devoted to the serial forms—adaptations and remakes, sequels, and series—which are continually present throughout cinema history, there is—as in Reynolds' account of the new millennial fad for sampling, mash-ups, and bootleg remixes (in part enabled by the compression of musical data and increased bandwidth)—an emphasis in this volume on remaking as an *audience* category. That is, alongside of discussions of adaptations and remakes of canonized classics of literature and film—*The Wizard of Oz, The Adventures of Sherlock Holmes, Wuthering Heights*—and "modern classics"—*Invasion of the Body Snatchers, The Manchurian Candidate, The Stepford Wives*—there is equal consideration given to non-commercial fan-made productions,—such as fan-films, fanvids, and mash-up or recut trailers,—which are gaining increased visibility in fan and media studies. This book falls into three interrelated sections—Adapt, Remake, Remodel—which together contain 12 original essays from leading and emerging scholars in the fields of film and media studies, fan studies, and American studies. The interdisciplinary backgrounds of these contributors bring diverse perspectives to the analysis of film remakes, adaptations, and fan productions to mark out new directions in media seriality.

Adapt

Part I of this volume takes particular interest in new theoretical perspectives on the study of film adaptations. Moving beyond the now much contested "fidelity approach" of adaptation studies which has typically focused on the "faithful" transformations of canonical literature into films,[3] the chapters of Part I broaden and expand the definition of adaptation to come to terms with the realities of industry, media, and cultural practices. They investigate, in other words, (1) *intertextual relationships* by putting literary source texts, film adaptations, remakes, series, and sequels into dialogue, and (2) *discourses* by linking these works to their specific socio-political, economic, and cultural contexts of production and reception. In doing so, they follow James Naremore's call to rethink the study of film adaptations. In a much quoted essay he writes: "The study of adaptation needs to be joined with the study of recycling, remaking and every other form of retelling in the age of mechanical reproduction and electronic communication" (15). In addition, each of the chapters in Part I challenges traditional notions when addressing questions of originality, repetition, and seriality, thus contributing to the theorization of film adaptations.

The first chapter of Part I, Frank Kelleter's "Toto, I think we're in Oz again (and again and again): Remakes and Popular Seriality," traces the proliferation of Oz adaptations within the framework of a theory of popular seriality. Kelleter introduces the term "popular seriality" to account for the seemingly endless repetitions and variations of a beloved classic of children's literature. The chapter concentrates on the publication and reception of L. Frank Baum's original novel *The Wonderful Wizard of Oz* (1900), its subsequent sequelizations and transmedia adaptations (as musicals and plays), translations and revisions, the MGM movie production (Victor Fleming, 1939), the sequel *Return to Oz* (Walter Murch, 1985), and the musical *The Wiz* (Sidney Lumet, 1978). Kelleter argues that Baum's original is, in a sense, already a remake because it draws on standard devices and situations of children's literature. Furthermore, it is a result of a particular mode of storytelling—serial narration— which is characteristic of American popular culture because, as Kelleter explains, the commercial organization of American popular culture encourages industrial reproduction and increased connectivity which in turn invites *serialization*: that is, a highly standardized and at the same time flexible form of serial storytelling. Kelleter goes on to propose two ways to study the textual sprawl of Oz stories, and in extension of adaptations and remakes in general: first, "to read these texts for the information they provide about historical change," and second, to examine "the dynamics of repeated popular narration itself—or put differently, [to investigate] the agency of remakes in an ongoing process of communicative modernization."

The concept of the textual sprawl of serial forms is taken up by Stephanie Sommerfeld in her chapter on Guy Ritchie's 2009 Sherlock Holmes-pastiche. "Series characters [like Sherlock Holmes] that undergo transmedial proliferation," Sommerfeld argues, "lend themselves to medial self-scrutinizing" because the medium's capacity of repetition and innovation can be measured against earlier renditions. In other words, each medium has to accept the challenge of remaking and remodeling a popular series character whose iconic status and memorable features it must simultaneously acknowledge. It is surprising, then, that Ritchie's Sherlock Holmes is deprived of elements—such as his most iconic sentences ("Elementary, my dear Watson") and ornaments (the deerstalker and meerschaum)—which were, in fact, added in previous adaptations of Arthur Conan Doyle's detective stories. Sommerfeld speaks of a "strategy of demonstrating innovation through authentication," designed to enhance Sherlock Holmes' appeal "by tying him more closely to his high cultural legacy and to outdo previous television and film productions." In what she terms a "resurrection" of the contested fidelity discourse of adaptation studies, *Sherlock Holmes* exchanges brand recognition for the cultural capital of Doyle's canonical literary work. In addition, the movie fully exploits the literary Sherlock Holmes' proto-superhero potential by infusing him with the traits of action heroes like James Bond, Indiana Jones, and *Die Hard*'s John McLane. Sommerfeld analyzes the promotional discourse of innovation and faithful adaptation as part of the movie's self-conscious investigation of its mediality.

If Sommerfeld's chapter provides a case study of a film that explicitly denies the influence of earlier adaptations and instead claims to be a faithful adaptation of a canonical literary work—in Thomas Leitch's words a "readaptation of a well-known literary work whose earlier cinematic adaptations [it] ignores or treats as inconsequential" ("Twice-Told Tales" 45)—Amy Martin's "A Battle on Two Fronts: *Wuthering Heights* and Adapting the Adaptation" explores what happens when a film adaptation of a novel becomes the canonical text. More precisely, the chapter is concerned with the enduring dominant cultural currency of one among three feature length films of Emily Brontë's *Wuthering Heights* (1847). Because William Wyler's 1939 film has become a "classic," Martin argues, subsequent adaptations have had to battle with its ingrained imagery which has in turn led to the enduring production of pop-cultural revisions and parodies of it. As Martin shows, the 1939 film as an adaptation is, however, a distant relative of the original text: barely half the chapters of the novel are covered and an entire generation of characters is absent. These omissions, and the stylistic choices of the production team, produced a film of such difference to the text, but of such popularity with its audience that its legacy remains in popular culture even now, hovering over any additional interpretations of the text, even those which strive to be more in keeping with Brontë's work. Martin examines how subsequent versions—Robert Fuest's 1970 adaptation and Peter Kosminky's 1992 adaptation—have served mainly to add to the lasting impressions of Wyler's 1939 film. She asks *how* the *Wuthering Heights* that 1930s Hollywood created remains firm in the popular culture of today by examining parody, music, and television interpretations, all of which reference the popular images of that film.

Birte Otten addresses very similar issues in her case study of *All the King's Men*, the last chapter of Part I. In contrast to Martin, who focuses on the dominant force of one particularly successful film adaptation, Otten approaches the subject from the angle of a "failed" adaptation. According to moviegoers and critics, Steven Zaillian's *All the King's Men* (2006) could not live up to either Robert Penn Warren's Pulitzer Prize-winning novel (1946) or Robert Rossen's Oscar-winning film version (1949). This leads Otten to the question of how to adequately judge Zaillian's adaptation of *All the King's Men*, a film that is inevitably viewed in connection to three earlier models: the 1949 version of the film, the 1946 novel on which both films are based, and the historical person Huey P. Long who served as a source for the main character in the novel. Departing from a value-driven assessment of the film's fidelity, Otten opts for a comparative approach which focuses on the narratological and cinematic elements of both film adaptations, and juxtaposes them with the political visions inherent in each text. The extent to which these films engage with American social, cultural, and political discourses at their respective times of production, Otten argues, suggests that the relative failure of the 2006 version, despite its impressive cast, may have less to do with its relation to past models than with its lack of regard for present concerns.

Remake

In "Remakes and Cultural Studies," Robert Eberwein points to the affinity between the terms "adaptation" and "remaking," defining the latter as "a kind of reading or rereading of the original [text]" (15). This definition seems equally applicable to each, but what typically distinguishes the concepts is the relation between the new version—adaptation or remake—and the medium of the original artifact. A remake is generally considered a version of *another film*, whereas one of the principal arguments of adaptation theory is concerned with the movement between *different semiotic registers*, most often between literature and film.[4] This seems simple enough when dealing with the matching of written and cinematic signs, but any easy demarcation between adaptation and remake is complicated when sources derive from other (visual) media, such as graphic novels, computer games, television programs, and experimental and animated films. Even more problematic is the fact—already demonstrated in Part I—that many literary adaptations have themselves been previously adapted to film, as in the case of the multiple versions of *The Wizard of Oz*, *The Adventures of Sherlock Holmes*, and *Wuthering Heights*. Moreover, as Lesley Stern points out, a chain of remakings often makes the more recent film version "by default a remake, and particularly in a case in which the source is not a classic [literary] text, the reference point will be the earlier film" (226).

Part II takes up some of these issues, adopting the terminology of translation studies employed by Robert B. Ray to suggest that a new film version—an adaptation and/or remake—is not "a faded imitation of a superior, authentic original ... [but] a 'citation' grafted into a new context and thereby inevitably refunctioned ... [and] disseminated" (127). While it might often be the case that "the critic treats the original and its meaning ... as a fixity, against which the remake is measured and evaluated" (Eberwein 15), each one of the chapters in Part II demonstrates that more interesting questions pertain to the *factors* (discourses) that enable the identification of the intertext, and to the nature of the *transformations* that are worked upon it. In this way the translation—adaptation or remake—is less interested in its fidelity to the original than in the potential of the precursor/s to generate further, and sometimes unpredictable, cultural production/s. As Eric Cazdyn points out, every remaking not only transforms the original but also its anterior adaptations: "each adaptation organizes the elements of the original literary text in a certain way in order to wrap it up with meaning" yet the notion of a *transformative* adaptation/remake "implies that the original is not only what it is, but also that it *exceeds* itself" (117, emphasis added).

The opening essay in Part II, Kathryn Schweishelm's "Remaking *The Stepford Wives*, Remodeling Feminism," interrogates the 2004 filmic readaptation of *The Stepford Wives* in view of the earlier 1975 version and the 1972 novel by Ira Levin. As in Francesco Casetti's recent assertion that the rejection of abstract claims to fidelity leads to an investigation of the *"reappearance, in another discursive field, of an element (a plot, a theme, a character, etc.) that has previously appeared elsewhere"* (82, emphasis in original), Schweishelm deals with the recontextualization of *The Stepford Wives*, "demonstrating how feminism is 'remade' at the same time as the film is remade [in 2004 to reflect] much broader changes in contemporary discourse surrounding the cultural status of the women's movement." The following chapter, Kathleen Loock's "The Return of the Pod People," similarly seeks to investigate the reformulation of a communicative situation but takes up the more expansive case of Jack Finney's serially published story "The Body Snatchers" (1954), made and remade four times over the past half-century *Invasion of the Body Snatchers* (Don Siegel, 1956), *Invasion of the Body Snatchers* (Philip Kaufman, 1978), *Body Snatchers* (Abel Ferrara, 1993), and *The Invasion* (Oliver Hirschbiegel, 2007). Loock adopts three approaches—repetition, variation, and continuation—to demonstrate how each film version (made at 15–20-year intervals) transforms the story within the limitations of a specific space-time (a historical and geographical situation), "absorbing and altering [as Robert Stam puts it] the genres and intertexts available through the grids of ambient discourses and ideologies, and as mediated by a series of filters: studio style, ideological fashion, political constraints, auteurist predilections, charismatic stars, economic advantage or disadvantage and evolving technology" (68–69). Examining, for example, the endings of different versions, Loock argues that each one of the films fulfills (then) current cultural needs, with the happy ending of the most recent version—*The Invasion*—working to restore stability and alleviate fears in a post-9/11 America, and post-SARS and avian flu context.

In the same way that Schweishelm's and Loock's chapters demonstrate that literary properties—*The Stepford Wives* and "The Body Snatchers"—are reprogrammed or repurposed for a new political situation, the following chapter—Sonja Georgi's "Cyber-noia?"—looks at the film remake in the context of US foreign and domestic policy following the events of 9/11 and through the contemporary filter of American "life during wartime." Specifically, Georgi argues that John Frankenheimer's *The Manchurian Candidate* (1962), adapted from a 1959 novel by Richard Condon, reflects Cold War-induced "public discourses of cultural anxiety about the political and cultural 'other'." As in the case of Loock's discussion of *The Invasion*, Georgi's account of the recent *Manchurian Candidate* remake (Jonathan Demme, 2004) is understood in relation to a post-9/11 political and cultural context. Georgi suggests that *The Manchurian Candidate*—a film that deals with a conspiracy theory about the Manchurian Global Corporation's illegal biotechnological experiments on American soldiers during the Gulf War—translates the Cold War anxiety of the earlier film to draw a portrait of a twenty-first century where multinational capitalism and international terrorism have formed an uneasy alliance. Additionally, in a move that demonstrates that "the intertext, the precursor text, is never singular and never a moment of pure origin" (Frow), Georgi analyzes Demme's version of *The Manchurian Candidate* as a work of cyberfiction, one that resonates with key elements—globalization, Orientalism, cognitive remapping—of early literary cyberfiction such as William Gibson's canonical *Neuromancer* (1984).

Like the majority of chapters in the Part II, the final essay, Constantine Verevis' "A Personal Matter," deals with a remake, *H Story* (Nobuhiro Suwa, 2000), which is at once a readaptation and a remake, in this case of the novella-screenplay, *Hiroshima mon amour* by Marguerite Duras and the film directed by Alain Resnais (1959). As in the previous chapter by Georgi, Verevis' work examines if and how the experience of a traumatic cultural moment—in this case, the effects of the atomic destruction of Hiroshima as presented in *Hiroshima mon amour*—can be re-presented to a new generation in and through the *H Story* remake. As Verevis demonstrates, *H Story* undertakes to do this by devising a scenario in which the film's director Nobuhiro Suwa plays a director (named Suwa) who brings a cast and crew to Hiroshima to film a (close) remake of *Hiroshima mon amour*. The self-reflexive, faux-documentary strategy of *H Story* not only enables Suwa to acknowledge the ongoing relevance of Resnais' modernist account of the ambiguities of historical representation, but also to challenge its cultural and generational authority. More broadly, *H Story*'s (ultimately abandoned) undertaking to copy *Hiroshima mon amour* faithfully (using the Duras screenplay as model) not only succeeds in demonstrating its immanent multiplicity (and difference) but also makes an ontological point about remakes and cinema in general: namely, "that each and every film is remade—that is, *dispersed and transformed*—in its every new context or configuration" (Verevis 75).

Remodel

If Part I and Part II of this volume focus on the production and reception of film adaptations and cinematic remakes, Part III engages with non-commercial fan-made productions such as fan-films, fanvids, mash-up or recut trailers, and machinima. The remixing and remodeling of commercial source texts in fandom settings is anything but new, and—even more importantly—is nowadays "anything but fringe or underground" (Jenkins, *Fans* 2). Fanvids are leaving their respective fan communities by "going viral" on YouTube, and semi-professional fan-films like the Lord-of-the-Rings inspired *The Hunt for Gollum* (Chris Bouchard, 2009) are receiving high media coverage.[5] The non-profit Organization for Transformative Works (OTW), founded in 2007, is building a fan archive and is supplying legal advocacy to protect and defend fan works. These recent developments have intensified academic interest in fandom. In fact, as Henry Jenkins has noted in *Fans, Bloggers, and Gamers: Exploring Participatory Culture*, "academic research on fan creativity, online communities, and participatory culture has [since the 1990s] become central to a range of different disciplines" (3). Notable scholarly publications in the area of fan production include Jenkins' seminal *Textual Poachers: Television Fans and Participatory Culture* (1992), Jenkins' *Convergence Culture: Where Old and New Media Collide* (2006), Lisa Lewis' edited collection *The Adoring Audience: Fan Culture and Popular Media* (1992), Matt Hills' *Fan Cultures* (2002), Jonathan Gray, Cornel Sandvoss, and C. Lee Harrington's collection *Fandom: Identities and Communities in a Mediated World* (2007), and studies devoted to specific media texts, such as *The Lord of the Rings: Popular Culture in Global Context*, edited by Ernest Mathijs (2006), *Reading Lost: Perspectives on a Hit Television Show*, edited by Roberta Pearson (2009), and Matt Hills' *Triumph of a Time Lord: Regenerating Doctor Who in the Twenty-first Century* (2010). Taking up and extending some of the lessons of these recent publications—namely, that fans as part of the media audience are often creative and engaged cultural producers—the chapters of Part III employ the rubric of *remodeling*. Specifically, Part III explores the idea that adaptation and remaking are not only industrial and textual categories, but also *reception* categories which depend upon the existence of audience activity: that is, not only prior knowledge of previous texts and intertextual relationships, but an understanding of broader generic structures and categories (see Altman 83–84; Grant 57).

In her chapter "Remaking Texts, Remodeling Scholarship," Robin Anne Reid situates the emerging scholarship on fan vidding in the historical development of academic scholarship on fan fiction. She foregrounds the extent to which scholarship focuses on gender and feminist analyses of fan vids and the ways in which they remake media texts. Given the growth of social justice work in online media fandom, Reid argues that fan fiction and fan studies need to acknowledge the distinct lack in the scholarship relating to race and ethnicity. The internet provides fans not only with the medium to share creative work but with opportunities for collaborative activities *and* scholarship, in the fan writings, meta-fan writings, fan communities, playlists, reviews, and in the wikis. Reid suggests that academic scholarship can benefit from considering the theories and practices of fan vidders in order to develop more general theoretical arguments. She fears that just as some academics privileged YouTube and machinima as being the origin of fan vidding, not knowing of the rich depth of cultural creations that preceded them, it is more than likely that academics may unknowingly perpetuate patterns of exclusion and marginalization if "gender" is the sole axis of analysis. According to Reid, that is the reason why the existence of critical creative and scholarly works on race that cross academic and fan boundaries should be acknowledged and be made a part of vidding scholarship (as well as other areas of fan studies). She draws on two transformative works, Shati's vid "Secret Asian Man" (2008) and Lierdumoa's vid "How Much Is That Geisha in the Window?" (2008), to illustrate how fans have commented on the racist cast and representation of characters in the television series *Firefly* (2002) and the later film *Serenity* (Joss Whedon, 2005).

If Reid calls for intersectional theoretical work and new perspectives on fan vidding—a fan practice that has existed since the 1970s—Sibylle Machat and Lili Hartwig turn to a specific fan practice of more recent origin in the next two chapters: the creation of trailers. Machat focuses on so-called fanfic trailers: that is, fanvids designed to advertise or promote a fan fiction story, while Hartwig examines recut trailers that appropriate footage from popular Hollywood movies and reassemble it, so that new and transformed meanings emerge. In the first of these two chapters, Machat comes to terms with the fact that fanfic trailers constitute a combination of fan fiction and fanvid practice. As she shows, the medial transformation of written fan fiction stories into audiovisual fan productions often results in curious and fascinating remodelings which not only consist of re-imagined and recontextualized scenes from the movie or series the fan fiction story is based on, but also from different media sources that are completely unconnected. Machat examines four sample fanfic trailers that advertise fan fiction stories based on the BBC television series *Merlin* (2008–) in order to explore the practice and politics of fanfic trailer vidding as well as the reception and discussion of these trailers within the fan community.

In the next chapter, Hartwig focuses on a different kind of fan-produced trailer which has quickly become one of the most popular kinds of online video parodies: that is, the several hundreds of recut trailers that can be found on the internet, some of which have attracted more than a million views. While some recut trailers parody the original genre of the feature film and re-examine the story through an affectively complementary genre, others fuse two or even more distinct films to create a mash-up. Hartwig argues that a closer study of these fan-made and semi-professional trailers can provide insight into new ways of storytelling and the corresponding reading strategies which span a complex web of intertextual references and reflexive modes. Discussing trailer parodies such as Robert Ryang's "Shining" (2005), which transforms Stanley Kubrick's 1980 horror classic *The Shining* into a family friendly comedy, Demis Lyall-Wilson's recontextualized "Sleepless in Seattle: Recut as a horror movie" (2006), Randy Szuch's critical "Avatar/Pocahontas Mashup" (2010), and others, Hartwig highlights the versatile aspects of online video culture and the importance of participation and active audienceship within the so-called "convergence culture" to explore cinephile media fandoms and the subversive potential of transformative works.

In the final chapter of this volume, Daniel Stein examines professional productions that in various ways remake and remodel fan practices. More precisely, Stein analyzes spoofs of the Batman and Spider-Man Hollywood franchises, in particular "The Dark Knight Is Confused" by the New York-based Key of Awesome comedy group from 2008 and the 2002 MTV Movie Awards Special Presentation on the first *Spider-Man* movie (Sam Raimi, 2002). These spoofs, he argues, are paradigmatic examples of a larger trend in American popular culture and, more specifically, in the evolution of American superhero comics. As "unauthorized" and "semi-authorized" productions, respectively, they are professional "fan-films" that want to participate in and remake the cultural discourse about superhero blockbuster movies. Moreover, they illustrate the centrality of fan practices and perspectives in the production of superhero narratives and indicate that fan productions, and parodies in particular, have played a significant role in the evolution of comic book seriality. This form of seriality is only inadequately captured by the resistance and opposition paradigms offered by the British Cultural Studies or by the Frankfurt School's pessimistic outlook on the culture industry. Rather, it is much better grasped by a sense of interaction and transposition according to which spoofs function as interventions into the serial continuity of comic book storytelling and as a creative practice that contributes to the dispersion—as well as the remaking and remodeling—of superhero narratives across multiple genres and media.

The three parts of this volume—Adapt, Remake, Remodel—thus aim to cover a broad range of creative and industrial practices that transform and appropriate existing texts (originals or earlier versions). By bringing film adaptations, cinematic remakes, and fan remodelings together this book contributes to an understanding of these diverse yet similar processes of cultural reproduction and the positive potential of "retromania" in our contemporary media climate.

Notes

1. There have also been special journal issues, including *Cinemascope* 2 (2005): special issue on "Versions"; *Journal of Romance Studies* 4.1 (2004): special issue

on "Film Remakes"; *The Velvet Light Trap* 61 (2008): special issue on "Remakes and Adaptations."
2. These themes have been previously discussed at the Remake | Remodel conference, an international conference on film remakes, adaptations, and fan productions, organized by Kathleen Loock, and held at the University of Göttingen (Germany) from 30 June to 2 July 2010. The event was closely related to and has featured various members of the Göttingen-based Research Unit "Popular Seriality: Aesthetics and Practice," funded by the German Research Foundation (DFG). The Research Unit brings together 15 researchers from the fields of American Studies, German Philology, Cultural Anthropology/European Ethnology, Empirical Cultural Studies, and Media Studies who are investigating the series as a narrative format that has become a defining feature of popular aesthetics; see http://popularseriality.uni-goettingen.de.
3. On recent discussions of the issue of "fidelity" to a precursor text in adaptation studies see, for example, Albrecht-Crane and Cutchins, Leitch ("Twelve Fallacies"), McFarlane, Naremore, and Stam.
4. See Andrew, "Adaptation" 32–34; and Ray, "Film and Literature" 121–23.
5. See, for example, the press section on *The Hunt for Gollum Movie Website*: http://www.thehuntforgollum.com/press.htm.

Works consulted

Albrecht-Crane, Christa, and Dennis Cutchins. "Introduction: New Beginnings for Adaptation Studies." *Adaptation Studies: New Approaches*. Ed. Albrecht-Crane and Cutchins. Madison, WI: Fairleigh Dickinson University Press, 2010. 11–22. Print.

Altman, Rick. *Film/Genre*. London: British Film Institute, 1999. Print.

Andrew, Dudley. "Adaptation." Naremore. 28–37. Print.

Casetti, Francesco. "Adaptation and Mis-adaptations: Film, Literature, and Social Discourses." *A Companion to Literature and Film*. Ed. Robert Stam and Alessandra Raengo. Malden, MA: Blackwell, 2004. 82–91. Print.

Cazdyn, Eric. *The Flash of Capital: Film and Geopolitics in Japan*. Durham: Duke University Press, 2002. Print.

Eberwein, Robert. "Remakes and Cultural Studies." Horton and McDougal. 15–33. Print.

Forrest, Jennifer, ed. *The Legend Returns and Dies Harder Another Day: Essays on Film Series*. Jefferson, NC: McFarland, 2008. Print.

——, and Leonard R. Koos, eds. *Dead Ringers: The Remake in Theory and Practice*. Albany, NY: State University of New York Press, 2002. Print.

Frow, John. Rev. of *Play It Again, Sam: Retakes on Remakes*, ed. Andrew Horton, and Stuart Y. McDougal. *Screening the Past* 7 (1999): Retrieved on 9 November 2011. www.latrobe.edu.au/screeningthepast/shorts/reviews/rev0799/jfbr7a.htm.

Grant, Catherine. "Recognising *Billy Budd* in *Beau Travail*: Epistemology and Hermeneutics of an Auteurist 'Free' Adaptation." *Screen* 43.1 (2002): 57–73. Print.

Gray, Jonathan. *Show Sold Separately: Promos, Spoilers, and Other Media Paratexts*. New York: New York University Press, 2010. Print.

——, Cornel Sandvoss, and C. Lee Harrington, eds. *Fandom: Identities and Communities in a Mediated World.* New York: New York University Press, 2007. Print.

Hills, Matt. *Fan Cultures.* London/New York: Routledge, 2002. Print.

——. *Triumph of a Time Lord: Regenerating Doctor Who in the Twenty-first Century.* London: I. B. Tauris, 2010. Print.

Hoberman, J. "Ten Years that Shook the World." *American Film* 10 (June 1985): 34–59. Print.

Horton, Andrew, and Stuart Y. McDougal, eds. *Play It Again, Sam: Retakes on Remakes.* Berkeley: University of California Press, 1998. Print.

Idato, Michael. "All Eyes on the Reprise." *Age* (10 March 2011): 12. Print.

Jenkins, Henry. *Textual Poachers: Television Fans and Participatory Culture.* New York: Routledge, 1992. Print.

——. *Convergence Culture: Where Old and New Media Collide.* New York: New York University Press, 2006. Print.

——. *Fans, Bloggers, and Gamers: Exploring Participatory Culture.* New York: New York University Press, 2006. Print.

Jess-Cooke, Carolyn. *Film Sequels: Theory and Practice from Hollywood to Bollywood.* Edinburgh: Edinburgh University Press, 2009. Print.

——, and Constantine Verevis, eds. *Second Takes: Critical Approaches to the Film Sequel.* Albany, NY: State University of New York Press, 2010. Print.

Leitch, Thomas. "Twelve Fallacies in Contemporary Adaptation Theory." *Criticism* 45.2 (Spring 2003): 149–71. Print.

——. "Twice-Told Tales: Disavowal and the Rhetoric of the Remake." Forrest and Koos 37–62. Print.

Lewis, Lisa A., ed. *The Adoring Audience: Fan Culture and Popular Media.* London/New York: Routledge, 1992. Print.

Mathijs, Ernest, ed. *The Lord of the Rings: Popular Culture in Global Context.* London: Wallflower Press, 2006. Print.

Mazdon, Lucy. *Encore Hollywood: Remaking French Cinema.* London: British Film Institute, 2000. Print.

McFarlane, Brian. *Novel to Film: An Introduction to the Theory of Adaptation.* Oxford: Clarendon Press, 1996. Print.

Naremore, James, ed. *Film Adaptation.* New Brunswick, NJ: Rutgers University Press, 2000. Print.

——. "Film and the Reign of Adaptation." Naremore 1–18. Print.

Pearson, Roberta, ed. *Reading Lost: Perspectives on a Hit Television Show.* London: I. B. Tauris, 2009. Print.

Perkins, Claire, and Constantine Verevis, eds. *Film Trilogies: New Critical Approaches.* London: Palgrave Macmillan, 2012. Print.

Rapold, Nicholas. "A Director's Toughest Competition." *New York Times* 13 March 2011: 10, 12. Print.

Ray, Robert B. "Film and Literature." *How a Film Theory Got Lost and Other Mysteries in Cultural Studies.* Bloomington, IN: Indiana University Press, 2001. 120–31. Print.

Reynolds, Simon. *Retromania: Pop Culture's Addiction to Its Own Past.* London: Faber and Faber, 2011. Print.

Stam, Robert. "Beyond Fidelity: The Dialogics of Adaptation." Naremore 54–76. Print.

Stern, Lesley. "*Emma* in Los Angeles: Remaking the Book and the City." Naremore 221–38. Print.

Verevis, Constantine. *Film Remakes*. Edinburgh: Edinburgh University Press, 2006. Print.

Part I
Adapt

1

'Toto, I Think We're in Oz Again' (and Again and Again): Remakes and Popular Seriality

Frank Kelleter

For example: the Wizard of Oz

You know the story—because it has been told many times. A little girl, perhaps nine years old, an orphan, lives with her aunt and uncle on a desolate, gray farm in desolate, gray Kansas. It is America's least fantastic place but it serves as the point of departure for one of America's most fantastic tales. A tornado destroys the farm and carries the little girl into a colorful land, which is the exact opposite of Kansas. There, far away from home, without the protection of parents or grown-ups, she makes new friends and learns something about herself.

The story was familiar even before L. Frank Baum published *The Wonderful Wizard of Oz* in 1900. Dorothy in the Land of Oz: retold many times, this story is itself a retelling of the traditional fairy tale in which a child is forced to leave home and confront an outside world that is both marvelous and dangerous. To be left to one's own devices, to face up to incomprehensible authorities, to discover the pleasures of self-sought companionship—these are standard situations in tales told about, and often for, children.[1]

In this sense, the original *Wizard of Oz* was already a remake.[2] Like any remake, however, it made a difference. We would not confuse the *Wizard of Oz* with *Alice in Wonderland*, *Peter Pan* or "Hänsel und Gretel," because Baum insisted on remodeling his familiar tale for a specific time and place, or more precisely, for a specific culture which is itself frequently regarded as the remake of an Old World. As Gerald Early notes, *The Wonderful Wizard of Oz*, published at the threshold of the twentieth century, "tried very hard to be an American book in its sensibility"

19

(456).[3] Consider what happens to Dorothy in her new world. Blown out of Kansas with her dog Toto, she meets three partners in misfortune, three inhabitants of Oz who are, however, equally forlorn in that foreign land: the Scarecrow whose head is filled with straw, the Tin Woodman who has no heart, and the Cowardly Lion, who looks frightful but lacks courage. The four of them and Toto set out for the Emerald City to ask a mysterious wizard for the things they want: brains for the Scarecrow, emotions for the Tin Woodman, self-confidence for the Lion and a return home for Dorothy. In addition to a wizard, Oz has witches in different sections of the land: the wicked Witch of the East, the wicked Witch of the West, the good Witch of the North, and Glinda the Good, living in the South. Except for the wicked Witch of the East, who is killed when the tornado drops Dorothy's house on her, these powerful women either impede or facilitate the companions' progress toward the Emerald City. But thanks to Dorothy's determination and her group's team spirit, the friends finally manage to destroy the wicked Witch of the West, as required by the Wizard in exchange for fulfilling their wishes. The Wizard, in turn, confronts them as "Oz, the Great and Terrible" (Baum, *Wonderful* 187) in various daunting incarnations: a ball of fire, a wild beast, a beautiful lady, a monumental levitating head, and a disembodied voice that announces its presence from all directions.

The true surprise, however, is still in store and it is quite an American surprise: toward the end of the tale, the God-like Wizard turns out to be a circus impostor from Omaha, Nebraska, whose hot-air balloon accidentally drifted into Oz some time ago. To protect himself from the truly gifted witches, this professional conman did what he does best and created a realm of illusions and simulations around himself. Even the astounding Emerald City owes its glamour to a ruse; everyone entering the city is required to wear green glasses. It is a humbug urban landscape, inspired by the White City of the 1893 World's Columbian Exposition in Baum's Chicago and in turn a source of inspiration for Walt Disney's amusement parks. Clearly, the Wizard of Oz stands in a long line of great American entertainers.[4]

Little wonder that this likeable charlatan does, in the end, manage to fulfill the wishes of Dorothy and her friends, even without magic, by making them understand that the things they are looking for are already in their possession. This quintessentially American insight—you can take on any identity if you only believe in it—previously transformed the man from Omaha into a powerful magician; now it turns the brainless Scarecrow into a philosopher, the heartless Tin Woodman into a sentimental soul, and the Cowardly Lion into the king of the animals. Dorothy and Toto, in turn, are supposed to fly back to Kansas with the Wizard's patched up balloon, but the balloon mistakenly ascends without them, so that Glinda's magic is needed to get them back home, even though Glinda reveals that Dorothy had it in her power to return all along.

What does it mean to say that this story is one of the most popular ever told in America? On the one hand, it means that this is a story *about* America, a story with which the culture describes itself. Baum's short introduction to the first edition of *The Wonderful Wizard of Oz* made it clear that Dorothy's tale was meant to establish a genuinely American children's literature. Baum explained that he wanted to invent "a modernized fairy tale." What he had in mind was a fairy tale without moralizing and cruelty, but with characters and incidents that "pleasure children of today" (Baum, *Wonderful* 4). In 1900, this repudiation of didacticism was visibly an American gesture—not in the sense that it did not exist in other literatures but in the sense of being a gesture by which American culture described and recognized itself after the Civil War.[5] Such anti-didacticism places *The Wonderful Wizard of Oz* in a framework of national self-conception sometimes subsumed under the name of pragmatism, with pragmatism understood in a wide sense, referring not only to a school of philosophy but to a set of cultural practices and values intent on (re)constructing national identity at a time of crisis. If we view *The Wonderful Wizard of Oz*, with its resolute heroine and its friendly conman title character, in the context of post-Civil War modernity, then Baum's book has more in common with the narratives of Mark Twain and the educational philosophies of John Dewey than with the subversive Victorian wit of Lewis Carroll.[6] Instead of nonsense, we get common sense, all the way down to style: the plain, unsentimental language of Baum's *The Wonderful Wizard of Oz*, so untypical of its period's children's literature, anticipates the mid-Western modernism of Ernest Hemingway.[7]

On the other hand, to say that Oz is one of the most popular stories ever told in America means that it is a story *of* America: the probable but stunning result of a particular mode of making stories. L. Frank Baum's *The Wonderful Wizard of Oz*, while remaking narratives long familiar, is a product and a force of American popular culture. This simple observation helps illuminate the terms and conditions of Dorothy's frequent return to Oz. There have been literally thousands of sequels to Baum's original novel, including adaptations, musicals, movies, games, and so on.[8] Making sense of these endless variations requires a theory of popular culture that can explain popular culture's affinity for serial narration.[9] Specifically regarding American popular culture, there are, at least, two features that elucidate its preference for serial forms: its fundamentally commercial organization and its need to address exceptionally diverse audiences, meaning audiences typical of modern immigration societies. The commercial foundation fosters standardization (that is, industrial reproduction), while mass-address, as maintained by various theories of the popular, demands multiple coding and polysemy (that is, increased connectivity).[10] Both features of popular culture—industrial reproduction and increased connectivity—encourage serialization.

Altogether, I argue that popular seriality, highly standardized and at the same time extremely flexible in terms of storytelling and usage, is best investigated as a commercially driven, largely self-reinforcing process of narrative and experiential *proliferation*. It is a process that produces its own follow-up possibilities, because structurally, a serial narrative is always open-ended, promising to constantly *renew* the ever *same* moment. More abstractly put, popular seriality promises to accomplish a paradox which may well be the structural utopia of all capitalist culture: it promises a potentially infinite innovation of reproduction.

I shall return to this concept of popular seriality and its relevance for the study of remakes. At this point, suffice it to say that Baum's original Oz narrative was immediately serialized and transposed into other media. The first major adaptation of Dorothy's story dates back to 1902 when the novel was made into a successful musical, for which Baum produced the script.[11] In turn, this success allowed, indeed necessitated, further continuations. Between 1904 and 1919, Baum wrote 13 more Oz novels and six shorter booklets for small children, the so-called "Little Wizard of Oz stories," then other authors took over.

Even if we adopt an author-centered perspective (which is never quite appropriate for popular series) and concentrate on Baum's personal involvement as a novelist, disregarding the activities of other players and media, as well as the internal productivity of serial texts, we find that the Oz narratives exhibit certain core features of American popular culture at large. These are, most importantly, a close interaction between producers and consumers (Baum received numerous letters from readers with queries, requests, and recommendations for further plot developments) and the organization of a more or less coherent narrative universe across different media (after the success of the first musical, Baum tried his hand at several theater and movie adaptations, including the traveling multimedia show *Fairylogue and Radio-Plays* in 1908, before he founded his own motion picture company in 1913).[12] Baum's consecutive forewords, in which he reflected on mail received from young readers, express his changing attitude toward the series.

From requesting a certain number of responses before he would produce another volume to adopting a playful tone of resignation about the inescapability of further sequels, Baum became increasingly aware that he was not master of his own story world. These forewords reflect an author's growing recognition of the inevitable division of labor in commercial serial storytelling.

In fact, the transmedia existence of the Oz universe was already evident in the 1902 musical, which was the first Oz text to mention Dorothy's surname, Gale, before it was picked up in the literary series. Already Baum's second novel, *The Marvelous Land of Oz* (1904), drew heavily on the musical. The book is dedicated to Fred A. Stone and David C. Montgomery, the actors who played the Scarecrow and the Tin Woodman in the stage production. The Cowardly Lion, who only had a minor part in the musical, was completely dropped from the book's cast of characters. Evidently, the relationship between Oz novels and Oz stage productions was not going to be one of original and adaptation. Rather, we find opportune serializations across different artistic channels. In fact, *The Marvelous Land of Oz*—with its army of girl soldiers, perfect for a chorus-line—was clearly written with an eye to being produced as a stage play (which happened in 1905, when Baum scripted the musical *The Woggle-Bug*) (see Riley 99–109).

In terms of content, Baum's *The Marvelous Land of Oz* continued the story of *The Wonderful Wizard of Oz*, using familiar characters such as the Scarecrow and the Tin Woodman, who had been particularly popular in the 1902 stage production, but also adding new figures and themes such as the immensely popular character of the Woggle-Bug, who in turn generated further publications.[13] The plot centered on a boy called Tip who, in the course of the story, transforms into the girl Ozma to become the princess ruler of Oz. A few years after *The Marvelous Land*, Baum followed the success of his first two books with the novels *Ozma of Oz* (1907), *Dorothy and the Wizard in Oz* (1908), *The Road to Oz* (1909), and *The Emerald City of Oz* (1910). This sixth novel was conceived as the final installment of the series; in it, Dorothy, Aunt Em, and Uncle Henry settle in Oz for good to escape an economic depression in their own world (the bank threatens to seize their mortgaged farm). The novel concludes with Dorothy informing her readers that a Barrier of Invisibility will henceforth protect Oz from visitors—and, presumably, from the curiosity and ongoing demands of customers of the franchise.

Three years later, Baum himself faced financial troubles and could no longer afford to ignore his readers' insistence that he produce new

Oz novels.[14] Once more, popular art rhymed with money—or the lack thereof. In fact, the publication of the *Little Wizard of Oz Stories* in 1914 had already been driven by commercial considerations; these simplified tales were supposed to familiarize a new generation of younger readers with the Oz universe after Baum had decided to launch a second series. The novels written after 1913—made possible, Baum explained, by his use of wireless telegraph to contact the cut-off land—did not restore his wealth but tied his financial lot to the series even more closely.[15] As if to mark this changed relationship to his creation, he now signed his books as "The Royal Historian of Oz," a title expressing his new understanding of popular authorship as a kind of commissioned office. (In a similar manner, John R. Neill, who succeeded W. W. Denslow as illustrator after the first book, became "The Imperial Illustrator of Oz.") To stay afloat Baum produced a new Oz book each year until his death: *The Patchwork Girl of Oz* (1913), *Tik-Tok of Oz* (1914), *The Scarecrow of Oz* (1915), *Rinkitink of Oz* (1916), *The Lost Princess of Oz* (1917), *The Tin Woodman of Oz* (1918), *The Magic of Oz* (1919), and the posthumously published *Glinda of Oz* (1920).

After Baum's death in 1919, Ruth Plumly Thompson, who as a child had been an avid reader of the Oz books, took over as Royal Historian of Oz and continued the series until 1939 with 21 further volumes. Later authors included John R. Neill, Jack Snow, Eloise McGraw, Lauren McGraw, and many others. Altogether, the fan website Books of Oz (Frodelius) lists 370 authors, among them Baum's sons Frank Joslyn and Kenneth Gage Baum as well as his great-grandson Roger S. Baum. Like many American entertainment industries, Oz is obviously also a family business, including grudges and legal battles.[16]

In addition to the authorized sequels, there are countless translations, adaptations, and revisions. Abroad, the series spawned its most curious spin-off in Russia, where Aleksandr Volkov loosely translated Baum's novels, then increasingly modified them (because American copyright did not extend to the Soviet Union) until there was an independent Russian series. Most of the Russian adaptations were in turn translated for publication in the German Democratic Republic so that after World War II there were two distinct Oz cultures in Germany: one following Baum's series, the other one ("Der Zauberer der Smaragdenstadt") based on Volkov's versions, which are also better known in China (see Wladimirski and Ernst).

And this is only the print sector. Like most popular series, the Oz narratives quickly spread through various media, generating radio shows, theater productions, musicals, movies, animations, television programs, comic books, and so on. Of all these remakes and transpositions, none has left a deeper impression on American culture than the 1939 MGM movie, *The Wizard of Oz*, with Judy Garland as Dorothy.[17] When the movie was first released, it was only mildly popular. Its cultural importance really dates back to the postwar decades, when it successfully crossed over into another American entertainment industry. In 1956 and 1959, the MGM *Wizard* was shown on television during the holiday seasons. Ever since, re-watching *The Wizard of Oz* has been part of the nation's cultural routines.

The MGM production may well be one of the most frequently and most intensively watched movies of all time. Its influence on twentieth-century literature and art is immense, probably exceeding the influence of Baum's original novel. Salman Rushdie declared that this movie (about which he published a book) made him want to become a writer. James Thurber, Ray Bradbury, Gore Vidal, John Updike, Stephen King, and others have written essays about the film or based novels or stories on it. Judy Garland's puzzled exclamation on her arrival in Oz, "Toto, I have a feeling we're not in Kansas anymore" (a sentence that does not appear in Baum's novel), has become a byword in American literature, serving, for example, as epigraph to the third part of Thomas Pynchon's *Gravity's Rainbow* in 1973.

Illustration 1.1 Dorothy (Judy Garland) upon her arrival in the Land of Oz in the 1939 MGM movie *The Wonderful Wizard of Oz*

Among more recent adaptations, Gregory Maguire's 1995 novel *Wicked: The Life and Times of the Wicked Witch of the West* has been the most influential. Maguire retells the stories of Baum's first Oz novel and the MGM movie from the perspective of the Witch: a revision made plausible by the original series' refusal to turn even its most villainous characters into figures of evil. In this sense, Maguire developed and radicalized an aspect of the Oz universe that was already contained within the initial texts, most likely through the influence of Baum's mother-in-law, Matilda Joslyn Gage, who published a feminist history of witch hunts in 1893, which argued that witches were killed for "crimes which never existed save in the imagination of [their] persecutors" (*Woman, Church, and State*, qdt. in Schwartz 279). Against this background it is noteworthy that the two killings of witches in *The Wonderful Wizard of Oz* are accidents and that Baum's wicked Witch of the West is herself a somewhat ambivalent character, deeply irritated by the death of her sister and untypically afraid of the dark (Baum, *Wonderful* 223; see also Hearn 222). By foregrounding these character options, Maguire's novel has retroactively impacted the reception and meaning of its source texts. Remakes and series often work this way: their narrative accomplishments are oriented backwards as much as forwards; they provide continuity by changing their own past.

In 2003, *Wicked* was turned into a successful musical, so that Maguire found it profitable to write two more revisionist Oz books. The first of these, *Son of a Witch* (2005), was supposedly inspired by the Abu Ghraib torture photographs. The novel is dedicated to the cast of the *Wicked* musical in much the same way in which Baum dedicated his second novel to the two actors who turned the 1902 stage extravaganza into a success. (In both cases the musical version took great liberties with its novelistic precursor.) The third novel, *A Lion Among Men* (2008), centers on the Cowardly Lion and reflects the difference between military and diplomatic methods of conflict solution. A fourth installment, "Out of Oz," appeared in November 2011. Evidently, Dorothy's tale has become a stable intermediary for American culture to measure its own instabilities and evolutions.

All of this is Oz as a piece of modern American popular culture: a wide and constantly expanding realm of interlocking, transmedially active, mass-addressed commercial stories. With their narrative sprawl and their openness to ever new uses, these serial products complicate traditional narratological notions of beginning, middle, and end, source and adaptation, original and copy. More than that, popular seriality complicates the very categories of author and reader. The importance of letters to the editor (or author) in the history of popular culture is paramount, starting with Eugene Sue's *Les mystères de Paris* (1842–43) and not ending with L. Frank Baum's reading of his readers' writing.[18] Of course, copyright and proper names remain crucially important in serial storytelling, but the Oz universe is clearly not authored by any *one* writer, producer, or company. Obviously, popular address always invites popular participation. Serial publication amplifies this process, making acts of writing and reading increasingly permeable, because serial publication by definition overlaps with serial reception. A series, in other words, can observe its effects on audiences while the narrative is still running and react accordingly. Conversely, audiences can influence a narrative's development if the narrative is still unfolding, that is, if it is a serial narrative.

In extreme cases—and with technologies such as the internet, the extreme is gradually becoming the rule—the distinction between producer and consumer, author and reader, is almost completely dissolved. As Michael Chabon suggests, popular culture eschews institutional control of author/reader roles. Instead of a canonical anxiety of influence, Chabon finds that popular aesthetics is ruled by what he calls the "bliss" of influence (57). Such enthusiasm may be overstating the case, but it helps explain the predominance of serial formats in popular art. Apparently, popular producers, whether corporate or private, are inclined to see themselves not so much as authors, creating more or less self-contained structures, but as *co*-producers in a literal sense, as reader-producers, *aficionados* or fans, inviting ever more recipients to *continue* a pleasurable game with narrative material that is familiar, shared, and easily accessible.

Similar observations have brought forth neologisms such as "wreading" (Landow) and "produsing" (Bruns) to describe the increasingly porous boundaries between popular production and popular reception. Even so, the dynamic of commercial proliferation consists in more than a de-hierarchization of cultural practices or academic concepts. In fact, it may be useful to move beyond the fashionable privileging of popular reception over popular production (with production usually framed as restrictive and reception as emancipatory) and the attendant populism that organizes much contemporary research on popular culture. The wide range of popular amateur or reader productions (from early unauthorized renderings of Sherlock Holmes, perhaps the first serial character in a modern commercial sense, to the manifold varieties of user creativity on the internet) express a fundamental feature of all modern popular aesthetics: its inherent tendency to produce, out of itself and by itself, ever more diversified continuations, spin-offs, revisions, and sub-genres. "All novels are sequels," says Chabon (57). If this is so, what is the best way to study this textual sprawl?

Remake: a change

There are at least two ways in which remakes can become fertile objects of cultural analysis, and insofar as American popular culture is a culture of remakes and serializations, this argument can be extended to this larger sphere. The first way to study commercial remakes, and by implication popular culture, is to read these texts for the information they provide about historical change. In one form or other, this is certainly the most common approach to popular repetitions today. Another approach, more rarely tried, examines the dynamics of repeated popular narration itself—or put differently, it examines the agency of remakes in an ongoing process of communicative modernization. I argue that these are distinct modes of analysis, both valuable, often mutually enhancing, but with different interests and demands.

The established approach is to utilize remakes as measuring devices for cultural transformations. Commercial remakes are particularly suited to this type of investigation because a remake always foregrounds a change, be it a change of narrative technique or a change of the context in which the narrative unfolds. Post-structuralism has taught us—if we did not already know it—that there is no such thing as an exact repetition. Iteration always takes place in time: something has changed between an act and its duplication. Indeed, change best reveals itself against the background of regularity. Paradoxically, then, commercial standardization provides an excellent opportunity to observe what is new. Serial narratives are especially useful for this kind of observation because a series is always structured as a constant with variables, reproducing the same situations or characters in ever new circumstances or constellations. In this sense, a serial analysis of, say, the James Bond movies would speak volumes about changing gender conceptions in the Western world between 1962 and today. The same can be said about remakes: it is precisely because a remake repeats a story that has already been told that the disparities between its own telling and a previous one are highly visible.

More abstractly put: serial texts and remakes (treated as similar modes at this point) indicate the *temporality* of culture more directly and more strongly than single texts are able to do. In fact, it would be possible to trace the evolution of twentieth-century American culture, or important strands of it, through a comparative reading of the Oz narratives. For instance, Baum's original novel, with its deficient but good-natured men, its imposing women, and its pragmatic heroine—a prototype of the American girl in numerous later popular novels and movies—obviously reflects the growing influence of feminism in the American public around the turn of the century. Baum dedicated *The Wonderful Wizard of Oz* to his wife Maud Gage, the daughter of Matilda Joslyn Gage, a prominent suffragette and co-author with Elizabeth Cady Stanton and Susan B. Anthony of the multi-volume *History of Woman Suffrage* (1881–86). From what we know, Matilda Gage was an active supporter of Baum's literary career and she was the one who first encouraged him to write down the bedtime stories he told his sons and send them to a publisher. (The result was *Mother Goose in Prose*, 1897, Baum's first bestseller.)[19]

However, as the series continued it became more focused on economic and political conditions in Oz. In their cumulative effect, Baum's 13 sequels paint a relatively coherent vision of social organization, offering an imaginative alternative to economic developments in the United States at the time. For many readers, therefore, these novels stand as major expressions of American utopian literature as it flourished between the Civil War and the First World War.[20]

These utopian tendencies allowed later critics to use the Oz novels to revitalize progressivist ideas for their own times. Often reading Baum's narratives as socialist parables or communitarian utopias in the vein of Edward Bellamy, such scholarly allegories can be included among the welter of time-bound retellings of the *Wizard of Oz*. In important ways, they *remake* Baum's largely matriarchal and feudal society as a collectivist paradise (while downplaying Baum's preference for deus-ex-machina solutions, so typical of children's literature).[21] By contrast, other scholars took note of Baum's talents as salesman and advertiser. Before turning novelist he was not only an oil salesman and a newspaper editor but also owned a variety store, founded a monthly journal on shop window dressing, and authored a book on the same topic, *The Art of Decorating Dry Goods Windows and Interiors*, published almost simultaneously with *The Wonderful Wizard of Oz*. Not surprisingly, a number of critics have therefore pointed to the commodity status of the Oz narratives and claimed the exact opposite of populist readings: Oz is a parable of capitalist consumption.[22] What both readings have in common is their interest in updating the Oz narratives for contemporary times and interests. They are, in every sense of the term, remakes: they exhibit a strong tendency to invigorate popular texts by instrumentalizing them;

they de-emphasize discordant proliferations in favor of current bina-ries.[23] Engaged scholarship *on* popular culture thus testifies to the cul-tural uses made *of* popular culture—in much the same way in which a comparative reading of Baum's Oz novels and, for instance, Volkov's Russian transpositions would shed some light on different conceptions of community, solidarity, and social morality in the United States and the Soviet Union.

In 1939, then, the MGM movie production made a difference in the emphatic sense of the term. Much has been written about this film. If studied as a remake, it offers insight into the cultural mood of America toward the end of the Great Depression. While remaining faithful to Baum's plot and character constellation, the MGM *Wizard* added musi-cal numbers and deviated in two significant ways from the novel and earlier adaptations. First, Judy Garland's Dorothy is more passive than Baum's protagonist. Given to tears and often dependent on the help of others, Garland spends much of the movie longing to return to Aunt Em and Uncle Henry. In this manner, the escapist swoon of her song "Somewhere Over the Rainbow" is ultimately neutralized by the defini-tive charisma of Dorothy's final words in Oz, "There's no place like home."

This sentimental reinterpretation of the protagonist is closely related to the second innovation offered by the MGM movie. The 1939 *Wizard* portrays Kansas in sepia tones and Oz in Technicolor, but Oz is not a parallel universe. Instead, the wonderful land is peopled with charac-ters that are obvious variations of Dorothy's real-life friends and foes. Oz, in other words, turns out to be the product of Dorothy's feverish dreaming. Far from offering a viable alternative to Midwestern gloom, as in Baum's novels, the marvelous land exists only in Dorothy's imagi-nation. Hence, it makes sense that all her adventures are headed for a family reunion. Doggedly the movie progresses towards a climax that is almost a template for narrative closure in American film. In the end, *the family* reconstitutes itself as the ultimate realm of solidarity and the lost child is restored to her kinfolk. If Judy Garland's Dorothy emerges from Oz matured, the lesson she has learned is to accept her living conditions, no matter how miserable and provincial they are. This is a story of the Great Depression indeed: there is no place like home, even if home is a rundown farm in the middle of nowhere.

Possible consequences of this kind of family contentment are shown 46 years later in a remarkable movie called *Return to Oz* (1985). It is a Walt Disney production that poses as the direct continuation of the 1939 film, as if it were the most belated sequel ever made for a movie.[24] Like most sequels, however, it is also a remake. Directed by Walter Murch, the film strongly re-emphasizes the feminist aspects of Dorothy's visit to Oz, but instead of Baum's turn-of-the-century concern with social equality we now get a feminism that is interested in the psychological demands of inhabiting a female body. *Return to Oz* begins with Dorothy being checked into a mental hospital where surgery is offered as the most modern tool to exorcise her childish fantasies about a marvelous land (so much for "There's no place like home"!). What follows is *The Wizard of Oz* as a horror movie. The prettiness of the MGM production has vanished, not only because an evil king has taken possession of Oz, but because in Dorothy's own world the twentieth century is dawning, as her dangerously understanding neurologist repeatedly emphasizes before he gets ready to chase electricity through her brain. The first 20 minutes of the movie are unremittingly dark, drawing a chilling image of bourgeois science. Women who dream of faraway countries, or girls who look in the mirror and see someone else instead of themselves, are promised shock treatments and lobotomies.

Fairuza Balk plays Dorothy accordingly, a trusting little girl who gradually learns that in the real world, outside her dreams, no one can be trusted. In the beginning, she innocently follows Aunt Em's advice, believing what all the loving grown-ups are telling her: always to mind the doctors and nurses—until it is no longer believable. So Dorothy escapes to Oz again. Much closer to Baum's practical heroine than sentimental Judy Garland, Balk's Dorothy always finds a way out when someone gets too close to her, which happens all the time. Once in Oz, she is confronted with the worst molestations the world holds in store for a girl, all of them faithfully adapted from Baum's novels *The Marvelous Land of Oz* and *Ozma of Oz*. And Dorothy prevails. Without compromising her childish heart, without turning shrill, vindictive or robust, she overcomes a gang of predatory youngsters (the rapist-like Wheelers), escapes mutilation in the name of beauty (Mombi's hall of severed female heads for all occasions), and tricks patriarchal know-it-alls (the surreal stone face of the Nome King). As with Huck Finn, that other pragmatic American dream character, this may be the most fabulous thing about her: that she learns to be clever without growing up, that is, without hardening or going crazy.

While repeating familiar motifs and characters, *Return to Oz* speaks to its time, as the MGM movie and Baum's novel did to theirs. Thus, when Dorothy's companions from the earlier film are dutifully restored at the end of the 1985 sequel, they look oddly out of place, like puppets from another show, shadows from another nightmare. It is a good thing no one is singing songs anymore—unlike in another remake, made eight years earlier, where song is inevitable: *The Wiz* is an African American musical, first performed on Broadway in 1975, then quickly released as a movie, a Motown production, in 1978, starring a full-grown Diana Ross as Dorothy. This version not only features an all-black cast; it transfers Baum's story to New York City. Dorothy is at home in Harlem, not Kansas, and her journey to Oz is a journey downtown, through parts of the city she never dared to visit before.

Dorothy's adventures in this fantasy Manhattan look like a wild inventory of inner city despair in the 1970s. We are in the era of Jimmy Carter's American malaise: there are children's playgrounds so run-down they look like frightful crime scenes; garbage bags are piled man-high to mark the yellow brick road; Dorothy tells the Scarecrow that he is just "a product of negative thinking"; the Tin Man is rusting away in a closed-down amusement park; the Lion's fur is dusty. At one point, Dorothy and her friends are attacked in a subway station by street peddlers and trash cans—and finally by the subway station itself coming alive. Baum's field of poppies has become a seedy nightclub, and there are yellow cabs on the yellow brick road but, unsurprisingly, the characters hail them in vain, because the cabs do not stop for black people.

Thus the marvelous land has turned into a post-apocalyptic landscape, New York as it might look after a nuclear attack, with an industrial drone always in the distance. And yet, the characters break out into song and dance, and not only because this is a musical but because they are determined to turn their hopeless surroundings into a decent living space. In a word, *The Wiz* is a true Motown production, turning urban gloom into golden entertainment. Fittingly, Michael Jackson portrays the Scarecrow as a pitiful drifter, crucified in the beginning but then dancing with the pure joy of being alive. The Wizard, played by Richard Pryor, resides as a media tycoon at One Liberty Plaza in the World Trade Center. Terrified of being found out as a fraud, he leaves it to Dorothy to explain to her friends that they already possess what they are looking for. This is only logical because the film's transposition of Baum's turn-of-the-century fairy tale into a story of African American urbanity endows the motif of companionship—the necessity of sticking together—with a new, no longer childlike urgency. But this also accounts for the nightmarish quality that permeates even the most carefree musical numbers, certainly a reason why *The Wiz*, which was intended to be the pinnacle of 1970s all-black cinema, flopped at the box office.

These are just a few examples and it continues. In the post-Cold War era, there are Gregory Maguire's parables about animal rights and terrorism. There is Shelley Jackson's *Patchwork Girl* from 1995, one of the early successes in hypertext fiction, inspired by Baum's 1913 novel, *The Patchwork Girl of Oz*.[25] There is the dystopian steam-punk of *Tin Man*, a 2007 mini-series on the Sci-Fi channel. There is going to be a CGI movie directed by John Boorman as well as a prequel feature film directed by Sam Raimi. And so on. Watching these remakes means watching cultural history at work. Since variation draws attention to itself, to remake a narrative is one of the strongest ways to make a point. Remakes lend themselves to media innovations as well as to political uses, as they invite us to reconsider the stories we tell ourselves, not only in commercial mass culture but also in more robustly canonized formats. Think of postcolonial literature and its affinity for revisionist retellings. Think Derek Walcott's *Omeros*, think Jean Rhys' *Wide Sargasso Sea*. But also think Dorothy in Oz, accompanying American culture from 1900 until today.

Thoughts on an alternative approach: popular seriality and American culture

Popular culture loves repetition, and repetition offers an excellent opportunity to measure temporal difference. Research that makes use of popular material in this manner is bound to come up with remarkable results. The method has merits, and I have tried to outline a few of its interpretive possibilities for the Oz narratives. However, because this is such a successful and widely established approach the challenge for future research may lie elsewhere. When we turn popular remakes into stable data material for the routine questions of Cultural Studies, tracing constellations of race, gender, or class in these texts, we certainly learn something important, but we learn little about why popular culture keeps generating such repetitions in the first place. We learn little about the conflict-ridden agency of specific serial texts, little about the narrative and media dynamics of commercial remakes, little about their differences from retellings in other fields of cultural practice. These questions are important, not only because they address the flexible doings of serial narratives, but because popular culture, despite our hopeful convergence theories, generates formal and experiential possibilities that are still distinct from those prevailing in, say, folk culture or artistic fields more strongly invested in notions of the closed oeuvre and non-commercial authorship. Hence it might be useful to shift our analytical interest to the terms and conditions of popular seriality itself.

Think about it: a scholar's life could be devoted to mapping the narrative sprawl set in motion by L. Frank Baum's original novel. But there is no need for that. Popular audiences are already doing it. The world of Oz has given rise to readers and fans who, in turn, have given rise to entire networked orders of knowledge about Oz. There are full-fledged schools of reading, especially on the internet, and the questions that divide them are usually not about the plausibility of this or that individual interpretation but concern the structure of the serial universe itself. In this fashion, exegetic problems abound *within* the Oz narratives. They are, in fact, driving forces *of* the narratives because the competing answers produced by different agents are of consequence for the ongoing self-description of the serial universe. For example, should the Oz novels be read as a consistent narrative? This question is raised not only by readers but inevitably by each new installment to the series. And how can we make sense of existing and ever growing inconsistencies? Readers and writers alike, often indistinguishable from each other, are engaged in the continual establishment of meta-narratives of order—canons, that is—which try to differentiate between legitimate and illegitimate, influential and non-influential contributions to the universe, even as they add further variations of their own: an almost inevitable consequence of any longer running series.[26]

Thus, personal variations and the search for means to integrate mushrooming installments into a more or less coherent sequence (or well-arranged network) increase the complexity of the series exactly by trying to reduce it. A case in point is provided by the manifold activities of the International Wizard of Oz Club, founded in 1957 by a 13-year-old Justin G. Schiller. The Club's journal, *The Baum Bugle*, like most such fanzines, has long crossed the boundary between parascholarly commentary and active contribution to the serial universe. Even before the Club's founding, many Oz authors typically started out as fans, including the "Royal Historians" Ruth Plumly Thompson and, especially, Jack Snow, who was also one of the first Oz scholars. But perhaps this way of phrasing it already obscures the author/reader relations operative in popular series: Thompson and Snow did not cease to be fans when they became official authors of the series; nor did their writing for OZ start only when they were paid for it by Reilly & Britton. The productivity of such career moves (their cultural work) consists in opening the field of organized fan activities to ever more controversial self-descriptions. Since the emergence of "acafandom," these self-descriptions can overlap with explicit scholarly conflicts about popular narratives.[27] In fact, self-aware performances of acafandom accelerate and radicalize a process of serial complexity management that generates more and more contested authorizations (including competing definitions and practices of egalitarian participation, gift-giving, community-building, identity politics, and so on, as well as rival critiques of supposedly restrictive but unavoidable hierarchies): paradoxical proliferations of serial order, increasingly complex reductions of complexity. What is more, complexity management of this sort unfolds itself in a serial fashion: again and again, in quick succession. In this manner, popular canons are distinguished from their counterparts in highbrow culture by their sheer number, volatility, and the velocity of their competitive moves. Not only do they consist of series, they come themselves in serialized form.

To put it in different terms: popular series have created countless strategies of simulating coherence and unity where, structurally, neither unity nor coherence is to be had. The best known devices in this context are probably the strategies of retrospective continuity (retcon) in American superhero comics. The Oz series has developed similar ploys. For instance, some of March Laumer's Oz novels work hard to assimilate Aleksandr Volkov's Russian versions into the narrative world invented by Baum. Laumer achieves this through an elaborate scheme that establishes Volkov's Oz as a parallel universe, but then he is also the author of some deliberately non-canonical and crypto-pornographic Oz novels published in Hong Kong and Sweden, such as *The Green Dolphin of Oz* (1978).

From a Cultural Studies perspective, it is easy to celebrate such developments as the cultural equivalent of grassroots democracy or, in Stuart Hall's and John Fiske's terms, as the subversive tactics of a readerly "people" undermining the authority of a writerly "power bloc." According to Hall and Fiske, a new globalized folk culture is at work in the realm of popular consumption, fighting capitalist technology with its own weapons. However, if the history of serial narratives illustrates anything, it is the difficulty of applying to modern popular culture the high-cultural dichotomy of author and reader, even in its neo-Marxist inversions, folksy repeals, or "participatory" blends.[28] I suggest, therefore, that we understand such appropriations and remakings as essential parts of commercial seriality itself. In an intensely networked media culture, serial narratives always tend to unfold in a self-reinforcing sprawl rather than in the consecutive manner typical of the field of restricted production. Usually produced in a division of labor, popular series inexorably complicate the authority of personal artistic control, subjective or collective. Serial narratives support little authorial commitment; instead, they foster a dynamic of continuous differentiation, provoking further concatenations in all directions. It is usually not "the people" who are doing this against a cabal of elitist authors or companies. Rather, what we can observe in these manifold reprises is the productivity of serial textuality itself: narrative entanglements that, in their sum, are never the result of intentional structuring, even as they invite ever more intentions and ownership claims to participate.

In this sense, what is remarkable about reader and fan participations, beyond the ideologically contested self-descriptions of the actors involved, is how such activities speed up a process of textual sprawl that exists independently of—and often in opposition to—the purposes of the people it engages. Obviously, there is no central management that would plan or guide such narrative proliferation. Rather than being determined by interests and identities, it deploys interests and enables identities to recognize and formalize themselves (see Kelleter, "Serial"). As a consequence, fan productions constitute a huge arena for popular culture to observe itself, an experimental field where serial narratives ceaselessly reflect on the possibilities of their continuation. Perhaps such self-reproduction is best conceptualized as an evolutionary process that makes use of an unprecedentedly high number of players and products, ambitions and commitments, ideological affiliations and sexual preferences, to generate variations or mutations (lucky accidents) for future employment and retroactive mobilization. From this perspective, the size of the experiment matters more than the participatory gratification of individual agents. In fact, the huge majority of fan actions, if approached as single contributions, are evolutionary dead ends in the sense that they have little or no impact on further variations. They might as well not have happened. However, in their sum total, they produce momentous effects, because even the most isolated posting on an internet blog feeds into a sizeable process of narrative trial and error. It may not seem to be an efficient process but in the absence of concentrated organization or stable authorization, the continual renewal of variable identities and volatile control claims proves to be an astonishingly reliable method of reproduction. The more variations there are, the higher the probability that the system will hit on sustainable ones.

If we begin to read popular texts from this perspective, we will be less ready to construct an evaluative contrast between popular reception and popular production. Reading popular texts within the framework of an overarching theory of seriality as a self-dynamic form, we will attend to amateur productions, fan fiction, letters to the editor, and so on, not as oppositional or idiosyncratic counter-discourses but as necessary features of popular seriality itself, even and especially when they generate oppositional self-descriptions. Furthermore, we will see narrative texts, both authorized and unauthorized, not as raw material for (dissident or complicit) uses but as prime actors in a larger historical process of communicative modernization that has been going on since at least the middle of the nineteenth century, transcending the agency of individual desires and even the remarkable power of economic ownership claims. On a formal level, we will read these texts with an interest in the specific possibilities and restraints of serial commercial narration, asking how each serial text refers back to earlier tellings and how it allows for future tellings, how it depends on mediation and prepares remediations.[29] As Ruth Mayer writes, popular seriality is "a principle rather than a technique" (n. pag.). It is, in other words, a dynamic of storytelling that is not only modern but modernizing: instead of merely reflecting history in narratives, it makes narrative history. Popular series are a currency of culture.

Understanding seriality as a principle that creates its own conditions of possibility—as an evolutionary process rather than a narrative device—helps us to make sense of numerous features of serial storytelling we would otherwise regard as epiphenomena, such as the high degree of self-reflection that is typical of serial formats. But auto-referentiality is not a gratuitous extra that can or cannot be affixed to serial texts. Interacting as commodities, popular series have a vital interest in monitoring their own development. Their recursive and competitive operations force them to pay constant attention to their own evolution as narrative forms and cultural forces. Consequently, commercial series offer one of the most compelling occasions to observe how popular culture observes itself.[30]

In conclusion (as far as the topic allows) I suggest that we not only ask how a given serial text reflects the cultural situation and intentional structures of its time but also what work it performs in enabling its own cultural realities and intentional follow-ups. I suggest we ask how a serial text *makes* popular culture: how it deploys multiple inter-actors both human and objective, both personal and aesthetic, to situate itself actively as a dependent but novel part within an ongoing set of narratives. Each serial text develops a previous text's openness for continuation into something concrete, if another suspended solution, while it suggests further continuations and remakes. It is in this sense that the cultural work of popular seriality knows no end, no conclusion. Once set in motion, it seems, these stories can always be continued, retold, revived. Perhaps they will only disappear when the culture they make disappears.

And so it goes, also with Oz: a scenario already familiar when it was first published in 1900 becomes a lucrative "storytelling engine" (Chabon 47) and a multi-auctorial shaping force of American culture. Are we surprised to learn that one of the earliest astronomical projects looking for extraterrestrial life was called Project Ozma (see Vidal 1096)? Or consider the invasion of other stories, Oz spilling over into distant narratives and looking strangely familiar there: John Boorman's dystopian movie *Zardoz* from 1974, starring Sean Connery, paints a totalitarian society founded on an esoteric reading of Baum's *The Wonderful Wizard of Oz*; David Lynch's *Wild at Heart* from 1990 features Glinda as goddess ex machina, together with numerous visual allusions to the MGM film; in the 1990s, a rumor circulated on the internet that Pink Floyd's 1973 album *The Dark Side of the Moon* is perfectly synchronized with MGM's *Wizard of Oz*, which prompted Turner Classic Movies to broadcast both works superimposed on each other as *The Dark Side of the Rainbow* in 2000; Alan Moore and Melinda Gebbie's graphic novel *Lost Girls* (1991–2006) devotes one of its parts to Dorothy's sex life; the HBO series *Oz* (1997–2003) tells about the brutal conditions in a high security prison, ironically calling on names and places from the Oz novels and films.

This is popular culture, often in its specific manifestation as American popular culture. And despite our justified qualms about American exceptionalism, it remains interesting to ask why so many of these texts actually reach us as "American" texts. Apparently, the function of mass-addressed commercial art in the United States is still a little different from its operations elsewhere, entangled histories and worldwide webs of communication notwithstanding. Apparently, the American *type* of culture—geographically extensive, socially incongruous, historically improbable, and inevitably multicultural—has a special need for serial media artifacts to get and keep a sense of its own coherence. Looking at this unlikely culture, perhaps we can say America would not even *be* a culture without its popular culture, meaning: without a self-perpetuating system of narrative trust created and insistently reproduced by serial narratives. Within the chaotic echo-chamber of self-references that is American popular culture, each remake not only introduces a change but also has a stabilizing function, as each new variation reinforces the entire system of cultural self-generation and furthers the culture's belief in its own existence and continuity. Many more Oz remakes and adaptations could be named by way of example, but ultimately Oz itself is more than just an example: it is an agent of cultural subsistence and renewal, an active network of variable iterations that make and remake American culture.

Notes

For suggestions and critique, I wish to thank Christy Hosefelder, Andreas Jahn-Sudmann, Alexander Starre, and Daniel Stein.

1. Baum's reliance on folklore and myth has been discussed in numerous publications; for a recent reading, see Tuerk.
2. At this point, I use the term "remake" in a literal sense, denoting the time-delayed retelling of a narrative within the same medium. In the following, a more restricted understanding of the term (referring to films that use the plot, character constellation, and often title of an earlier film as resource material for narrative modernizations and revisions) will be related to the overarching logic of popular seriality.
3. Like Early, I will use the term "America" in a non-normative manner, i.e. in accordance with effective self- and hetero-descriptions of United States culture (see Kelleter, "Transnationalism").
4. On the White City, see Badger; Böger; Burg; Harris et al; Hollweg; Larson; Muccigrosso. For its influence on Baum, see Hearn 176; Schwartz 212–27. The term "humbug"—reminiscent of P. T. Barnum, the self-proclaimed Prince of Humbugs—is used by the Wizard to describe himself. Famously, Thomas A. Edison, often dubbed the Wizard of Menlo Park, illuminated the White City with electric light (on these and other sources, see Hearn 261–62; Schwartz 82–92).
5. The historical context is important to distinguish Baum's search for an American fairy tale from earlier attempts such as Washington Irving's transposition of European folklore into American landscapes or Nathaniel Hawthorne's metaphysical reinterpretation of local legends (see Hearn xlix). As Hearn points out, Baum's understanding of what constitutes American literature was strongly influenced by discussions of this topic at the 1893 Columbian Exposition, in particular Hamlin Garland's "Literary Emancipation of the West."
6. The standard discussion of pragmatism in these terms is Menand. On Dewey and Baum, see Zipes, "Explanatory Notes" 359.
7. See Vidal on the novel's opening sentences as "the plain American style at its best" (1105).
8. See Snow: "It is interesting to note that the first word ever written in the very first Oz book was 'Dorothy.' The last word of the book is 'again'" (59). Some transmedia descendants of Baum's novel are discussed in Durand and Leigh; on adaptations prior to the 1939 movie, see Swartz.
9. Many of the themes discussed in the following have been developed in the six-project Research Unit "Popular Seriality: Aesthetics and Practice" at the University of Göttingen (Germany): see http://popularseriality.uni-goettingen.de. In accordance with this research group, I use the adjective "serial" as a general term for all types of commercial seriality, not just for narratives extending story arcs over many episodes, as in

the series/serial distinction common in Anglo-American media studies (see Williams). The present approach—and the set of studies linked to it—assumes that the difference between what television scholars call a "series" and a "serial" is not as clear-cut as often suggested; see Kelleter, "Serial Agencies," "Populärkultur und Kanonisierung." On the relationship between sameness and renewal in serial forms, see Kelleter and Stein, "Great."

10. On the connection between popular culture and American multiculturalism, see Fluck; the classic statement of popular polysemy can be found in Hall, "Encoding."

11. The standard study of the musical is Swartz.

12. On the interaction between Baum and his readers, see Westbrook.

13. Apart from the (unsuccessful) stage play mentioned above, the Woggle-Bug appeared in a series of 27 syndicated Sunday newspaper comic pages, "Queer Visitors from the Marvelous Land of Oz" (1904–5), written by Baum with Walt MacDougall and followed by Baum's *The Woggle-Bug Book* (1905).

14. For biographies of Baum, see Baum and MacFall; Rogers; Schwartz.

15. See Hearn, "Introduction": "Because of the onset of World War I and changing conditions at home, the later titles did not sell as well as the earlier ones. Reilly & Britton suspected that the decrease was due largely to the flood of cheap Baum books now on the market. ... Baum in effect was competing with himself" (lxxiii–lxxv).

16. On Ruth Plumly Thompson, see Gardner 40. Frank Joslyn Baum's publication of *The Laughing Dragon of Oz* in 1934 was followed by a lawsuit between Frank and the publishing house Reilly & Lee which represented the interests of Frank's mother Maud. The case was decided in favor of Maud Baum (see Hearn, "Introduction" lxxxvi–lxxxvii).

17. The best introduction to the film is still Fricke et al.; also see Rushdie.

18. On the influence of readers' letters on *Mystères de Paris*, see Thiesse. On the relation of serial authorship and serial readership, see the project "Authorization Practices of Serial Narration: The Generic Development of Batman and Spider-Man-Comics," directed by Daniel Stein and myself as part of the Research Unit "Popular Seriality" (n.9 above).

19. The feminist aspects of *The Wonderful Wizard of Oz* and Matilda Gage's influence in this regard are stressed by Lurie.

20. On Oz as a utopia, see Sackett; Wagenknecht. For a critique of utopian readings, see Vidal 1103.

21. On feudalism in Oz, see Bewley (261) and Vidal about Oz's "minuscule countries ... governed by hereditary lords" without "parliaments or congresses" (1103). Examples of progressivist interpretations are Littlefield; Ritter; Rockoff; Zipes, "Introduction." For a survey, see Dighe; Parker.

22. On Baum's career in shop window dressing, see Schwartz 128–50. For (anti-) capitalist interpretations, see Culver; Leach.

23. What both positions also have in common and what organizes their disagreement is the underlying assumption that the commercial dimension of popular storytelling exists in opposition to its praxeological openness. My decision to include scholarly readings among the cultural activities of a series (in other words, to treat interpretations as serial effects) is discussed in more detail in Kelleter, "Serial." It is indebted to the description of Actor-Network-Theory in Latour.

24. The official sequel to the MGM production is *Journey Back to Oz* (1971), an animated movie produced by Filmation.
25. On Jackson's work, see Hayles.
26. For an (openly involved) perspective on canon formation in the Oz universe, see Durand.
27. On the term "acafan" (academic fan), see Hills.
28. For the term "participatory culture," committed less to Marxist preconceptions and more to democratic ideologies, see Jenkins. For an approach that seeks to make the intuitions of the participatory paradigm fruitful without perpetuating its populism, Kelleter and Stein, "Autorisierungspraktiken."
29. On the interplay of seriality, mediation, and popular narration, see the project "Serial Figures and Media Change," directed by Shane Denson and Ruth Mayer as part of the Research Unit "Popular Seriality" (n.9). The term "remediation" is borrowed from Bolter and Grusin.
30. In this context, it is particularly promising to investigate the logic of serial contest, which is perhaps best expressed by the tendency of serial narratives to outbid, surpass, or competitively circumvent each other. See the project "The Dynamics of Serial Outbidding *(Überbietung)*: Contemporary American Television and the Concept of Quality TV," directed by Andreas Jahn-Sudmann and myself as part of the Research Unit "Popular Seriality" (n.9).

Works consulted

Badger, R. Reid. *The Great American Fair: The World's Columbian Exposition and American Culture.* Chicago: Nelson-Hall, 1979. Print.

Baum, Frank Joslyn, and Russell P. MacFall. *To Please a Child: A Biography of L. Frank Baum, Royal Historian of Oz.* Chicago: Reilly & Lee, 1961. Print.

Baum, L. Frank. *The Wonderful Wizard of Oz.* Annotated Centennial Edition. Ed. Michael Patrick Hearn. New York: Norton, 2000. Print.

——. *The Marvelous Land of Oz.* New York: Books of Wonder/Harper Collins, 1985. Print.

Bewley, Marius. *Masks and Mirrors: Essays in Criticism.* New York: Atheneum, 1970. Print.

Böger, Astrid. "(Re)Visions of Progress: Chicago's World Fairs as Sites of Transnational American Memory." *Transnational American Memories.* Ed. Udo Hebel. Berlin: de Gruyter, 2009. 311–31. Print.

Bolter, Jay David, and Richard Grusin. *Remediation: Understanding New Media.* Cambridge, MA: MIT Press, 1999. Print.

Bruns, Axel. *Blogs, Wikipedia, Second Life, and Beyond: From Production to Produsage.* New York: Lang, 2008. Print.

Burg, David F. *Chicago's White City of 1893.* Lexington: University of Kentucky Press, 1976. Print.

Chabon, Michael. *Maps and Legends: Reading and Writing along the Borderlands.* San Francisco: McSweeney's, 2008. Print.

Culver, Stuart. "What Manikins Want: *The Wonderful Wizard of Oz* and *The Art of Decorating Dry Goods Windows.*" *Representations* 21 (1988): 97–116. Print.

Dighe, Ranjit S., ed. *The Historian's Wizard of Oz: Reading L. Frank Baum's Classic as a Political and Monetary Allegory.* London: Praeger, 2002. Print.

Durand, Kevin K. "The Emerald Canon: Where the Yellow Brick Road Forks." Durand and Leigh 11–23. Print.

Durand, Kevin K., and Mary K. Leigh, eds. *The Universe of Oz: Essays on Baum's Series and Its Progeny.* Jefferson, NC: McFarland, 2010. Print.

Earle, Neil. *The Wonderful Wizard of Oz in American Popular Culture.* Lewiston: Edwin Mellen, 1993. Print.

Early, Gerald. "1900: L. Frank Baum Publishes a New Type of 'Wonder Tale'." *A New Literary History of America.* Ed. Greil Marcus and Werner Sollors. Cambridge, MA: Harvard University Press, 2010. 455–59. Print.

Fiske, John. *Reading the Popular.* London: Routledge, 1989. Print.

Fluck, Winfried. "California Blue: Amerikanisierung als Selbstamerikanisierung." *Amerika und Deutschland: Ambivalente Begegnungen.* Ed. Frank Kelleter and Wolfgang Knöbl. Göttingen: Wallstein, 2006. 54–72. Print.

Fricke, John, Jay Scarfone, and William Stillman, eds. *The Wizard of Oz: The Official 50th Anniversary Pictorial History.* London: Hodder & Stoughton, 1989. Print.

Frodelius, Blair. *Books of Oz.* Blair Frodelius & Air Gap Firewalls, 2002. Retrieved on 3 June 2011. http://ozproject.egtech.net/.

Gardner, Martin. "The Royal Historian of Oz." Gardner and Nye 19–45. Print.

Gardner, Martin, and Russel B. Nye, eds. *The Wizard of Oz and Who He Was.* East Lansing, MI: Michigan State University Press, 1984. Print.

Hall, Stuart. "Encoding/Decoding." *Culture, Media, Language: Working Papers in Cultural Studies, 1972–1979.* Ed. Stuart Hall, Dorothy Hobson, Andrew Lowe, and Paul Willis. London: Hutchinson, 1980. 128–40. Print.

——. "Notes on Deconstructing 'The Popular'." *People's History and Socialist Theory.* Ed. Raphael Samuel. London: Routledge and Kegan Paul, 1981. 227–40. Print.

Harris, Neil, Wim deWit, James Gilbert, and Robert W. Rydell, eds. *Grand Illusions: Chicago's World Fair of 1893.* Chicago: Chicago Historical Society, 1993. Print.

Hayles, N. Katherine. *My Mother Was a Computer: Digital Subjects and Literary Texts.* Chicago: University of Chicago Press, 2005. Print.

Hearn, Michael Patrick, ed. "Introduction to *The Annotated Wizard of Oz.*" *Centennial Edition: The Annotated Wizard of Oz.* Ed. Michael Patrick Hearn. New York: Norton, 2000. xi–cii. Print.

——. "Annotations." *Centennial Edition: The Annotated Wizard of Oz.* Ed. Michael Patrick Hearn. New York: Norton, 2000. 3–356. Print.

Hills, Matt. *Fan Cultures.* London: Routledge, 2002. Print.

Hollweg, Brenda. *Ausgestellte Welt: Formationsprozesse kultureller Identität in den Texten zur Chicago World's Columbian Exposition (1893).* Heidelberg: Winter, 2001. Print.

Jenkins, Henry. *Textual Poachers: Television Fans and Participatory Culture.* New York: Routledge, 1992. Print.

Kelleter, Frank. "Transnationalism: The American Challenge." *Review of International American Studies (RIAS)* 2.3 (2007): 29–33. Print.

——. "Populärkultur und Kanonisierung: Wie(so) erinnern wir uns an Tony Soprano?" *Wertung und Kanon.* Ed. Matthias Freise and Claudia Stockinger. Heidelberg: Winter, 2010. 55–76. Print.

——. "Serial Agencies: *The Wire* and Its Readers." Unpublished manuscript, partial publication as: "*The Wire* and Its Readers." '*The Wire*': Race, Class, Genre. Ed.

Liam Kennedy and Stephen Shapiro. Ann Arbor: University of Michigan Press, 2012 (forthcoming).

——. and Daniel Stein. "*Great, Mad, New*: Populärkultur, serielle Ästhetik und der amerikanische Zeitungscomic." *Comics: Zur Geschichte und Theorie eines populärkulturellen Mediums*. Ed. Stephan Ditschke, Katerina Kroucheva, and Daniel Stein. Bielefeld: transcript, 2009. 81–117. Print.

——. and Daniel Stein. "Autorisierungspraktiken seriellen Erzählens: Zur Gattungsentwicklung von Superheldencomics." *Populäre Serialität: Narration— Evolution—Distinktion*. Ed. Frank Kelleter. Bielefeld: Transcript, 2012. 259–90. Print.

Landow, George. "What's a Critic to Do? Critical Theory in the Age of Hypertext." *Hyper/Text/Theory*. Ed. George Landow. Baltimore, MA: The Johns Hopkins University Press, 1994. 1–48. Print.

Larson, Erik. *The Devil in the White City: Murder, Magic, and Madness at the Fair that Changed America*. New York: Crown, 2003. Print.

Latour, Bruno. *Reassembling the Social: An Introduction to Actor-Network-Theory*. Oxford: Oxford University Press, 2005. Print.

Leach, William. *Land of Desire: Merchants, Power and the Rise of a New American Culture*. New York: Pantheon, 1993. Print.

Littlefield, Henry. "*The Wizard of Oz*: Parable of Populism." *American Quarterly* 16 (1964): 47–58. Print.

Lurie, Alison. "The Oddness of Oz." *The New York Review of Books* 47.20 (21 December 2000): 16–24. Print.

Mayer, Ruth. "Machinic Fu Manchu: Popular Seriality and the Logic of Spread." *Journal of Narrative Theory* 43 (Fall 2013): forthcoming.

Menand, Louis. *The Metaphysical Club: A Story of Ideas in America*. New York: Farrar, Straus and Giroux, 2001. Print.

Muccigrosso, Robert. *Celebrating the New World: Chicago's Columbian Exposition of 1893*. Chicago: Ivan R. Dee, 1993. Print.

Parker, David B. "The Rise and Fall of *The Wonderful Wizard of Oz* as 'Parable on Populism'." *Journal of the Georgia Association of Historians* 15 (1994): 49–63. Print.

Return to Oz. Dir. Walter Murch. Perf. Fairuza Balk, Nicol Williamson, and Jean Marsh. Walt Disney/Buena Vista, 1985. DVD.

Riley, Michael O. *Oz and Beyond: The Fantasy World of L. Frank Baum*. Lawrence: University Press of Kansas, 1997. Print.

Ritter, Gretchen. *Goldbugs and Greenbacks: The Anti-Monopoly Tradition and the Politics of Finance in America*. New York: Cambridge University Press, 1997. Print.

——. "Silver Slippers and a Golden Cap: L. Frank Baum's *The Wonderful Wizard of Oz* and Historical Memory in American Politics." *Journal of American Studies* 31 (1997): 171–202. Print.

Rockoff, Hugh. "The 'Wizard of Oz' as a Monetary Allegory." *Journal of Political Economy* 41 (1990): 739–59. Print.

Rogers, Katharine M. *L. Frank Baum, the Royal Historian of Oz: A Biography*. New York: St Martin's Press, 2002. Print.

Rushdie, Salman. *The Wizard of Oz*. London: British Film Institute, 1992. Print.

Sackett, S. J. "The Utopia of Oz." *The Georgia Review* 14 (1960): 275–90. Print.

Schwartz, Evan I. *Finding Oz: How L. Frank Baum Discovered the Great American Story*. Boston, MA: Houghton Mifflin Harcourt, 2009. Print.

Snow, Jack. *Who's Who in Oz.* Chicago: Reilly & Lee, 1954. Print.

Swartz, Mark Evan. *Oz Before the Rainbow: L. Frank Baum's* The Wonderful Wizard of Oz *on Stage and Screen to 1939.* Baltimore, MA: The Johns Hopkins University Press, 2002. Print.

The Wiz. Dir. Sidney Lumet. Perf. Diana Ross, Michael Jackson, and Nipsey Russell. Motown/Universal, 1978. DVD.

The Wizard of Oz. Dir. Victor Fleming. Perf. Judy Garland, Frank Morgan, and Ray Bolger. MGM/Warner Bros., 1939. DVD.

Thiesse, Anne-Marie. "L'éducation sociale d'un romancier: Le cas d'Eugène Sue." *Actes de la recherche en sciences social* 32–33 (1980): 51–63. Print.

Tuerk, Richard. *Oz in Perspective: Magic and Myth in the L. Frank Baum Books.* Jefferson, NC: McFarland, 2007. Print.

Vidal, Gore. "The Oz Books." 1977. *United States: Essays 1952–1992.* New York: Broadway, 1993. 1094–119. Print.

Wagenknecht, Edward. *Utopia Americana.* Seattle: University of Washington Book Store, 1929. Print.

Westbrook, M. David. "Readers of Oz: Young and Old, Old and New Historicist." *Children's Literature Association Quarterly* 21 (1996): 111–19. Print.

Williams, Raymond. *Television: Technology and Cultural Form.* London: Fontana, 1974. Print.

Wladimirski, Leonid, and Hans-Eberhard Ernst. *Überall ist Zauberland: Die Märchenreihe von A–Z.* Leipzig: LeiV, 1998. Print.

Zipes, Jack. "Introduction." *The Wonderful World of Oz.* Ed. Jack Zipes. Harmondsworth: Penguin, 1998. ix–xxix. Print.

——. "Explanatory Notes." *The Wonderful World of Oz.* Ed. Jack Zipes. Harmondsworth: Penguin, 1998. 359–89. Print.

2
Guy Ritchie's Sherlock Bond, the Deerstalker and Remediation

Stephanie Sommerfeld

In the featurette "Sherlock Holmes: Reinvented" on the 2009 Blu-ray disc of *Sherlock Holmes*, director Guy Ritchie and producer Lionel Wigram are intent on selling their version of the odd couple of 221B Baker Street as both the most original and most authentic Holmes and Watson to date. The film crew repeatedly stress how markedly their Sherlock Holmes diverges from what Joel Silver calls "the dusty old chestnut" all too familiar from previous productions, and they keep reminding the audience that this movie is fresh, dynamic, and modern. In the additional bonus material, Guy Ritchie informs us that his Holmes is much more "streetwise" than the "lofty toff" he used to be ("Not a Deerstalker Cap in Sight"). In short, Ritchie's[1] Sherlock Holmes is presented as a hero of modernity, much like the James Bond of the 1960s whom Tony Bennett and Janet Woollacott describe as "a cultural marker of the claim that Britain had escaped the blinkered, class-bound perspectives of its traditional ruling elites and was in the process of being thoroughly modernized" (34–35). Although Ritchie creates a Holmes whose shabby chic and readiness for physical combat indeed knock him off his pseudo-aristocratic high horse, I am less interested in how the movie or the discourse surrounding it reflect and define Englishness than in considering this rhetoric of innovation as part of the movie's self-conscious investigation of its mediality.

Much more than in previous Holmes television or movie productions, media technologies take center stage in Ritchie's *Sherlock Holmes*. With oedipal insistence, this action movie is set apart from earlier productions involving Holmes,[2] and self-reflexively[3] exhibits the technological achievements of digitally enhanced film while simultaneously staging its indebtedness to traditional media. Surrounding itself with a discourse of nostalgia and faithful adaptation, it thus turns itself into "a complex hybrid of the high-tech and the traditional" (Morley 216). Much like a netbook camouflaged as a mechanical typewriter with the help of a plastic skin, *Sherlock Holmes* embodies a media nostalgia particularly attractive to a relatively young high-tech-wise audience[4] and presents its technological advancements in the guise of familiar media.

Against the backdrop of the promotional discourse surrounding the movie, I will read the film's negotiation of media nostalgia and innovation as an illustration of the fact that, in spite of the utopian and dystopian rhetoric recurring at "moments of cultural and technological transition" (Thorburn and Jenkins 1), new technologies do not simply replace their predecessors but trigger complex processes of co-existence, competition, collaboration, and hybridity that potentially restructure media relations (cf. Thorburn and Jenkins 2–3). To explore the ways in which *Sherlock Holmes* self-consciously explores its status as a digitally improved action film,[5] I will start out by highlighting how the movie's character conception caters to the twin demands of authenticity and innovation and thereby works to infuse the pop cultural genre of digitally embellished action film with the high cultural capital of Doyle's canonical prose.[6]

In the second part of my chapter, I will use Jay David Bolter and Richard Grusin's concept of remediation to show how *Sherlock Holmes* attends to the "contradictory imperatives for immediacy and hypermediacy" (Bolter and Grusin 5). That is, I will investigate how it moves between veiling the act of mediation and making the medium invisible to the viewer on the one hand and foregrounding the presence of the medium and its work of mediation on the other hand. The film's computer-generated imagery, its appropriation and refashioning (that is, remediation) of television and paper, and its aesthetics of "Holmes-o-vision" all negotiate the relationship between immediacy and hypermediacy, self-reflexively mirror seriality,[7] and play an important part in the aforementioned strategy of simultaneous authentication and medial self-monitoring.

The series character itself is but the movie's most obvious site of remediation and, consequently, media competition. Series characters that undergo transmedial proliferation lend themselves to medial self-scrutinizing as they offer a straightforward backdrop against which the respective medium's capacity of facing the challenge of simultaneous innovation and repetition can be measured. Each medium that remakes and remodels such a popular series character has to face up to its iconic status and has to come to terms with trademark accessories and features. The film crew working on the 2009 *Sherlock Holmes* put great emphasis on the benefits of reducing these particular ornaments. The film's avoidance of the iconic Holmes costume is one of its most obvious claims to both innovative power and authenticity. The mere title of another featurette on the Blu-ray disc, "Not a Deerstalker Cap in Sight," illustrates the great liberation that Ritchie and the producers profess to achieve through freeing Holmes from unnecessary décor. Their main strategy of "reinventing an iconic English figure" (Ritchie, "Sherlock Holmes: Reinvented") and "weed[ing] out all that old fashioned cliché" (Strong) while at the same time guaranteeing its status as a faithful adaptation of Arthur Conan Doyle's prose manifests itself in four major changes to the original formula which are repeatedly mentioned in press interviews with cast and crew and in the bonus material: no deerstalker, no meerschaum, no Watson as a corpulent fool, and no "elementary, my dear Watson." While these were in fact elements added by illustrator Sidney Paget, actor William Gillette, and the first Holmes movies[8] (cf. Leitch, *Film Adaptation* 208–9; Oudin 28–29), it is remarkable how confidently the filmmaker and producers imply that eliminating these ingredients of the Sherlockian cosmos necessarily entails a faithful adaptation of the stories. This resurrection of the fidelity discourse, the classic and by now outdated topos of adaptation studies,[9] bespeaks a strong desire to sacrifice the value of brand recognition, which the hero's pop cultural trademark accessories would secure,[10] in order to cash in on the cultural capital of Doyle's canonical literature.

The strategy of demonstrating innovation through authentication to enhance the popular hero's appeal by tying him more closely to his high cultural legacy and to outdo previous television and film productions further pervades the film's character conception. Ritchie clearly distances his own detective and doctor from those of earlier productions[11] while at once stressing his movie's indebtedness to the literary original. The only impersonation that is openly associated with a specific actor when being attacked is that of Watson in the Nigel Bruce and Basil Rathbone movies. *The New York Times'* Charles McGrath reminds us that:

> the most influential, the one whose Holmes lingers in the mind as an anti-version of Mr Downey's, is Basil Rathbone, who was a movie Holmes from 1939 to 1946, and who imprinted on us such seemingly essential Holmesian traits as the high, brainy forehead; the slick, swept-back hair; the languid, aristocratic bearing; the supercilious putdowns.

Rathbone's physique—together with that of Jeremy Brett of the Granada television series, which was produced by Michael Cox between 1984 and 1994 and followed by five movies—can be equated with the buttoned-up "lofty toff" that Ritchie wants to rid the Holmes canon of. Still, Nigel Bruce is the only actor starring in a previous production who is referred to by name on the Blu-ray and DVD where he functions as the textbook example of Watson's depiction as an ignorant, clumsy clown. Director and producers take pride in having left the Nigel Bruce legacy behind and deny their movie's indebtedness to the Rathbone and Bruce films, although Universal's *Sherlock Holmes and the Voice of Terror* (John Rawlins, 1942) and *Sherlock Holmes and the Secret Weapon* (Roy William Neill, 1943) are important predecessors in that they attempt to make Holmes into something of an action hero. Instead of Bruce's overweight fool, we are presented with a properly dressed and groomed Jude Law who, during the production, acquired the name "Hotson" as we learn from "Sherlock Holmes: Reinvented" (Ritchie). However, as much as the movie makers claim the opposite, the buffoonery is still retained and simply projected onto Inspector Lestrade who thus becomes Ritchie's Nigel Bruce.

In addition to reducing Holmes' trademark features and ridding them-selves of Bruce's influential Watson cliché, Ritchie's second strategy of simultaneously achieving authenticity and displaying the innovative and modernizing impact of his appropriation is to transform Holmes into what *New York Times* critic A. O. Scott calls "a brawling, head-butting, fist-in-the-gut, knee-in-the-groin action hero." Ritchie's *Sherlock Holmes* presents itself as modern by being faithful to the literary original: this is the film's "narrative image" (Ellis 30). This rhetoric continues through the various interviews with the actors, directors, and producers, the pro-motional material, the official website, the trailer, and the dust jacket. The various epitexts conform to the process identified by Constantine Verevis. First, the earlier text—that is, Conan Doyle's prose—is praised and this gesture of appreciation is followed by the illustration of the filters employed in its transfiguration (cf. Verevis 134). As the fusion of Sherlock Holmes with the popular genre of action film most bla-tantly betrays the movie makers' (legitimate) commercial interests, the promotional discourse aims at counterbalancing this genre's popular culture appeal by adorning it with high cultural, "literary" prestige.[12] Applying the strategy that Thomas Leitch calls "selective fidelity" (*Film Adaptation* 231), Ritchie tells the story of Conan Doyle's Sherlock Holmes as the first martial arts hero in Western culture (cf. Ritchie, "Ba-Ritsu: A Tutorial") whose true action hero nature all previous productions have ignored. His Holmes is infused with the hard-boiled traits of the bankable action hero à la Indiana Jones, John McClane, and James Bond.[13] Consequently, 2009's action Holmes is "born for dangerous adventures, bred to take hardship, pain and fearful threats with cold courage, trained till his six senses respond instantly to the menace of a situation" as the 1964 fanzine description of Bond has it (qtd. In Bennett and Woollacott 12) has it. Due to the limited number of martial arts scenes in Doyle's novels and stories, Ritchie's movie has to resort to remaking prototypical action movie scenes, but although the film team presents Holmes as the Ur-action hero, it avoids naming the popular heroes to whom Holmes served as a hypotext[14] and who now become part of his updated identity. Two such texts that prepare the ground for the "Bondification" of Ritchie's Holmes are Barry Levinson's *Young Sherlock Holmes* (1985)[15] and Steven Spielberg's *Indiana Jones and the Temple of Doom* (1984). This is apparent if one compares two scenes revolving around occultist rituals in the latter movies and compares them to the scene in which Lord Blackwood performs a ritual in *Sherlock Holmes*. In both *Indiana Jones and the Temple of Doom* and *Young Sherlock Holmes,* the protagonists are sitting inside giant animal statues while watching the ritual. In both scenes, the villains enter their "stages" in ritualistic costumes, there is diegetic singing[16] as well as an almost constant camera movement, and the protagonists are shown in reaction shots in an elevated position (while their actual point of view is never given). The structural similarities between these scenes and the ritual performed by Lord Blackwood cast doubt upon the film crew's claim that it was merely Conan Doyle's interest in spiritualism that made them incorporate occultist practices in a temple (Wigram, "Powers of Observation & Deduction"). In the Blackwood scene, we again have an almost constant camera movement, except when the villain is shown and the female victim is forcibly tied to the altar, which also mirrors *Indiana Jones and the Temple of Doom* where the ritual scene is followed by a sequence where Willie, Indiana's female friend, is supposed to be sacrificed and thus tied to a machine that slowly lowers her towards hot lava.

By simply obliterating or denouncing all cinematic Holmes predecessors in their promotion of the film, Ritchie obscures the fact that especially Levinson's *Young Sherlock Holmes*, which was heavily influenced by the Indiana Jones movies—which, in turn, drew from James Bond (Paramount)—had already paved the way towards a renewed attempt at actionizing Holmes and injecting him with all the qualities of a virile action and adventure hero who has nothing to do with aristocratic haughtiness, provides the audience with quotable lines, and gets physical and dirty in the seedy streets of a computer-animated London. Rather than merely fitting into the Bond scheme, Ritchie's *Sherlock Holmes* thus belongs in the group of action and adventure movie series of the 1980s and early 1990s like *Die Hard* or *Indiana Jones*, which have recently witnessed their latest sequels.[17] Instead of acknowledging this legacy or stressing the fact that the literary original "is only one element of the film's intertextuality" (McFarlane 27), the film's cast and crew insist on presenting their film as what Leitch calls a "readaptation of a well-known literary work whose earlier cinematic adaptations [it] ignores or treats as inconsequential" ("Twice-Told Tales" 45). As such, its goal is "fidelity (however defined) to the original text, which it undertakes to translate as scrupulously as possible (presumably more scrupulously than earlier versions) into the film medium" (45). Using the fidelity argument thus helps Ritchie and his crew to endow an action movie with a remarkable claim to high cultural credibility and prestige. The success of this measure can be judged by the degree to which press coverage, reviews, blogs, and fan forum comments echo this marketing strategy.

Blending the popular hero's mass appeal with that of the action genre also prepares the ground for the film's conspicuous remediation. As action movies have a reputation of being audiovisual spectacles to be enjoyed at least as much for their special effects and sensory appeal as for the stories they tell, they offer a fertile ground for medial self-monitoring. In its use of computer-generated imagery (CGI) both in action scenes and in the recreation of Victorian London, the film conspicuously displays its technological potential. At first glance, the main aim and effect of CGI in both of these cases is immediacy, as technological innovation and a big budget enable digital graphics which render action scenes and Holmes' London realistic and credible. As in the case of their Holmes, who openly displays his physicality, Ritchie's team claim that rendering London more physical contributes to the fidelity of the adaptation (cf. Wigram; Law, "Future Past"). However, it is not only the look behind the scenes in the bonus material that stresses the mediality of the action scenes and creates awareness for the remarkable efficiency of computer graphics. The panoramic images of Victorian London that are highlighted by the majestic Hans Zimmer soundtrack present themselves as visual spectacles that invite the audience to immerse itself at least as much in the digital images as in the storyline and to appreciate the computer graphics' finesse and detail. These scenes invite the viewer to get absorbed in "a celebration of graphic technology" (Bolter and Grusin 153) and to enjoy "the oscillations between immediacy and hypermediacy produced by the special effects" (157). In other words, they make the audience waver between media transparency, "the feeling that the medium has disappeared" (70), and media opacity, the experience "in and of the presence of media" (71). As in the early film that Tom Gunning describes as a "cinema of attractions," the emphasis is not on narrative but on having the audience experience "the marvel of realistic moving images," and making it become "conscious of its desire for immediacy" (Bolter and Grusin 155) and of digital cinema's potential of creating it.

When *Sherlock Holmes* thus foregrounds its capacity to create immediacy and hypermediacy at the same time, it also explores its own distinctive features as a digital film that can be watched on Blu-ray players and high definition television. In the advertisement for the Blu-ray combo pack, the voice-over tries to attract potential buyers by announcing the following: "Rebellious—Dangerous—Reckless. Witness the crime in such detail on Blu-ray it's shocking. Unleash the power of your HDTV and see what you've been missing. You'll get so close to the action it will leave you breathless." The shock and awe rhetoric that this ad employs betrays the imprint of how the rhetoric of sublimity still informs the discourse about new technologies today[18] and highlights that the digital action film seeks to specify its own idiosyncrasies. It thus exemplifies that "a deep and even consuming self-consciousness is often a central aspect of emerging media themselves. Aware of their novelty, they engage in a process of self-discovery that seeks to define and foreground the apparently unique attributes that distinguish them from existing media forms" (Thorburn and Jenkins 4). Although the digitally enhanced action film itself is certainly no newly emerging medium in 2009, Ritchie's film is prompted to inspect its own mediality because it is the first digital action film to confront a series character inscribed in the contemporary collective memory not least for its early cinematic and televisual manifestations.

As indicated earlier, the film's self-monitoring in the promotional discourse is characterized by an odd anxiety of influence when it comes to its film or television precursors whose deerstalkers, aristocratic implications, and clumsy clowns have to be eliminated. In addition to struggling with the Bruce/Rathbone legacy, *Sherlock Holmes* tries to come to terms with the aforementioned Granada television series. The fact that the Granada series is an important hypotext to Ritchie's film becomes evident if one compares the opening credits of the television series with the beginning of the new Holmes movie. Both show the "Baker Street" sign, track a carriage, have extradiegetic music as well as ambient sound and they both exhibit a slight yellowish color dominance. In both cases, the camera, in a dolly shot, moves down and follows a carriage by tracking backward and slightly panning to the left at the same time. This shot overtly quotes the television series' opening credits and reveals that we are by no means dealing with a readaptation that completely ignores its cinematic precursors. In fact, Ritchie's film even revives Granada's Holmes as impersonated by Jeremy Brett who, together with Rathbone, is most certainly the second "dusty old chestnut" Ritchie is trying to get rid of. Unsurprisingly, Nigel Bruce is not alone in making his way back into this alleged readaptation of Conan Doyle's stories, in spite of the fact that the original stories are the only material that is credited at the end of the film.

Jeremy Brett's Holmes impersonation manifests itself in the guise of Lord Blackwood, the villain of aristocratic descent. Downey's Holmes is constructed in opposition to this pseudo-occultist "nazi-ish" character[19] (cf. Beavan; Ostwald) and looks like a rough and ready Indiana Jones fighting against organized fascists in *Raiders of the Lost Ark* (1981) or *Indiana Jones and the Last Crusade* (1989). On the diegetic level, this opposition reenacts the struggle insinuated by the epitextual[20] discourse about Ritchie's rebellion against outdated Holmes models. What the movie is doing by turning the villain Blackwood, whose appearance is always accompanied by that of a Poeesque raven, into a Jeremy Brett character, is to enact the oedipal revolt of a physically fit, disheveled, cool youngster Holmes against the evil but groomed gentleman of the past. Just like Blackwood who is hanged but, having been prematurely buried in Poeesque fashion, resurrects himself from the grave, the Rathbone/Brett-Holmes gets a show killing by being pushed into the supporting role of the villain while at the same time satisfying audience expectations by providing the "lofty toff" that Downey is not allowed to be. These references to previous Holmes productions are part of the movie's high degree of intertextuality, whose decoding obviously relies on the skills of a media-literate audience. More importantly, they also bespeak the film's attempt of coming to terms with its own mediality by negotiating it against the backdrop of television aesthetics. The critically acclaimed Granada series offers a suitable object of comparison and competition, as it offers the cultural prestige and the highly praised fidelity that Ritchie strives for.[21]

In spite of its simultaneous emphasis on its idiosyncratic features, *Sherlock Holmes* as digital action film can thus be located on the second level of medial evolution that Lorenz Engell describes: as the unacknowledged remake of Granada's opening credits illustrates, *Sherlock Holmes* imitates older, established media, aims at acquiring their cultural prestige, and tries to present a technologically enhanced continuation of what these older media have achieved (cf. 50). With this remade sequence, the film demonstrates that, in spite of its leaning towards hypermediacy, a digitally enhanced, postmodernist movie "for a whole new generation" (*Sherlock Holmes* Blu-ray Combo Pack) can achieve the same kind of immediacy that television could produce at the climax of its medial evolution career as the "window on the world"[22]—if only for a short sequence.

This short remake of the Granada series also quotes the look of the so-called British heritage television productions, or, more specifically, of "relatively faithful adaptations of classic, mostly nineteenth-century works of literature" (Cardwell 181) which were very much in demand until the mid-1990s (cf. 283) and gained particular prominence because they were often advertised as adaptations and seemed to share a common "look" (cf. 181). As Christophe Gelly illustrates, Granada's Holmes series, with its attention to historical accuracy, certainly exhibits these "heritage" aesthetics (cf. 160–61). Through its effort to reconstruct Holmes' Victorian reality as faithfully as possible, the series provides "comfortable images of a literary past [which] often represent a therapeutic nostalgia for 'traditional' national values, while at the same time marketing those values to foreign audiences as a self-contained, stable, and unified vision of another culture" (Corrigan 36).

Ritchie's team thus appropriates these television adaptations' nostalgic value and, by doing so, adds another dimension to the consolation that its own format as part of a series offers (cf. Eco 168; Hickethier 402). Even before the sequel *Sherlock Holmes: A Game of Shadows* was announced for December 2011, Ritchie's first movie left no doubt that the case of Sherlock Holmes is not closed. The film starts with the provisional solution of a case which, however, is already part of the new one—a fact that Susan Vahabzadeh traces back to the Bond patterns that the film rehashes—and it ends with the revelation that the current case was nothing but a deliberate diversion designed to cover up the next and, of course, even more momentous case revolving around Moriarty. If we apply Umberto Eco's terminology, the sequel will be a retake that "recycles the characters of a previous successful story in order to exploit them, by telling what has happened to them after the end of their first adventure" (167) and offers the reassuring force of serial reiteration.

In addition to fortifying the consoling effect of their product by offering the nostalgic fiction of a comfortable, stable, and readily accessible past, Ritchie's remaking of Granada's series also allows him to heighten the status of his own movie by summoning the prejudices against this kind of television adaptation: that is, the common idea that such adaptations reflect "television's tendency towards conservative, staid, and unimaginative programming in contrast with cinema's more vibrant, eclectic, and innovative offerings" (Cardwell 182). By imitating television's capacity to create the impression of media transparency and providing the nostalgic gaze of the 1980–90s British heritage television series, digital action film thus mimics and rivals television, and makes its presence felt to negotiate its own medial features, advantages, and desiderata. In this act of remediation, it also pays homage to television's special relationship with domesticity and its particular compatibility with seriality (cf. Cardwell 186–87). Both of these television-specific features are also reflected in how the Holmes-Watson relationship in *Sherlock Holmes* is infused with the character constellation of Neil Simon's *The Odd Couple* (1968). In spite of the fact that, in accordance with Ritchie's hard-boiling of his characters for the action genre, Watson is presented as a tough soldier, a gambler, and virile ladies' man, he frequently functions as Sherlock's Felix Ungar. This is mostly due to the fact that Holmes is depicted as a disheveled man in a patchwork rug whose room is a mess and who needs to be reminded to wash himself. Like Felix's Oscar, Sherlock is constructed as the alpha dog and draws part of his eccentricity and coolness from his refusal to care about domestic duties or hygiene. Injecting Holmes and Watson with the social dynamics of Felix and Oscar thus not only allows Ritchie to retain television's "emphasis on writing high-quality dialogue" (Cardwell 194) but also pushes the question of domesticity into the limelight[23] and simultaneously provides and rebuffs the domestic intimacy that television serials offer. As the movie's remediation of television illustrates, "self-reflexivity and imitation are contrasting aspects of the same process by which the new medium maps its emergent properties and defines a space for itself in relation to its ancestors" (Thorburn and Jenkins 10).

Another ancestral medium that features prominently in Ritchie's film is paper. In the Granada series, the audience is frequently invited to witness how Watson transforms his experiences with Holmes (cf. Gelly 163–64) into writing, and another close tie with the medium is established when Jeremy Brett and his Watson reenact Sidney Paget's illustrations (cf. Gelly 161). In a Sherlockian essay,[24] Kate K. Redmond praises this appropriation:

> Holmes and Watson become a *tableau vivant* in the railway carriage, as they assume the famous and favorite Paget illustration pose. There are many such other stagings, but none quite so striking. Slowly but

surely the Granada series is building up a visual archive of Canonical [sic] images that are faithful representations of the original tales. (79)

Redmond's hope for a completely faithful representation of the literary original through a faithful enactment of Paget's illustrations (which, of course, are only translations and interpretations themselves) bespeaks the Sherlockian longing for a uniform collective vision of Doyle's texts, a desire to counteract the fact that "every reading of a literary text is a highly individual act of cognition and interpretation" (McFarlane 15). Much like selling Ritchie's Holmes as a most faithful readaptation of Conan Doyle's prose, Redmond's praise of Granada's fidelity illustrates the wish to access the essential meaning of an original text and the true nature of the popular hero Sherlock Holmes, who has a striking tendency to be treated as a real person.[25] Granada's animated illustrations thus cater to the nostalgic fantasy of stability and accountability that characterizes the Sherlockian fan community, whose insistence on the sovereignty of the original paper version is a way of counteracting the sprawling nature of Holmes as a series character. The same goal of authentication is achieved by Granada's remediation of photography through the transformation of single shots into sepia-tinted photographic images in the opening titles, by the use of Paget's illustrations as the backdrop for the end credits in most episodes of *The Adventures of Sherlock Holmes*, and the transformation of the last shot of Moriarty's head into an apparently hand-drawn, non-Pagetian illustration for the end credits of "The Red-Headed League." Ritchie emulates this strategy and strives to profit from the prestigious literary original by staging the nostalgic value of the paper medium itself, as especially the main titles and the end credits reveal.

The main titles comprise a fast ride through different media: a photographer intends to capture Lestrade, Holmes, and Watson for a newspaper announcing Scotland Yard's latest success. The last reverse shot of the group is transformed into a photograph which then transfigures into the front page of *The Penny Illustrated Paper* whose headline is subsequently isolated and blown up to constitute the movie's title. The latter is shown in the kind of flickering reminiscent of old movies and, after another flashlight sound that reminds the viewer of the diegetic photographer, cuts to the "Baker Street" sign, which is first presented in the same hue as the paper, and is then desaturated before it sets off the Granada sequence. This ride through media history illustrates that "remediation is a defining characteristic of the new digital media" (Bolter and Grusin 45) as the older media photography, print, early film, and television are at once absorbed and conspicuously exhibited. The showcasing of the visual and acoustic materiality of paper continues in the first part of the end credits, where the last shot of Robert Downey Jr. is transformed into an unfinished hand-made illustration on stained paper with hardly decipherable handwriting and ink sprayed on it. The same procedure is applied to the shot previously used for the main titles, which presents the first end credit in legible handwriting and is accompanied by the sound of paper being crumpled or at least shuffled. Subsequently, ten shots are treated equally and are followed by close-ups of the handwritten title "Sherlock Holmes," which create the impression that we are witnessing how the words are being written. This is again followed by 15 shots that, like their predecessors, are less saturated than in the film itself, and whose last frames turn into paper illustrations animated by ink stains, which sometimes function as stand-ins for blood, red wine, or gunpowder. Especially the artwork crediting the executive producers renders evident that the soiled paper is supposed to be read as being part of a book. Before the paper is wiped off screen and is followed by the rolling titles, we are thus confronted with a self-conscious act of mediation that foregrounds the materiality of writing, drawing, and the production processes associated with the medium of paper.[26] The original medium of the literary model is taken up in this act of hypermediacy and is literally absorbed by the digital action film. The rugged, "used" look of the untidy paper (which parallels Holmes' vintage look) accentuates its analogue character and allows the film to counterbalance the potentially sterile look of "perfect" CGI. Main and end titles exemplify that older media's "original functions are adapted and absorbed by newer media, and [that] they themselves may mutate into new cultural niches and new purposes" (Thorburn and Jenkins 12). By equipping itself with the "human touch" of analogue predecessors, which are nostalgically associated with a past that produced the literary original allegedly readapted by the film, digital action film adorns itself with the aura of an authentic, hand-crafted product.[27] Like a car made to look like a horse-drawn buggy (cf. Thorburn and Jenkins 7), it carries its ancestral media with it; and like the aforementioned netbook disguised as a typewriter, it strives to downplay its technological innovation, following the "drive to make the techno-future safe, by incorporating it into familiar formats, icons, symbols" (Morley 212).

An emblem for how *Sherlock Holmes* thus inscribes itself into the material mediality of the nineteenth century can be found in the fusion of the Warner Brothers, Village Roadshow Pictures, and Silver Pictures logos with London's computer-generated fin de siècle cobblestone in the opening sequence. In this case, however, we again witness the oscillation between immediacy and hypermediacy already discussed in the case of the digital recreation of Victorian London. Here, the digital graphics aim at achieving the effect of immediacy by recreating the cobblestone as realistically as possible but the mediality of this potentially transparent image is disrupted by the logos, that is, the self-reflexive exposition of the film's mediality. The same mixture of immediacy and hypermediacy can be discerned in the subsequent camera movement. First, the camera travels forward and simultaneously tilts up while the intradiegetic sound sets in. It then presents the viewer with a static shot of a carriage moving down a London street in which the mediality of the shot becomes invisible. The hypermediacy sets in when the camera openly makes its presence felt in the next tracking shot, which accelerates while following the carriage down the road and only comes to a halt when it meets the barred window of the police carriage. As in early film, the camera is used "to dramatize the shift from still to moving pictures" (Thorburn and Jenkins 4) to foreground the film's mediation.

In the name of hypermediacy and of distancing the film from the transparency of television and cinematic "heritage" productions, the camera even becomes something of a protagonist in what cast and crew affectionately term "Holmes-o-vision" (cf. Lee), that is, Sherlock's way of processing information. While in the Granada series, the Watsonian gaze predominated (cf. Trembley 13), which entailed an external perspective on Holmes' ratiocination, forcing the viewer to read Jeremy Brett's face and physique for signs, Ritchie uses virtual cinematography to turn thought processes into his most defining feature. Thus compensating for the lack of trademark costume accessories, "Holmes-o-vision" offers a means of hypermediacy that reflects on the status of digitally improved film's own status as a medium of enhanced visual and auricular experience.

In the Granada series, the hallucination scene of "The Devil's Foot" has attracted some attention because it interrupts the linear storytelling as well as the series' Watsonian gaze. According to Elizabeth Trembley, the fact that "the camera rolls to disrupt the parallel between the matched horizontal axis of the horizon and of the lens" (22) produces the impression that a hallucination is depicted. As in classic Hollywood style, "the camera is a transparent lens on the world" when the characters are in mental balance, whereas "when something is wrong (when they are drunk or physically or mentally ill), the subjective camera offers a distorted view that makes us aware of the film as medium" (Bolter and Grusin 152).

The harsh transition from the series' predominant medial transparency to marked hypermediacy only underlines television's (and heritage film's) proneness for creating immediacy. Although Ritchie's film also uses this kind of hypermediacy for a hallucination scene (thereby again remaking the Granada series), the fact that "Holmes-o-vision" gets a much smoother introduction into the movie illustrates that digital action film as a genre is characterized by the aforementioned simultaneity of immediacy and hypermediacy.

When Holmes is waiting for Watson and his bride-to-be to join him for dinner at the Royale, he spends his time observing customers and staff members at the restaurant, and "Holmes-o-vision" sets in. The point of view shots that portray his observations minimize the distance between him and the scrutinized parties. When Holmes moves from collecting visual data to processing it in his mind, the camera tracks in on him until we have a close-up of his face with his eyes shut while the sound of his ticking watch is amplified. Whilst his sensory capacities are already shown to be enhanced, the level of detail in the close-ups of his memory is even higher and the images he takes in succeed at an increased speed. "Holmes-o-vision" consequently fulfills at least two purposes: it showcases the particular proneness of digital film to create visual and audio spectacles and it mirrors its own and Holmes' serial status. When Holmes' sensory capacities are applied with a difference (that is, when he closes his eyes), the structural principle of seriality is mimicked. To the same effect, "Holmes-o-vision" is deployed in the boxing match of what blogs and forums have come to call "the *Fight Club* scene": as in the restaurant sequence, Holmes' sensory acuteness is portrayed with the help of close shots. When Holmes recognizes Irene Adler, a voice-over informs the viewer that Holmes decides to focus on the fight and the diegetic sound fades out and stops. While Holmes' voice-over continues to announce his next moves, slow motion alternates with normal speed and accelerated motion in the depiction of Holmes' anticipation of the fight. During the extra slow motion we hear the amplified sounds of the calculated actions. In the accelerated sequences the (slightly muted) ambient noise of the cheering crowd sets in. This scene, where internal focalization and auricularization as well as external ocularization predominate,[28] is consequently repeated without the voice-over, the differences in motion, and the associated sounds. Holmes' machine-like ratiocinative abilities are combined with pre-calculated physical moves which are, in turn, mechanistically repeated with slight differences—which literally turns Holmes into a fighting machine (Ostwald) thinking like a computer (Vahabzadeh).

Illustration 2.1   Sherlock Holmes (Robert Downey, Jr.) in what blogs and forums have come to call "the *Fight Club* scene" of Guy Ritchie's *Sherlock Holmes* (2009)

"Holmes-o-vision" imitates the structural principle of seriality in its ever new combinations of a fixed inventory of perceptive possibilities and of the means of their depiction.[29] It visually enacts Norbert Bolz's assessment that digital technology mirrors human modes of perception (cf. 63–64) and, in an act of hypermediacy, highlights the narrative possibilities of digital effects. Furthermore, it illustrates the driving force behind Holmes' seriality: the serial Holmes-machine, which fuels the "storytelling engines" that Michael Chabon (47) describes, will always find a new case where the same deductive steps can be taken and order will finally be established—if only provisionally.

It comes as no surprise that a character conceived in the age of industrialization produces the kind of technological sublimity that Warner Brothers' Blu-ray combo promises: at once unfathomable, uncanny genius who, even in the most "homely" domestic setting, "does not permit [him]self to be read"—to use Poe's phrase from "The Man of the Crowd" (388)—and as an untiring executor of the ever-same deductive patterns that he applies to ever-changing cases, Holmes himself bears the imprint of technological, serial mass-production[30] and carries with him the latter's utopian promises and dystopian nightmares.[31] Like Doyle's stories, which self-consciously examine their own seriality by thematizing productivity, serial behavior, and addiction as Ed Wiltse has shown (cf. 106), "Holmes-o-vision" thus stages the processes of serial narration and it does so by exploring the particular narrative possibilities that virtual cinematography offers. As if to counteract Knut Hickethier's claim that the more cinema becomes the medium of audiovisual spectacles, the less it invites seriality (398), Ritchie uses the most proliferated series character of all times to create a cinematic series that allows digital action film to display its ability to encourage audiovisual immersion by creating moments of media transparency. At the same time, Ritchie's first Holmes movie further contributes to repositioning digitally enhanced film as a medium by striving for authentication through the remediation of its ancestral media and by foregrounding its unique capacity to create moments of hypermediacy that self-consciously examine the defining feature of serial narration: that is, the interplay of repetition and variation.

Notes

1. Whenever I refer to *Sherlock Holmes* and its protagonist as Guy Ritchie's creations, I do so merely for the sake of abbreviation, using the film's director as a synecdoche for the collaboration of the film's cast and crew.
2. The cast and crew are reluctant to identify the various Holmes productions that they feel to be antiquated. The only films that they specifically refer to are the Nigel Bruce and Basil Rathbone movies, released between 1939 and 1946 (Katz 1177). In addition to analyzing the film team's anxiety of influence as displayed in the bonus material, I will shed light on the film's unacknowledged remaking of scenes from the Granada Television Series *Sherlock Holmes* (1984–1994) and Barry Levinson's *Young Sherlock Holmes* (1985).
3. For a specification of the term self-reflexivity cf. Kay Kirchmann who is arguing against the simplistic equation of any kind of cinematic self-reflexivity with cinematic modernism.
4. For different examples of this media nostalgia cf. Morley 212–13.
5. While Ritchie's film was shot on both celluloid and digital support (cf. Price), it is ostentatiously promoted as an action film that features remarkable digital special effects, as the plethora of green screens in the bonus material and especially the featurette "Future Past" illustrate. Whenever I talk about "digital action film," I thus do not mean to suggest that the film has been shot with digital cameras only but am highlighting that the promotional material presents the film as an audiovisual spectacle made possible by the use of the latest technology in its production and consumable through the use of advanced digital technology in its reproduction at home.
6. If I am using the Bourdieuian concept of high cultural capital, I do not do so to insist on the border between high and low culture but to convey that the notion of a gap between the two is a prominent driving force behind the film team's strategies of authentication.

7. Martin Priestman suggests that the term *seriality* should be replaced with *seriesicity* to refer to the particular qualities of the series (cf. 50). I will, however, use the broader term *seriality* when analyzing Ritchie's film as part of the Holmes series to denote the interplay of redundancy and variation (cf. Blättler 512) which is at work in all serial artifacts, for example, in both the serial and the series.

8. William Gillette's stage performances of Sherlock Holmes between 1899 and 1932 had a lasting effect on Holmes' iconic accessories (cf. Pohle and Hart 65–68). Frederic Dorr Steele's illustrations for *Collier's* (cf. 67) as well as Holmes' first appearance on the film screen in 1903 (cf. 24) attest to how Gillette's additions of the dressing gown and the curved pipe shaped the detective's public image.

9. On the issue of fidelity in adaptation studies cf. McFarlane and Corrigan.

10. Wiltse shows that Doyle's creation of the Holmes series was founded on "a frank, market-driven pragmatism" that succeeded in turning Sherlock Holmes into "a far more effective 'brand name' than either author or title" (108).

11. Ritchie thus makes the spirit of competition for economic success, cultural impact, and popularity between his and other Holmes versions explicit and participates in what Martin Priestman, referring to Holmes' scornful remarks about the detectives Dupin and Lecoq in *A Study in Scarlet*, calls "the oedipal predecessor-bashing which is one of the ritual pleasures of series detection" (55).

12. Corrigan illustrates how, at the beginning of the twentieth century, the film industry used adaptations of canonical literature to elevate itself to a high cultural branch of the arts (cf. 34). Ritchie follows the same strategy in that he aims at acquiring this kind of (high) cultural capital to balance the obvious commercial promise of action movies designed for serialization.

13. Joel Silver spells out that *Sherlock Holmes* borrows from Bond and describes that "it feels like a 1891 version of a Bond film." Loaded with references to the serial heroes Indiana Jones and John McClane, with which various generations have grown up, Ritchie's Holmes speaks to a large, action-film savvy target audience that would not ordinarily be interested in adaptations of canonical literature.

14. Gérard Genette's term *hypotext* designates any text that functions as the anterior text to another text (called *hypertext*) that "attaches" itself to this hypotext in any other way than by commenting on it (cf. Genette, *Palimpsestes* 11). Through Conan Doyle's stories, novels, stage adaptations, and the first Holmes movies, Sherlock Holmes became a precursor to serial characters such as James Bond and Indiana Jones. In Genettian terms, an Indiana Jones movie, for example, can thus be considered as a hypertext that partly derives from anterior textual elements of the late nineteenth- and earlier twentieth-century Holmes multiverse, which can thus be labeled as hypotexts. The same Indiana Jones movie might then be read as a hypotext to Ritchie's 2009 (hypertext) *Sherlock Holmes*.

15. In "Sherlock Holmes: Reinvented," Ritchie curtly acknowledges that he knows that this movie exists, but he does so only to signal that he discarded his initial idea of portraying a slightly younger Holmes.

16. For a definition of *diegesis* cf. Genette, *Discours du Récit* (237).

17. The latest sequels are *Live Free or Die Hard* (Len Wiseman, 2007) and *Indiana Jones and the Kingdom of the Crystal Skull* (Steven Spielberg, 2008).
18. For discussions of technological sublimity cf. Leo Marx's *The Machine in the Garden*, John Kasson's *Civilizing the Machine* and David E. Nye's *The Technological Sublime*. David Morley (235–72) uses the term (originally coined in Perry Miller's *The Life of the Mind in America*) to investigate the utopian claims made on behalf of the progressive and metaphysical potential of new technologies.
19. On the tradition of imbuing Holmes' antagonist with Nazi features cf. Leitch, *Film Adaptation* 223.
20. For Genette's definition of *epitext* as a paratext located *"anywhere outside of the book"* (or, in our case, outside of the film proper), cf. Genette, *Seuils* 316.
21. Illustrating how television aesthetics are shaped by its ideals and institutions, Cardwell argues that television's goal of public education decisively influenced its leaning towards the "faithful" adaptation of classic literature (cf. 188). This is certainly an important factor in accounting for Granada's acclaimed attempt to stay faithful to the literary original. For how the Granada series' lighting and set decoration create its image of a faithful adaptation, cf. Gelly 160–61. For an example of the critical praise of Granada's fidelity to the original cf. Trembley.
22. Cf. Engell on the medium's third evolutionary phase in which it is taken for granted and in which its mediality becomes invisible (51–52).
23. Of course, domesticity has always been an important ingredient of Doyle's stories, whose interest in domestic seclusion partly derives from Poe's Dupin trilogy.
24. On the use of Sherlockiana in academic criticism cf. Wiltse 119–20. As the interest in fan productions and their role in complicating notions of authorship and authority increases, it becomes obvious that Sherlockian publications are indispensable resources for academic research.
25. Ever since the stories were published in *The Strand*, letters have been sent to 221B Baker Street, on which the resident Sherlock Holmes Museum has bestowed the title of "the world's most famous address" (Riley). On the Sherlockian and pre-Sherlockian inclination to treat Holmes and Watson as real-life persons, cf. Wiltse 109; and Leitch, *Film Adaptation* 211.
26. Originally, the stress on the production processes associated with the medium was supposed to be even more emphatic, as creative director Danny Yount explains in an interview: "We also wanted to show part of the printing process of that time period using the linotype machine and wood block type headline compositions."
27. Danny Yount stresses this "human touch" when he explains that what was needed to create the main and end titles were "[a] lot of human hands, a photocopier, ink footage and a few photoshop filters."
28. For an approach that uses François Jost's terminology to analyze fictional films, cf. Schlickers.
29. This fixed inventory is also singled out and conveniently applicable in the film's accompanying game, "Unlock Your Sherlock: A Modern Mystery Revealed," which can be accesses through Warner Brothers' official movie site for *Sherlock Holmes*.

30. Christine Blättler investigates the relationship between industrial mass-production and seriality in her essay on the aesthetics of seriality (cf. 505).
31. The film's multi-layered and self-conscious investigation of technological innovation is also reflected in its diegetic preoccupation with "magical," potentially world-shaking technological devices and its steampunk aesthetics that infuse the Victorian heritage look with the aura of sci-fi technology.

Works consulted

Beavan, Jenny. "Not a Deerstalker Cap in Sight." *Sherlock Holmes.* Dir. Guy Ritchie. Warner Bros. Entertainment, 2010. Blu-ray.

Bennett, Tony, and Janet Woollacott. *Bond and Beyond: The Political Career of a Popular Hero.* New York: Methuen, 1987. Print.

Blättler, Christine. "Überlegungen zu Serialität als ästhetischem Begriff." *Weimarer Beiträge* 49.3 (2003): 502–16. Print.

Bolter, Jay David, and Richard Grusin. *Remediation: Understanding New Media.* Cambridge, MA: MIT Press, 2000. Print.

Bolz, Norbert. "Die Zukunft der Zeichen: Invasion des Digitalen in die Bilderwelt des Films." Karpf, Kiesel, and Visarius 57–65. Print.

Cardwell, Sarah. "Literature on the Small Screen: Television Adaptations." Cartmell and Whelehan 181–95. Print.

Cartmell, Deborah, and Imelda Whelehan, eds. *The Cambridge Companion to Literature on Screen.* Cambridge: Cambridge University Press, 2007. Print.

Chabon, Michael. "Fan Fictions: On Sherlock Holmes." *Maps and Legends: Reading and Writing along the Borderlands.* San Francisco: McSweeney's, 2008. 35–57. Print.

Corrigan, Timothy. "Literature on Screen, a History: In the Gap." Cartmell and Whelehan 29–43. Print.

Eco, Umberto. "Innovation and Repetition: Between Modern and Post-Modern Aesthetics." *Daedalus* 114.4 (1985): 161–84. Print.

Ellis, John. *Visible Fictions: Cinema, Television, Video.* Rev. ed. London: Routledge, 1992. Print.

Engell, Lorenz. "Die genetische Funktion des Historischen in der Geschichte der Bildmedien." *Archiv für Medienschichte* 1 (2001): 33–56. Print.

Gelly, Christophe. "Adaptation télévisuelle et problématique de l'énonciation: Le cas de la série 'Sherlock Holmes' réalisée pour Granada Television (1984–1994)." *Études britanniques contemporaines* 36 (2009): 159–70. Print.

Genette, Gérard. *Discours du récit: Essai de méthode.* Paris: Seuil, 2007. Print.

——. *Palimpsestes: La littérature au second degré.* Paris: Seuil, 1982. Print.

——. *Seuils.* Paris: Éditions du Seuil, 1987. Print.

Hickethier, Knut. "Serie." *Handbuch Populäre Kultur: Begriffe, Theorien und Diskussionen.* Ed. Hans-Otto Hügel. Stuttgart: Metzler, 2003. 397–403. Print.

Jost, François. "Narration(s): en deçà et au-delà." *Communications* 38 (1983): 192–212. Print.

Karpf, Ernst, Doron Kiesel, and Karsten Visarius, eds. *"Im Spiegelkabinett der Illusionen": Filme über sich selbst.* Marburg: Schüren, 1996. Print.

Kasson, John F. *Civilizing the Machine: Technology and Republican Values in America, 1776–1900*. New York: Grossman, 1976.

Katz, Ephraim. *The Film Encyclopedia*. Rev. by Ronald Dean Nolen. 6th ed. New York: HarperCollins, 2008. Print.

Kirchmann, Kay. "Zwischen Selbstreflexivität und Selbstreferentialität: Überlegungen zur Ästhetik des Selbstbezüglichen als filmischer Modernität." Karpf, Kiesel, and Visarius 67–86. Print.

Law, Jude. "Future Past." *Sherlock Holmes*. Dir. Guy Ritchie. Warner Bros. Entertainment, 2010. Blu-ray.

Lee, Chris. "Enter Holmes-o-vision in 'Sherlock.'" *The Olympian* 31 December 2009. Retrieved on 13 January 2011. www.theolympian.com/2009/12/31/1086540/enter-holmes-o-vision-in-sherlock.html.

Leitch, Thomas. *Film Adaptation and Its Discontents: From* Gone with the Wind *to* The Passion of Christ. Baltimore, MA: Johns Hopkins University Press, 2007. Print.

——. "Twice-Told Tales: Disavowal and the Rhetoric of the Remake." *Dead Ringers: The Remake in Theory and Practice*. Ed. Jennifer Forrest and Leonard R. Koos. Albany, NY: State University of New York Press, 2002. 37–62. Print.

Marx, Leo. *The Machine in the Garden: Technology and the Pastoral Ideal in America*. New York: Oxford University Press, 1964.

McFarlane, Brian. "Reading Film and Literature." Cartmell and Whelehan 15–28. Print.

McGrath, Charles. "Sherlock Holmes, Amorphous Sleuth for Any Era." *New York Times* 5 January 2010. Retrieved on 29 June 2010. www.nytimes.com/2010/01/06/books/06holmes.html.

Morley, David. *Media, Modernity and Technology: The Geography of the New*. New York: Routledge, 2007. Print.

Nye, David E. *American Technological Sublime*. Cambridge, MA: MIT Press, 1994.

Ostwald, Susanne. "CSI: London." *NZZ Online* 20 January. 2010. Retrieved on 29 June 2010. www.nzz.ch/nachrichten/kultur/film/csi_london_1.4665741.html.

Oudin, Bernard. *Enquête sur Sherlock Holmes*. Paris: Gallimard, 2009. Print.

Paramount Pictures. "Making Raiders of the Lost Ark." *Indiana Jones* 23 September 2003. Retrieved on 13 January 2011. http://web.archive.org/web/20031207015023 /www.indianajones.com/raiders/bts/news/news20030923.html.

Poe, Edgar A. "The Man of the Crowd." *Poetry and Tales*. Ed. G. R. Thompson. New York: Library of America, 1984. 388–96. Print.

Pohle, Robert W., Jr., and Douglas C. Hart. *Sherlock Holmes on the Screen: The Motion Picture Adventures of the World's Most Popular Detective*. South Brunswick, NJ: Barnes, 1977. Print.

Price, Stephen. "Shooting with the Sherlock And Slumdog Camera." *HD Magazine* 30 April 2010. Retrieved on 13 January 2012. www.definitionmagazine.com/journal/tag/sherlock-holmes.

Priestman, Martin. "Sherlock's Children: The Birth of the Series." *The Art of Detective Fiction*. Ed. Warren Chernaik, Martin Swales, and Robert Vilain. New York: Palgrave Macmillan, 2000. 50–59. Print.

Redmond, Kate Karlson. "Granada Television's *Adventures of Sherlock Holmes*: I." *The Baker Street Journal: An Irregular Quarterly of Sherlockiana* 35.2 (1985): 75–79. Print.

Riley, Grace, ed. *The Sherlock Holmes Museum*, n.d. Retrieved on 13 January 2011. www.sherlock-holmes.co.uk/.

Ritchie, Guy. "Ba-Ritsu: A Tutorial." *Sherlock Holmes*. Dir. Guy Ritchie. Warner Bros. Entertainment, 2010. Blu-ray.

——. "Not a Deerstalker Cap in Sight." *Sherlock Holmes*. Dir. Guy Ritchie. Warner Bros. Entertainment, 2010. Blu-ray.

——. "Sherlock Holmes: Reinvented." *Sherlock Holmes*. Dir. Guy Ritchie. Warner Bros. Entertainment, 2010. Blu-ray.

Schlickers, Sabine. "Focalization, Ocularization and Auricularization in Film and Literature." *Point of View, Perspective, and Focalization: Modeling Mediation in Narrative*. Ed. Peter Hühn, Wolf Schmid, and Jörg Schönert. Berlin: de Gruyter, 2009. 243–58. Print.

Scott, A. O. "The Brawling Supersleuth of 221B Baker Street Socks It to 'Em." *New York Times* 25 December 2009. Retrieved on 29 June 2010. http://movies. nytimes.com/2009/12/25/movies/25sherlock.html?partner=rss&emc=rss&pa gewanted=print.

Sherlock Holmes. Blu-ray Combo Pack. Advertisement. *The Official Movie Site for Sherlock Holmes*. Warner Bros. Entertainment, 2009. Retrieved on 13 January 2011. http://sherlock-holmes-movie.warnerbros.com/dvd/index.html.

Sherlock Holmes. Dir. Guy Ritchie. Perf. Robert Downey Jr., Jude Law, Rachel McAdams, Mark Strong, and Eddie Marsan. Warner Bros. Entertainment, 2010. Blu-ray.

Sherlock Holmes and the Secret Weapon. Dir. Roy William Neill. Perf. Basil Rathbone, Nigel Bruce, and Lionel Atwill. Universal Pictures, 1943.

Sherlock Holmes and the Voice of Terror. Dir. John Rawlins. Perf. Basil Rathbone, Nigel Bruce, and Evelyn Ankers. Universal Pictures, 1942.

Sherlock Holmes: The Complete Granada Television Series. Prod. Michael Cox. 1984–94. Granada Television, 2007. DVD.

Silver, Joel. "Ba-Ritsu: A Tutorial." *Sherlock Holmes*. Dir. Guy Ritchie. Warner Bros. Entertainment, 2010. Blu-ray.

——. "Sherlock Holmes: Reinvented." *Sherlock Holmes*. Dir. Guy Ritchie. Warner Bros. Entertainment, 2010. Blu-ray.

Strong, Mark. "Sherlock Holmes: Reinvented." *Sherlock Holmes*. Dir. Guy Ritchie. Warner Bros. Entertainment, 2010. Blu-ray.

Thorburn, David and Henry Jenkins. "Introduction: Toward an Aesthetics of Transition." *Rethinking Media Change: The Aesthetics of Transition*. Ed. Thorburn and Jenkins. Cambridge, MA: MIT Press, 2003. 1–16. Print.

Trembley, Elizabeth A. "Holmes Is Where the Heart Is: The Achievement of Granada Television's Sherlock Holmes Films." *It's a Print!: Detective Fiction from Page to Screen*. Ed. William Reynolds and Elizabeth A. Trembley. Bowling Green, KY: Bowling Green State University Popular Press, 1994. 11–30. Print.

Vahabzadeh, Susan. "Darauf wäre Watson nie gekommen." *sueddeutsche.de* 28 January 2010. Retrieved on 29 June 2010. www.sueddeutsche.de/kultur/im-ki no-sherlock-holmes-darauf-waere-watson-nie-gekommen-1.61043.

Verevis, Constantine. *Film Remakes*. Edinburgh: Edinburgh University Press, 2006. Print.

Warner Bros. Entertainment. *Sherlock Holmes*. 2009. Retrieved on 13 January 2011. http://sherlock-holmes-movie.warnerbros.com/dvd/index.html.

Wigram, Lionel. "Future Past." *Sherlock Holmes*. Dir. Guy Ritchie. Warner Bros. Entertainment, 2010. Blu-ray.

——. "Powers of Observation & Deduction." *Sherlock Holmes*. Dir. Guy Ritchie. Warner Bros. Entertainment, 2010. Blu-ray.

Wiltse, Ed. "'So Constant an Expectation': Sherlock Holmes and Seriality." *Narrative* 6.2 (1998): 105–22. Print.

Young Sherlock Holmes. Dir. Barry Levinson. Perf. Nicholas Rowe, Alan Cox, and Sophie Ward. Paramount Pictures, 1985.

Yount, Danny. "A Q&A with Danny Yount of Prologue Films." *The Art of the Title Sequence* 21 January 2010. Retrieved on 13 January 2011. http://www.artofthetitle.com/2010/01/21/sherlock-holmes/.

3
A Battle on Two Fronts: *Wuthering Heights* and Adapting the Adaptation

Amy Martin

> [Holly] "I read that story twice ... It doesn't *mean* anything."
> "Give me an example," I [Fred] said quietly, "Of something that means something. In your opinion."
> "*Wuthering Heights*," she [Holly] said, without hesitation. ...
> [Fred] "But that's unreasonable. You're talking about a work of genius."
> [Holly] "It was wasn't it? *My wild sweet Cathy.* God, I cried buckets. I saw it ten times."
> [Fred] said "Oh" with recognizable relief, "oh" with shameful, rising inflection, "the movie."
>
> —Truman Capote, *Breakfast at Tiffany's* (59)

This discussion from Truman Capote's novella *Breakfast at Tiffany's* (1958) goes some way to showing the nature of the dual legacy of Emily Brontë's *Wuthering Heights* (1847). Fred—educated, a writer—is horrified to think he could be asked to produce something on par with a canonical text of English literature. He is calmed, however, when he realizes that Holly is asking for the *Wuthering Heights she* knows: the model love story of the cinema. Though a memorable image to her, it is not one she is afraid to recommend for repetition; it is not the impenetrable work that "Fred" believes the novel to be. Capote's characters represent the polar views on *Wuthering Heights*: on the one hand, that of popular culture, which has elevated the version of the novel associated with the 1939 adaptation over the novel itself; and on the other, a more academic view that Emily Brontë's 1847 work eludes easy definition and therefore must be considerably altered, and possibly traduced, when it is reworked

67

for the screen. It is a novel that has endured peaks and troughs in criticism in the 150 years since its publication; a novel that has inspired films, plays, music, and comedy; a novel that has been integrated into popular culture so deeply that its title conjures up particular images recognizable by those who have not read the text itself.

The enduring legacy of Brontë's novel as that of a conventional love story, of the romantic hero Heathcliff and the tragic heroine Cathy, is undoubtedly attributable to the 1939 cinematic adaptation.[1] The 1920s saw a silent version, now lost, of *Wuthering Heights* that depicted both generations of characters and was billed: "Emily Brontë's tremendous story of hate" (Stokes). Though this primary attempt to translate the novel to the screen sought to remain faithful to the text, it was not until the adaptation almost 20 years later, directed by William Wyler, and starring Merle Oberon and Laurence Olivier, that a mass audience embraced *Wuthering Heights*, and it is the images created in that film that have had cultural reverberation. It is estimated that by 1948, 22 million people had seen Wyler's *Wuthering Heights* (Ingham 228). Examining this film and highlighting the features from the original text that it maintains, alters or fabricates gives some understanding of the ways in which *Wuthering Heights*—its plot and characters—have been both remembered and misunderstood.

Wuthering Heights was adapted for the big screen for a third time in 1970 and the stark contrast—in terms of presentation and innuendo—between the 1939 and the 1970 films is significant. The changes in society by 1970 and the fully British undertaking of the production led to a more aggressive and explicit, though still much altered, interpretation of the novel. This third treatment on film led to its further establishment in popular culture: music, both on stage and in the charts, seemed suddenly relevant while at the same time the images of the story had become so familiar that parody also became common. It was not until 1992 that a more "faithful" adaptation was attempted by Peter Kosminsky at a time when literature was again being treated with reverence on the screen. As recently as 2011, critically acclaimed, Academy Award winning director Andrea Arnold adapted Brontë's novel in the style of her previously off beat and artistic films (*Red Road*, 2006; *Fish Tank*, 2009) but fell into similar tracks as her predecessors, eliminating half the plot and focusing intently on the scenery surrounding her characters. This novel's translation into the entertainment culture has been essential for its survival. Yet it is important to gauge just what its prolonged popularity through adaptation has taken from the original, and what has been altered by Hollywood interpretation.

Since its publication in 1847, both *Wuthering Heights* and its author, have proved enigmatic. Brontë's depiction of an unrequited love between the orphan Heathcliff and socially ambitious Cathy which descends into madness, violence, and revenge on each other and their subsequent generations was an oddity when it first appeared. Brontë's protagonists and their spouses and children thrash out an unforgettable, if unfathomable story set on the stormy Yorkshire moors which makes this novel stand starkly apart from the other Brontë sisters' work, leaving Emily shrouded in a darker reputation than her sisters. Emily Brontë's reputation as the "sphinx" of English literature has grown steadily since her death in 1848, perpetuated by her elder sister Charlotte's ambiguous "Biographical Notice" to the second edition of *Wuthering Heights*, published in 1850 (Miller 171). Charlotte tried to defend and explain the peculiarities of her sister and her novel, though by trying to excuse the brutality of Emily's characters by depicting her as inexperienced and simple minded, she only achieved in forming further mystery around them both. As Lucasta Miller explains, Charlotte Brontë was Emily's first mythographer (174). The "simultaneous admiration and repulsion" that *Wuthering Heights* garnered immediately after its publication gave way to a debate by critics as to whether the woman Charlotte Brontë had described was even capable of writing such a text; some believed her brother Branwell was the chief author behind it (206–7). The novel's reputation for being ignored for the decades after this interest subsided was, as Miller argues, due to a combination of Emily's posthumous elusiveness and Charlotte Brontë's more commercial success, so that for the latter half of the nineteenth century *Wuthering Heights* still occupied a place in the alternative, rather than mainstream, culture of the day (210). The dawn of the twentieth century, however, brought a change amongst women and their literary idols: their search for a new, more meaningful place in society left them jaded with Charlotte Brontë's work and made the peculiarities of Emily's more appealing. May Sinclair's 1912 biography, *The Three Brontës*, went far in igniting the new intrigue in Emily and served to promote *Wuthering Heights* as an established text of English literature. This increased female interest in the story of Cathy and Heathcliff paved the way for the new medium of cinema to embrace the story but it would be a development in the novel's history that would only serve to embolden the "myth" of *Wuthering Heights*. Using this term herself, Ingham argues that through the cinematic adaptations of the text "frequent second-hand knowledge of [the] plot has become widespread and has reached mythic status" (216). The image that Charlotte Brontë began in trying to defend the novel has been continued by filmmakers who have attempted to commercialize it.

"The true field of the movies is not *art* but *myth*... A myth is a specifically free, unharnessed fiction" (Tyler 748). This statement describes the product that all cinema produces, but in adapting a product already linked with "myth" the outcome is doubly enigmatic. Examining the process and outcome of adapting the novel *Wuthering Heights* for the screen means looking at the concept of adaptation in general. Although often considered problematic, theorists of the art form are quick to defend it. As humans, we are attracted to repetition, argues Linda Hutcheon, "the comfort of ritual combined with the piquancy of surprise" (4). This is a point worth taking further. In choosing to see an adaptation of a loved (or hated) text, we are subjecting ourselves to a second-hand interpretation, an opinion that is not our own. We are opting to be told a story we already know; the only elements that can possibly produce a sense of amazement are those that we do not recognize from the familiar. Of course, the very essence of adaptation is change, since regardless of what a written text is adapted into—film, play, painting—it changes its vehicle of presentation. Hutcheon boils conflict between the "original" and the "adaptation" down to the wonderfully simple definition of "Telling—Showing," two actions that describe something in completely different ways. "Showing" deals with specific people, places, and things, providing us with precise images so our own interpretations are not needed. "Telling," however, allows for individual imagination and can be vague and symbolic (38–39). The two separately pose no problem; we can be *told* what a character looks like and let the image form in our imagination, or we can be shown the actor who is portraying a character who will then become our only image of it. But when we are shown something we have first been told, the provided reproduction is subject to a personal reaction. Having formed individual imagery in response to a description, to be provided with a physical interpretation of that image may cause conflict with what has been established in the mind. Though, as mentioned above, we may be attracted to familiarity of a plot or character, we may then be abashed to discover unanticipated differences or changes in what we have imagined and therefore reject the adaptation.

In applying the differences in "Telling-Showing" to *Wuthering Heights* a film adaptation of this novel seems immediately problematic as it is a novel with a plot that is quite literally being told (narrated). Brontë's famously layered narrative has Mr Lockwood telling us a story that Nelly Dean has told him and, occasionally, a story that Isabella or Zillah has told her. Descriptions of people and events are therefore second, even third, hand. There is no omniscient narrator able to follow the characters on their private exploits or who is privy to their thoughts, and as neither narrator is one of the focal characters, to tell their story on screen means showing much which is only alluded to in the text. Though adapting any novel into a film means that the images on screen are inventions of the filmmakers, in the case of *Wuthering Heights* they must also invent parts of the plot. Dealing with two characters who conduct much of their relationship "off-page" means that instead of having Lockwood or Nelly sit and tell the audience, through the screen, of Cathy and Heathcliff's actions, they must be fabricated to be shown by the characters themselves. Robert Stam shows his sympathies for adaptations, as a brand of film that can never seem to win: "a 'faithful' film is seen as uncreative, but an 'unfaithful' film is a shameful betrayal of the original" (8). Adaptations, he argues, lose on two counts: they are films and therefore subjected to subliminal class prejudice, pleasing the "great unwashed popular mass audience, with its lower-class origins in 'vulgar' spectacles" (7). Film adaptations do not have the same intellectual approbation as novels, either for critics or the general public. Yet as Kamilla Elliot also argues, adaptations are also "less" than true films, unoriginal and parasitic, taking from another source, stealing ready-made popularity. Adaptations, for all their relevance in the media industry, are very much in a category of their own, second class entities, neither literature nor true film (27). It is the lasting effect that they have on their "feeder" texts that is of most relevance as they bring "classic" literature to a mass audience, so cultivating it for popularity rather than integrity. In the case of *Wuthering Heights*, Miller argues that our image of the novel today is so influenced by Hollywood's 1930s "repackaging" of it as a "conventional love story" that it is easy to forget the darkness and controversy of Brontë's characters and plot (189). Hollywood has created the myth of *Wuthering Heights* that has lasted until today.

An unconscious cooperation

In 1938, as the script for *Wuthering Heights* was being circulated in Hollywood, worldwide problems were adding to the internal tensions of the industry. War was looming over Europe, leaving Americans uncertain of the political climate, while filmmakers, struggling to reflect the international context that monopolized current news and with it their audience, also found themselves under strict scrutiny and censorship. Since 1930, the Hollywood Production Code, enforced by the

Production Code Administration (PCA), had been clamping down on sexual innuendo and violence in Hollywood's product. John Izod notes that by 1935, every producer kept in touch with the PCA at every stage of production to ensure no extra expense would be incurred, meaning that for two decades "sexuality was replaced by coyness and controversy by blandness" (106). With this need for repressed sexuality on screen, it is easy to see why period dramas were becoming appealing to producers. Canonical works of literature were favorites for the movie treatment, as they often had familiar plot lines and so brought with them a ready-made audience. Scripts based on "classic" literature usually needed little cleaning up due to their restrained sexual or violent content and also had the appeal of their often distinguished literary status.

Producer Samuel Goldwyn was, nonetheless, at first unsure about *Wuthering Heights*. Though he understood the success elsewhere of literary adaptations, he did not see how a script so "relentlessly grim" could be a success with audiences (Berg 320). As a result he tried everything he could to brighten the story, throwing around title changes like "The Wild Heart," "He Died for Her" and "Bring Me the World" (321), even while his director William Wyler remained stubbornly intrigued by the darkness in the story. Though Goldwyn lost his battle to change the name of the film, he did win other fights. Feeling worried after test audience reactions, he edited the ending to show the ghostly figures of Cathy and Heathcliff reunited on Peniston Crag, a choice Wyler point-blank refused to take part in, claiming it "violated the nature of the film" (328). Goldwyn also approved the change of time period by around half a century for the purely aesthetic reason that the costumes of the regency period would look more sumptuous and show off Merle Oberon's shoulders to their best advantage (322).

However, the two most important aspects of the 1939 film are its alterations to the novel's plot and setting. The most obvious and resounding change is that the second half of the novel is missing: film audiences only encountered the first generation of Earnshaws and Lintons. In doing so, the characters of Cathy and Heathcliff were able to be shown with all of their tragedy and love but with none of the hatred and revenge that dominated the latter parts of the novel. Cathy and Heathcliff, and with them the entirety of *Wuthering Heights*, is normalized, now a conventional love story: passionate, unrequited, and tragic.

In disposing of the second half of the novel the production team eliminated the half of Bronte's story that is most illuminating, the half of the story that shows the aftermath of the love, and the repercussions of the death scene that begins the end of the film. Writers Ben Hecht and Charles MacArthur decided to "telescope the passage of time" in the novel and concentrate solely on the first generation of characters, leaving their buyer, Goldwyn, with a sellable love story which could now be compacted into a 90-minute run time (Berg 320). It was an economic, as well as artistic, decision to work with a smaller screenplay, yet it was a decision that changed the very meaning of the novel.

Dealing with two characters who conduct much of their relationship "off-page" meant that Cathy and Heathcliff's actions had to be fabricated

Illustration 3.1   Cathy (Merle Oberon) and Heathcliff (Laurence Olivier) out on the moors in the 1939 adaptation of *Wuthering Heights*

to be shown by the characters themselves. As mentioned above, the novel never makes it entirely clear how Cathy and Heathcliff behaved when alone, or even where they were during these times, since neither of them gets to narrate the story, but the producers and directors of the film adaptations had to provide a backdrop, not to mention action, for their plot despite the danger of conflicting with what was envisaged by the reader and meant by the author. Goldywn and Wyler then made a decision that would change the nature of *Wuthering Heights* forever: they created an outside. Throughout the novel, there is not one scene in which we see Cathy and Heathcliff alone outside. In truth, there is not one scene set outside in the entire first part of the novel that the film-makers interpret. Choosing to use the moors surrounding Wuthering Heights as the backdrop for the lead character's illicit love made those moors the biggest symbol of Emily Bronte's novel. Cathy running into the rain shouting "Heathcliff!" does not happen in the text because the novel's narrator is not there. Yet this is the iconic scene that is now associated with the novel. This film conventionalized Bronte's novel and turned it into another "love story with genuine mass appeal," an interpretation that would dominate any future adaptations. Subsequent directors have been unable to shake off this interpretation despite using their own contextual devices.

Adapting the adaptation

Twenty years passed before the next attempt to translate *Wuthering Heights* to the screen and the film industry had changed a great deal. According to Peter Biskind it was the 1960s that "saved Hollywood," providing the restless offspring of the "baby boomers" with young, rebellious heroes who channeled their frustrations and aspirations to change society (7). *A Streetcar Named Desire* (Elia Kazan, 1951), *On the Waterfront* (Elia Kazan, 1954), *Rebel Without A Cause* (Nicholas Ray, 1955), and *East of Eden* (Elia Kazan, 1955) brought glamorous rebels Marlon Brando and James Dean to the forefront of Hollywood cool by the end of the 1950s. They led the way for the success of films such as *Bonnie and Clyde* (Arthur Penn, 1967), *The Dirty Dozen* (Robert Aldrich, 1967), and *Easy Rider* (Dennis Hopper, 1969), which exemplified the appeal of those on the edge of society. Of *Easy Rider*, Eric Rhode writes: "Its two leading characters maintain a paradisal innocence by display-ing their aggression to the adult world" (631). This is a sense of detached togetherness that Cathy and Heathcliff also exemplify. Freedom, even with aggression, was now offbeat but appealing and as the 1960s came to an end, this meant that film had a freer rein than ever before. As the first English-language adaptation of *Wuthering Heights* since 1939 went into production, the changes made to the characters and story were significant, though gratuitous, as though taking advantage of the new freedom. It is with sexual freedom that Robert Fuest turns his back on Wyler and Goldwyn in 1970. His interpretation of Brontë's lovers would appear more believable as an account of the lives of contemporary rock stars: wild, sexual, and flouting the society that ensnares them. Fuest keeps the decision of the 1930s filmmakers to transplant the plot from the inside of Wuthering Heights to the countryside surrounding it, primarily in the physical scenes between Cathy and Heathcliff (now played by Anne Calder-Marshall and Timothy Dalton). His characters graduate from an enclosed box bed where they lie entwined with each other, to a draughty stable where they kiss, to a sprawling meadow where we leave them about to engage in sex. But the outside world becomes significant for Heathcliff purely because of that final conquest. Where in the novel, the moors around Wuthering Heights were Cathy and Heathcliff's refuge—a place where the reader never followed, a place where we are led to believe they bonded in a spiritual sense—the moors now become merely a canvas to express their sexuality and a symbol of their rebellion.

It is the fact that Cathy and Heathcliff are rarely seen together in a physical sense in the book that makes Fuest's film so redundant. Brontë's literary creations display a notoriously unfathomable connection that seems to boil down to a spiritual mirroring. Cathy herself struggles to articulate her relationship with the man who was raised as her brother but who became something like a soul mate. "I cannot express it; but surely you and everybody have a notion that there is or should be an existence of yours beyond you...I *am* Heathcliff! He's always, always in my mind: not as a pleasure, any more than I am always a pleasure to myself, but as my own being" (Brontë 82). Similarly, Heathcliff never describes Cathy as a lover despite clearly loving her. When he learns of her death he cries: "I *cannot* live without my life! I *cannot* live without my soul!" (168). Brontë goes to great lengths with her characters' dialogue to depict an unfathomable relationship between them. Theirs is a connection that surpasses the physical that Fuest appears determined to concentrate on. Fuest escalates from Calder-Marshall and Dalton embracing with surprising familiarity in bed, to the sexually charged violence between them in the stable mentioned above. When they finally meet in an openly sexual encounter in the land around Thrushcross Grange it becomes a humorous event for Heathcliff. When he is told that Cathy is expecting a child, whom we never see, he smirks knowingly when he is told that Edgar is "waiting to see the color of its eyes" before celebrating. Far from the inexplicable, spiritual relationship that Brontë's Cathy and Heathcliff share, we are now given characters whose relationship is motivated by sex, or rather the thrill of illicit sex. Heathcliff's rude question to Isabella—"Do you fancy a tumble then?"—shows how lightly he views physical relationships and that his actions are primarily for his own amusement. Although Wyler too took the interior plot of *Wuthering Heights* to the outside in 1939, he still used caution in portraying intimacy between the characters; the one kiss we do see between Cathy and Heathcliff fades quickly off the screen and caution over physical proximity is evident between them on Peniston Crag. The Heathcliff of the novel, and indeed the 1939 film, also gives the impression of indifference, even repulsion, towards being in a physical relationship with Isabella as he is so consumed by his love for Cathy.

Explicit sexual references are not limited to the two leading characters, however. An unexpected, and pointless, addition to the film's sexual element is the randomly placed romantic allusions between Nelly Dean and Hindley Earnshaw. This is arguably the most violent departure from both the novel and the previous film, which shows Nelly as the staid narrator of the story. Nelly's stern voice throughout the text is one of cautious vigilance over the souls of the Earnshaw and Linton families, and she berates all the characters' behavior at one point or another, including Hindley's. After her childhood shared with the Earnshaw children, she holds fast to the role of servant and, at times, substitute parent, especially for Cathy. This film's decision to add something more youthful and suggestive to her position in the story does nothing to enhance, or diminish, her character. It adds merely to the gratuitous play on sex throughout, boiling every relationship down to one of physical desire. Of course, we must bear in mind that in the context that surrounded the making of this film, coming out of the "Swinging Sixties" with music and film stars flaunting their "rebellious" attitudes to sex, Fuest has gone some way to updating Bronte's story from the grainy black and white images of the 1930s. But in doing so he loses some of the mystery of the plot and merely serves to further ingrain the iconic images created by those before him. He provides a similar landscaped background for Cathy and Heathcliff's meetings to that first introduced in Wyler and Goldwyn's 1939 classic serving to promote *Wuthering Heights* as an exterior plot—a direct opposition to its original source—once more.

When fidelity strikes

By the time the next English-language film adaptation of *Wuthering Heights* was made in 1992, the film culture surrounding literature adaptations was changing. At this time "period films" were enjoying a newfound prestige in the industry, thanks to a growing trend both for more critically acclaimed "faithful" adaptations and to the other extreme of innovative modernist interpretations. Baz Luhrman's 1996 success in transplanting Shakespeare's *Romeo and Juliet* to contemporary America sparked a trend in modernizing classic literature in films such as *Great Expectations* (Alfonso Cuaron, 1998) and *Hamlet* (Michael Almereyda, 2000), both starring Ethan Hawke, and even Shakespearean aficionado Kenneth Branagh embraced the contemporary trend for his 2000 adaptation of *Love's Labour's Lost*, choosing to shoot this film in the style of a 1930s musical. *The Taming of the Shrew* was also updated to an American High School in *10 Things I Hate About You* (Gil Junger, 1999). Whilst "updating" the classic appealed to the "pop culture" generation of the 1990s, there was also a growth in more "high-brow," faithful interpretations of literature. *Howards End* (James Ivory, 1992), *The Remains of the Day* (James Ivory, 1993), and *The English Patient* (Anthony Mighella, 1996) were all critically successful adaptations of period literature which not only lifted the reputation of this film genre, but also exemplified the strength of their UK cast: Anthony Hopkins, Emma Thompson, and Ralph Fiennes, to name a few. British television was also providing acclaimed adaptations of Jane Austen in the 1990s, adding to the popularity of lavish period productions. *Pride and Prejudice* (Simon Langton, 1995) and *Emma* (Diamuid Lawrence, 1996) were BBC successes, with Austen's *Emma* also receiving Hollywood treatment with Gwyneth Paltrow in the lead role (Douglas McGrath, 1996), and *Sense and Sensibility* (Ang Lee, 1995) winning the Oscar for Best Adapted Screenplay.

Although the 1990s version of *Wuthering Heights* includes much of the novel's plot that previous films had neglected, it still cannot escape the shadow cast by the "original" adaptation. While director Peter Kosminsky does fall into some of the same patterns as Wyler and Fuest, mainly the removal of the plot from the interiors of Wuthering Heights and Thrushcross Grange to the surrounding countryside, he does lend a new and individual claim to the iconic scenes. His interpretation of Peniston is a combination of them both into a barren landscape, the harsh stone of the crags laid flat where meadows would be expected. As Cathy and Heathcliff (this time played by Juliette Binoche and Ralph

Fiennes) huddle together under the bare tree that looms lonely over the rocky terrain, they are transported out of the romance of windy hilltops and the innuendo of rolling in lush grass. Kosminsky uses this setting to a new advantage to show the lifelessness of their relationship and their peculiar solidarity, both of which echo in the strangeness of their surroundings. Taking the predictable setting away gives leniency to the departure from the plot that cinematic audiences are accustomed to. Moreover, this film includes the second generation of Earnshaws and Lintons, allowing Heathcliff's behavior after Cathy's death to be seen in full for the first time on screen. Juliette Binoche becomes young Cathy by adorning a blonde wig, and Heathcliff and Isabella's son is subjected to the calculating cruelty of his father. As seen in the novel, a feeling of closure comes over the plot in the eventual union of young Cathy and Hareton after Heathcliff's death.

Ralph Fiennes hits closer than his predecessors to Brontë's Heathcliff with his interpretation: roughness without vulgarity, cruelty without logic, love without pomp. He cannot, however, fully portray the subversive character that the novel implies. As seen in both the previous adaptations, the ghostly apparitions alluded to in the novel make their way on to the screen. For Wyler in 1939, the specters of Cathy and Heathcliff at the end of the film spoiled any ambiguity to the film's ending. Similarly, Cathy's ghost appearing to Heathcliff in Fuest's film is relatively eerie and hypnotic, but as it leads him to be shot by Hindley, it completely rewrites the novel's ending. Although in the text we are told only of how Heathcliff was found dead in his room, Kosminsky, not content with showing the final shot of Heathcliff's dead body after his descent into madness, also shows us the specter of Cathy, leading him into the box bed where he is found. His decision to make the image that of Cathy as a child makes the scene slightly bizarre and yet entirely unbelievable. The insistence of the filmmakers in showing what is alluded to ambiguously in the text takes a degree of the appeal out of it. As Hutcheon points out, this can be the difficulty with adaptations. They take something we are told, and so left to interpret for ourselves, and *show* us it, leaving no room for imagination or questions (38–40). Though Kosminsky has tried to remain faithful to the text, he has made his own judgments as to what Brontë has hidden behind the narration and displayed that singular view to his audience.

The narration as a device within this film is another departure from the novel and previous films: "Emily Brontë" is incorporated into the film. Though she is not actually narrating the film, she begins and ends it, with small refrains in between, describing the inspirations behind the plot, wandering around the ruin of an old building, presumed to be The Heights. Boiling Brontë down to a gratuitous introduction detracts from, rather than adds to, Kosminsky's adaptation and simultaneously removes one of the most prominent characters from her well-informed perch. Though Nelly Dean is in the film (played well by Janet McTeer), she does not have the same effect as she does when the audience knows that she is telling the story. As the full title of the film reads *Emily Brontë's Wuthering Heights* it suggests that in including Brontë, the film would earn greater esteem, when in truth, it adds little to the film's impact. This film remains as much an adaptation of the images created by the 1939 classic, as it does Emily Brontë's novel, despite trying to remain more faithful to the text.

A cultural short cut?

There is no doubt that the cinematic attention paid to this nineteenth-century Gothic novel has kept it alive in a new age, but at what cost? In April 1999, the children's television program *Sabrina the Teenage Witch* (1996–2003) opened with the eponymous character reading *Wuthering Heights*. Finding the book difficult to get through, Sabrina asks her aunts to tell her what happens, but being strict guardians they tell her not to take "short cuts." Ignoring them, Sabrina casts a spell that sends her into the book. The scene then cuts to an exterior of a dark, stormy moor where Sabrina, clad in a formal period dress, runs through the marsh, grabs hold of a lone tree and shouts "Heathcliff!" in melancholy tones. She soon, however, exclaims "Dang, these moors are cold!" and transports herself home, telling her aunts through chattering teeth, "All right, you're right, I'll read the book" ("The Long and Winding Short Cut"). Sabrina had, of course, not sent herself into Brontë's novel, but into its "simplest memorable pattern" (Stoneman 129), an imprint created by the numerous film adaptations of the book. So well known has the imagery projected by the original film and its later imitators become, that popular culture is now able to reference scenes that never occurred in Emily Brontë's text, but that have now become synonymous with its meaning. The question is now, however, whether this ability for modern day pop culture to reference *Wuthering Heights* with such inaccurate ease is a good thing: a welcome modern promotion of one of literature's great works; or a bad thing: proof that the drive for popularity and profit in the film industry has changed the meaning of the original. Or indeed has film and its inevitable partner, pop culture, influenced *Wuthering Heights* so much that others like Sabrina are returning to the original decision to read the book?

The "boiled down" imagery of *Wuthering Heights* promoted by the film adaptations of the twentieth century not only made it easy to be remembered and therefore portrayed in popular culture, but it also became so clichéd that it was susceptible to comedic parody. Within three months of each other in 1970, two of the most scathing comedy acts on popular television had used *Wuthering Heights* in their sketch shows. In July, the *Morecambe & Wise* show (1968–77) staged a play called *Wuthering Heights*, crediting Ernest Wise as the writer with "additional material by Emily Brontë" (Ernest Wise Players). This humorous nod to how little Brontë's work has contributed to its adaptations serves to make the sketch that follows all the more ludicrous: for example, Mr Earnshaw riding in on a bicycle after hoofs have signaled his approach; the flamboyant gypsy garb of Eric Morecambe as Heathcliff; the main drive of the plot trying to trick Heathcliff into marrying Cathy. The typical slapstick of the duo's act is there, but the comedy in this sketch lies with the reversal of a plot that they assume the audience to be familiar with. The words "Wuthering" and "Heights" immediately trigger an idea of the intense love between Cathy and Heathcliff: that he would have to be deceived into marrying her makes their interpretation immediately comedic. Similarly, *Monty Python's Flying Circus* (1969–74) featured a sketch in their second series (September 1970) in which it is announced: "for the first time on the silver screen, from two books that once shocked a generation: Emily Brontë's *Wuthering Heights* and *The International Guide to Semaphore Code*." The banality suggested by a book about semaphore code adds humor to the contemporary interpretation of *Wuthering Heights* as a conventional love story. As the film interpretations of the novel have become more widespread and popular, the controversy that the novel originally experienced has disappeared; to some viewing this sketch, *both* books being described as shocking could seem funny. The sketch then goes on to mimic that same memorable pattern that *Sabrina* used, showing Cathy and Heathcliff on windy hilltops, signaling each other in semaphore whilst the subtitles below show "Catherine!" and "Heathcliff!" with increasing exclamation marks as the sketch progresses. The writers behind this show find the comedy in twisting what has become the obvious example of the story: they assume their audience will know the original image that they are mocking.

Benefitting from prior knowledge exemplifies the notoriety of the subject, but as Steven Johnson argues, it also rewards viewers in their understanding. In his defence of popular culture, Johnson argues that television comedies of the late twentieth century were both more intelligent than the programming that came before and more stimulating for the viewer (84). He points out that the growth in the "external information" that viewers must draw upon in order to "get" the jokes in their entirety means a more demanding experience for the audience (84). The *Morecambe & Wise* sketch mentioned above is funny for those not familiar with *Wuthering Heights* as it contains all the trademarks of the duo's usual comedic style, mainly Eric Morecambe's humorous deviations from the script, but it is *more* rewarding for those familiar with the popular images of *Wuthering Heights* on film and doubly so for those with knowledge of the novel as well. This is in accordance with Johnson's argument that:

> For decades, we've worked under the assumption that mass culture follows a steadily declining path towards lowest-common-denominator standard, presumably because the "masses" want dumb, simple pleasures and big media companies want to give the masses what they want. But in fact, the exact opposite is happening: the culture is getting more intellectually demanding, not less. (9)

Though not speaking about *Wuthering Heights* specifically, Johnson's point rings true in the shows mentioned above: a parody is more rewarding when the audience knows the full extent of what is being caricatured. Curtis White, however, argues the opposition to the effect of popular culture. White believes that reproducing "high culture" for a mass audience takes away the intellectual validity of the source, leaving us a "Done-Elsewhere-by-Somebody-Else Culture" (10). He argues that the media entertainment industry has become the "imagination industry," effectively doing our imagining for us and "managing" creativity in well-packaged, profit making products, which turn real culture into "mush" (9–10). What White fails to mention, however, is that with the popularity of the "created" images can come a misunderstanding of the subject and so a resurgence of an appreciation for what was portrayed in the original can occur. In terms of adaptation this inevitably leads to the question of fidelity to the original source. As mentioned in the beginning of the chapter, recent scholars have argued sympathetically for the plight of film adaptations and how they seem to be consistently considered "less" than their source novels. Despite this current attempt at an understanding for adaptations to be their own individual creation, though, the specter of the previous medium still lingers over them. As Thomas Leitch describes:

> the challenge for recent work in adaptation studies, then, has been to wrestle with the un-dead spirits that continue to haunt it however often they are repudiated: the defining context of literature, the will to taxonomize and the quest for ostensibly analytical methods and categories that will justify individual evaluations. (65)

In the case of *Wuthering Heights* the fidelity argument becomes less clear-cut as after three relatively successful films it is hard to differentiate between what is being adapted: the novel, the previous films or both? As the novel suffered a prolonged absence from the public eye until the early twentieth century, which coincided with the beginning of its appearance on film, it seems correct to assume that cinema will have had just as much influence on contemporary assumptions as the novel itself. With the images of *Wuthering Heights* becoming as important as the written text the two can become interchangeable and at times misrepresented. The parts of the plot made famous by the cinema at times misconstrued the more subversive details of the original prose. For example, the end of the decade that featured the *Morecambe & Wise* and *Monty Python* sketches saw the release of Kate Bush's single *Wuthering Heights* which went to number one in the British charts in 1978. An interview with Bush behind the inspiration for the song reveals that she had not read the book when she wrote it, saying: "It's one of those classic stories you vaguely know. I knew there was Heathcliff and Cathy and that she died and came back. It just fascinated me" (Martin n. pag.). Though Bush went on to read the book, saying she was "amazed" by it, her influential song was based on the backlog of images inspired by the Hollywood film. The lack of knowledge Bush had of the novel about which she wrote a song seems to have affected the understanding of the song itself. Though a popular hit when released, and memorable even now, it seems that the lyrics of the song have been fundamentally misunderstood for around 20 years. A survey featured on Sky News in August 2008 about songs whose lyrics are most misunderstood placed Bush's song at number 10, as listeners claimed to hear her singing: "Heathcliff! It's me; I'm a tree, I'm a wombat. Oh, so cold at the end of your winter" instead of the actual line: "Heathcliff! It's me, Cathy and I've come home oh, so cold, let me in your window" (Stam, "Sting Top"). The popularity of this song, despite its misconstrued meaning has allowed further disorderly interpretations of the characters and plot to be linked with the text.

Unhappiness at musical interpretations of Emily Brontë's novel continued beyond Kate Bush's pop song and raised considerable fervor towards the concept of "adaptation" when Cliff Richard was presented as Heathcliff in the stage musical of the same name. Writing for *The Independent* in 1994, Sandra Barwick claimed it would require "a suspension of sanity" to accept the singer as Heathcliff. Richard's clean-cut, Christian image provoked a debate on what was needed to portray Brontë's Heathcliff correctly. Critics such as Patricia Ingham take Olivier in the 1939 version to task, claiming he appears as nothing more than "a matinee idol with a pleasing touch of bohemian" instead of the violent anti-hero of Brontë's text (229) but at the time he proved a popular choice for the film audiences. As the twentieth century progressed, however, Heathcliff was portrayed increasingly more realistically and faithfully to Brontë's creation, particularly in Kosminsky's 1992 film which depicted the cruel treatment of his own son, and he has also been portrayed in a somewhat more subversive way in Arnold's 2011 version which chooses to show Heathcliff as black. Expectations of Heathcliff are now unable to be filled by the polite and well-to-do Cliff Richard, as Barwick's article demonstrates. She argues that Richard would be better suited to playing mild-mannered Edgar Linton but "not—never—Emily Brontë's incarnate hobgoblin," and that playing Heathcliff would probably be "the first gross perversion of his life," which is ironic as Heathcliff is a character full of gross perversions.

The continuing battle

The decision to include no musical soundtrack in the 2011 adaptation of *Wuthering Heights*, instead using the sounds of the weather and the creatures of the surrounding countryside to create a backing track for the characters, shows the continuing importance placed on this outside world that the Hollywood Golden Age created for the "original" adaptation. Whilst many critics compliment Arnold for attempting the "shock of something new" with her adaptation (Bradshaw), mainly by casting Heathcliff as a young, black male, her debt to the previous filmic interpretations is as clear as those that came before her. In fact, she too, as mentioned above, eliminates the latter half of the novel which contains the more controversial behavior from Heathcliff—it is hard to forget that he hanged Isabella's puppy (150) or dug up Cathy's corpse (288)—in favor of concentrating on the "love story."

The tragedy of unrequited love is the lasting image of *Wuthering Heights*, thanks to the success of William Wyler and Samuel Goldwyn's film at the height of the Hollywood Golden Age. Cathy and Heathcliff have been immortalized in popular culture as characters not only of a "typical" love story, but characters that can be understood, even related to. British Prime Minister Gordon Brown made such a gaffe in July 2008 as he described himself as an "older Heathcliff, a wiser Heathcliff" ("I'm an Older Heathcliff"). Clinging to the romanticized version of the character established by cinematic interpretations, Brown clearly considered this a modest compliment to himself, seeing himself as a wounded hero, unappreciated by those around him. He was, of course, quickly corrected by Ann Dinsdale, collections manager of the Brontë Parsonage Museum, who specifically blamed the film adaptations for the misconstrued image of Emily Brontë's character: "Is this the role model we want for our Prime Minister? There's this romanticized gloss that comes from the film versions of Heathcliff. When you look at the book, he's not an ideal role model" ("I'm an Older Heathcliff"). When a person in Brown's position, whose every word in public is recorded, can reference something easily and assume a certain interpretation of it, popular culture has made its mark. Though the film adaptations of *Wuthering Heights* have popularized the novel and have created certain ingrained images which are mainly misunderstandings of the text, they have also kept it alive. They have allowed it to be digested by modern culture, complimented by familiar humor and known to those whose knowledge of literature may be limited. Although each adaptation has been influenced by the period it was produced in, and exploited by filmmakers for prestige, profit or propaganda, these versions have ultimately kept a novel of a nineteenth-century recluse alive in the minds of the twenty-first-century masses. Differences between the adaptations and the novel are inescapable, and may never be resolved, but with the over-familiarity that the films have produced has become the start of correcting the predisposed assumptions. As the recent revelations on Kate Bush's pop song, and the commentaries on what "makes" Heathcliff have shown, the looser the references to the original, the quicker the corrections seem to come. The importance of the novel is creeping back in as we perhaps start to learn, like Sabrina the Teenage Witch, not to rely too much on short cuts.

Note

1. For a recent account of various adaptations—English-language and cross-cultural—of *Wuthering Heights* see Jenkins, "Heights of Fashion."

Works consulted

Barwick, Sandra. "Cathy Loves Heath-Cliff. Crikey." *Independent* 16 April 1994. Retrieved on 21 June 2011. www.independent.co.uk/opinion/cathy-loves-heathcliff-crikey-1370342.html.

Berg, A. Scott. *Goldwyn: A Biography*. New York: Alfred A. Knopf, 1989. Print.

Biskind, Peter. *Easy Riders, Raging Bulls: How the Sex 'n' Drugs 'n' Rock 'n' Roll Generation Saved Hollywood*. London: Bloomsbury, 1999. Print.

Bradshaw, Peter. Rev. of *Wuthering Heights* (2011). *Guardian* 10 November 2011. Retrieved on 18 January 2012. www.guardian.co.uk/film/2011/nov/10/wuthering-heights-film-review.

Brontë, Emily. *Wuthering Heights*. London: Bloomsbury Classics, 1996. Print.

Capote, Truman. *Breakfast at Tiffany's*. 1958. London: Penguin, 2000. Print.

Elliot, Kamilla. *Rethinking the Novel/Film Debate*. Cambridge: Cambridge University Press, 2003. Print.

Ernest Wise Players. "Morecambe and Wise Present *Wuthering Heights*." *Online Posting*. YouTube, 20 May 2008. Retrieved on 21 June 2011. www.youtube.com/watch?v=ya55rwvT1zY.

Hutcheon, Linda. *A Theory of Adaptation*. New York: Routledge, 2006. Print.

"I'm an Older Heathcliff, says PM." *BBC News* 10 July 2008. Retrieved on 21 June 2011. http://news.bbc.co.uk/go/pr/fr/-/2/hi/uk_news/politics/7497903.stm.

Ingham, Patricia. *The Brontës*. Oxford: Oxford University Press, 2006. Print.

Izod, John. *Hollywood and the Box Office, 1895–1986*. London: Macmillan, 1988. Print.

Jenkins, David. "Heights of Fashion." *Sight and Sound* 21.12 (December 2011): 37. Print.

Johnson, Steven. *Everything Bad is Good for You*. London: Penguin, 2006. Print.

Leitch, Thomas. "Adaptation Studies at a Crossroad." *Adaptation* 1.1 (2008): 63–77. Print.

"The Long and Winding Shortcut." *Sabrina the Teenage Witch: The Third Season*. Writ. Nell Scovell. Dir. Gary Halvorson. Warner Brothers, 2008. DVD.

Martin, Brendan. "Konversation with Kate Bush." *brendanmartin.tripod.com*. 30 June 1998. Retrieved on 21 June 2011. http://brendanmartin.tripod.com/.

Miller, Lucasta. *The Brontë Myth*. London: Vintage, 2002. Print.

Monty Python's Flying Circus. "The Semaphore Version of Wuthering Heights." *Online Posting*. YouTube, 15 September 2008. Retrieved on 21 June 2011. http://www.youtube.com/watch?v=kqiUGjghlzU.

Rhode, Eric. *A History of the Cinema from its Origins to 1970*. Middlesex: Penguin, 1976. Print.

Sinclair, May. *The Three Brontës*. Charleston, SC: BiblioBazaar, 2007. Print.

Stam, Robert. "The Theory and Practice of Adaptation." *Literature and Film*. Eds. Robert Stam and Alessandra Raengo. Oxford: Blackwell, 2005. 1–52. Print.

"Sting Top of Confusing Pop Songs." *Sky News* 22 August 2008. Retrieved on 21 June 2011. http://news.sky.com/skynews/Home/Showbiz-News/Sting-And-Police-Top-Confusing-Lyric-Chart-Beating-The-Beatles-The-Bee-Gees-and-U2/Article/200808315083681.

Stokes, Paul. "Only a Few Photos Reveal the Existence of the First Wuthering Heights Film." *Telegraph* 7 November 2005. Retrieved on 22 June 2011. http://

www.telegraph.co.uk/news/uknews/1502376/Only-a-few-photos-reveal-the-existence-of-the-first-Wuthering-Heights-film.html.

Stoneman, Patsy. *Brontë Transformations: The Cultural Dissemination of Jane Eyre and Wuthering Heights.* Hertfordshire: Prentice Hall/Harvester Wheatsheaf. 1996. Print.

Tyler, Parker. "Film and Society." *Film Theory and Criticism: Introductory Readings.* Ed. Gerald Mast and Marshall Cohen. Oxford: Oxford University Press, 1979. 747–53. Print.

White, Curtis. *The Middle Mind: Why Consumer Culture Is Turning Us into the Living Dead.* London: Penguin, 2005. Print.

Wuthering Heights. Dir. William Wyler. Perf. Merle Oberon, Laurence Olivier, and David Niven. 1939. MGM Home Entertainment, 2004. DVD.

Wuthering Heights. Dir. Robert Fuest. Perf. Anna Calder-Marshall, Timothy Dalton, and Harry Andrews.1970. MGM Home Entertainment, 2005. DVD.

Wuthering Heights. Dir. Peter Kosminsk. Perf. Juliette Binoche, Ralph Fiennes, and Janet McTeer. 1992. Paramount Home Entertainment, 1992. DVD.

Wuthering Heights. Dir. Andrea Arnold. Perf. Kaya Scodelario, Nicola Burley, and James Howson. Ecosse Films, Film4 et al., 2011.

4

Of Political Visions and Visionary Politicians: Adapting *All the King's Men* to the Big Screen

Birte Otten

When Steven Zaillian's film adaptation of Robert Penn Warren's Pulitzer Prize-winning novel *All the King's Men* was released in 2006, the reactions were reserved at best. Mostly regarded as a badly narrated and miscast remake of Robert Rossen's Oscar-winning 1949 film version, it disappointed moviegoers and critics alike. With a high-budget production, an impressive cast (including Sean Penn, Jude Law, Kate Winslet, James Gandolfini, Mark Ruffalo, Patricia Clarkson, and Anthony Hopkins), and a director and scriptwriter (Zaillian) who had already received an Academy Award for his screenplay for *Schindler's List*, expectations were admittedly high. But although the 2006 version of *All the King's Men* was praised by some reviewers for its "earnestness" (*Groucho*) and its being "true to the essence of its source" (*LA Times*), Zaillian's close adherence to the novel could not prevent the film from being mostly regarded as a failure, as Stanley Kauffmann's assessment exemplifies: "The film isn't dreadful: it is just generally disappointing" (22).

There are several difficulties pertaining to these reactions. First, considering the 2006 version as a remake might be surprising to some viewers since Zaillian was quoted in a *New York Times* article by David M. Halbfinger as not having seen the original version. Disregarding the reliability of such a statement, the question remains of how to assess the 2006 version of *All the King's Men*, a film which critics inevitably view in connection to three earlier sources: the 1949 version of the film, the 1946 novel on which both films are based, and the former governor of and Senator from Louisiana, Huey P. Long, who served as an inspiration for the main character in the novel. In addition, the story of *All the King's Men* exhibits analogies to various other sources, among them Southern plantation writing, philosophical idealism, the Bible, and the well-known nursery rhyme Humpty Dumpty. Thus, not only does Zaillian's film raise questions about its categorization as a remake, it also problematizes the reviewers' comments about the degree of fidelity and originality the 2006 adaptation exhibits towards its assumed source text.

It is probably safe to say that many viewers, including journalists, judge literary adaptations by comparing them to the original text. This is a typical reaction and (in some sense) constitutes a "logical" approach. Nevertheless, such value-driven assessments of adaptations that rely on a film's fidelity to its source text have been largely discredited by the academic community. Instead of presupposing a superiority of the literary source over the adaptation, an increasing number of scholars in recent years have tried to provide the field of adaptation studies with a solid theoretical basis that allows for a more informed analysis of film adaptations. Referring to the poststructuralist concepts of intertextuality and hypertextuality, these scholars move beyond the "fidelity approach" by foregrounding a variety of issues pertinent to a constructive assessment of adaptations. Thus, they point to the inherent differences of the two media of literature and film, the specificities of the production process (budget, studio style, technological innovations, cast, etc.), and to historical and cultural contexts at the time of both the source text(s) and the adaptation. Adaptation theorists have also recognized the influence of theoretical developments in other disciplines on adaptation studies and the impossibility of disentangling both adaptation and source text(s) from innumerable other texts that always already inform and impact them.[1]

Yet, as becomes clear from many viewers' tendency to evaluate adaptations on the basis of their fidelity, studying adaptations always involves a comparative approach. As Brett Westbrook suggests, instead of buying into simplistic judgments of two texts, "the best question film adaptation studies can ask itself is, 'What can we learn *through* a comparison that cannot be learned via a single text?'" (43). The different versions or "readings" of *All the King's Men*, to borrow from Christa Albrecht-Crane and Dennis Cutchins' terminology (18), thus exemplify the problems connected to the debate around fidelity and originality. As Albrecht-Crane and Cutchins puts it, "adaptations are dialogues with other texts, including the texts upon which they are based, and those texts are in dialogue with adaptation" (19). By linking them through comparison we enable them to communicate with each other and thus give us information that goes beyond the individual text. In so doing, these texts point to their situatedness in a specific time and place. To put it in Robert Stam's words:

> Each re-creation of a novel for the cinema unmasks facets not only of the novel and its period and culture of origin, but also of the time and culture of the adaptation. ... Adaptation, in this sense, is a work of reaccentuation, whereby a source work is reinterpreted through new grids and discourses. Each grid, in revealing aspects of the source text in question, also reveals something about the ambient discourses on the moment of reaccentuation. By revealing the prisms and grids and discourses through which the novel has been reimagined, adaptations grant a kind of objective materiality to the discourses themselves, giving them visible, audible, and perceptible form. (45)

Since it is nearly impossible to focus on all the aspects pertaining to the making of an adaptation, this chapter examines the narratological and cinematic elements of Steve Zaillian's 2006 adaptation in its relation to Robert Rossen's 1949 version and Robert Penn Warren's 1946 novel. A starting point might be to ask what is achieved by producing another adaptation of what is generally considered one of the foremost novels about American politics 60 years after the novel and the first film were released. The following analysis will show how closely the 2006 film adhered to Warren's novel, especially when compared to Rossen's film. "Why," to ask with Thomas Leitch's words, "does this particular adaptation aim to be faithful?" (127). This chapter aims to shed light on what the different texts of *All the King's Men* can tell us about their "historical angles" (Scholz 658). Focusing on the political dimension of the texts, this analysis investigates to what extent they engage with American social, cultural, and political discourses at the time of their creation.

Remodeling the story

Being first and foremost a political novel, Robert Penn Warren's *All the King's Men* narrates the story of Willie Stark, the son of a backwoods farmer (from the South) who is elected governor on the basis of a populist agenda during the 1930s. As governor, Willie aims to speak for the common people, but he abuses the power handed to him in order to install a near-dictatorial government which is characterized by graft, corruption, and outright coercion. The story about Willie's personal and political development is told by the character-narrator Jack Burden, the son of an old Southern family, who works as a reporter for a newspaper but is missing a clear direction in life. Through his job Jack gets to know Willie and, being attracted to both his strength and political vision, ends up as his close assistant. His job is to "do research," to find compromising information about people in order to force them into compliance when necessary. When the pressure on the administration increases, Willie orders Jack to dig up information about his surrogate father, Judge Irwin, who still exerts influence on the state's elite. But when Willie orders Jack to use the information, the Judge kills himself rather than comply. Too late, Jack learns that the man he has driven to death was in fact his biological father. At the same time, Jack's involvement in state politics draws his childhood friends Adam and Anne Stanton into the mix. Willie appoints Adam, a successful surgeon and an idealist believer in the good in people, as director of the new medical center he intends to build. Anne, Jack's former girlfriend and still the love of his life, meanwhile becomes Willie's mistress. Everything culminates when Adam is offered a bribe by Willie's opponents and finds out about his sister's affair. Deeply shaken in all is beliefs, he kills Willie and is in turn shot by his bodyguard Sugar-Boy.

All in all, Warren's novel constructs a story that is much more than merely a political commentary. By making Jack the disillusioned and idealist character-narrator of a story set in the South, Warren also deliberates about the link between past and present, the shadow of history, the concept of original sin, the interrelationship of good and evil, and the question of individual and collective responsibility in a democratic society. On a formal level, these various themes intricately interweave in a narrative that frequently moves between different temporal levels. Hence, adapting a text like this to film automatically requires medium-specific innovations: how, for instance, should one remodel the first-person narrative, which is so crucial for the tone of the novel, within film? How does one insert the various flashbacks, if at all? What should one do with those long passages in the novel in which Jack ponders about his family's history, his inner struggles concerning Anne, or his theory about the Great Twitch?[2] In addition to these aspects, there remains the specifically cinematic problem of how to "flesh out" characters, settings, and props. As the following analysis of the two films reveals, Rossen's and Zaillian's adaptations differ to a large degree in their approach to and function of the source material.

Rossen's democratic vision

Rossen makes it clear from the very beginning that Willie Stark, played by Broderick Crawford, has never been naïve and innocent "cousin Willie," as he is portrayed in the novel. Rather, he is presented as a person whose ideas might have been good, but who has always been naturally depraved. Several key scenes in the novel support this interpretation. Within the first 20 minutes of the film it becomes clear that Willie is a self-absorbed husband and a careless father. When Jack Burden (John Ireland) visits him at his father's house, Willie doesn't pay attention to what his wife is saying and ignores the physical injuries his son received for handing out his leaflets. The close-up of Willie ferociously gnawing on a chicken's leg furthermore underlines the impression of an untamed man whose ambition will not allow him to rest. Fittingly, this scene concludes with Willie threatening a group of troublemakers: "I'm going to run. You're not going to stop me."

This first impression is expanded upon in the scene of Willie's political "awakening." Having been informed by his assistant Sadie Burke that he has been used by the Harrison gang to split the "hick vote," his political ambition becomes supplemented by a rampant recklessness. Almost the entire scene (meaning the shots on Willie as well as on the crowd) is filmed from a low camera angle. This angle could be interpreted as fortifying both Willie and the people. However, since Willie is positioned on a stage, the camera rather takes the perspective of the people as they are looking up at him. Read metaphorically, this camera angle implies that the people are not only physically looking up *at* him, but also looking up *to* him. However, the crowd of people listening to Willie is also filmed from a low camera angle, which in turn implies a certain reverence for them. Finally, this scene is followed by a sped-up narration of his campaign trip: the viewer sees the close-up of his almost manic face surrounded by torchlight (all complemented by menacing music) before he turns his back to the camera (as if already having turned his back to the people he represents) and violently threatens his political opponents. The scene does not leave any doubt that this man is out of control.

Meanwhile, the people depicted both here and in the rest of the film remain a rather passive mass which is being manipulated by the rising star Willie Stark. The only time the people move out of the shadow of Willie Stark is when they are being represented by an upright man who defies Willie's bribe and pays for it with his life, a passage not included in Warren's novel. This upright character, named Mr Hale, the father of a girl who loses her life due to Warren's son, Tom's, drunk driving, obviously becomes the spokesperson for the majority of people who believed in Willie but were disappointed by him. Mr Hale's significant response to Willie's bribe might function as the synopsis of the film: "I believed in you, I followed you, and I fought for you. Well, the words are still good. But you're not. And I don't believe you ever were." Here the film clearly implies that Willie's over-ambitious personality and his lust for power have always been a part of him. Warren's deliberations about original sin and civic responsibility and his hesitance to provide a definitive answer to these issues do not feature prominently in this film version. Instead, Willie is portrayed as the villain who abuses the power handed to him. The people, on the other hand, remain innocent and morally upright. As a result, the film also implies that the existent political and social structures have made his abuse of power possible in the first place. The question of individual responsibility which resonates so loudly in Warren's novel is thus muted.

But how does Rossen conclude his political vision? Not surprisingly, the ending of the film offers an unambiguous outlook. While Jack Burden starts to turn away from Willie relatively early, Anne becomes the one responsible for the Judge's suicide in this reading of *All the King's Men*. Interestingly, Jack and Anne are grouped in such a way that they form an opposition to Adam and the Judge. Whereas the latter stand for the virtuous and upright elite of the state, Jack and Anne take the role of the spineless and impressionable educated (middle) class (cf. Castille 178). Witnessing Adam's and Willie's deaths, Jack realizes that he and Anne need to continue what Adam and the Judge started, as becomes clear through Jack's melodramatic pleading, "Our life has to give his death meaning." After years of looking the other way, they now need to regain their personal integrity, which, however, also seems to lead them back to their hometown, Burden's Landing (cf. Davis 41, 42). In this calculation, the rest of the people, most notably the farming population, seem to remain passively in the background. They are absolved from all responsibility, but are neither vilified nor celebrated. Instead, they appear as the innocent mass which needs to be guided by an elite which distinguishes itself through personal achievements and integrity instead of money and ancestry. Only then, the film implies, can the likes of Willie Stark be prevented from gaining power.

Without returning to the fidelity model, it is still safe to say that this depiction of Willie Stark deviates from the Warren novel in significant ways—as it must. Most of Rossen's critics, indeed, reached the same conclusion, however using it as a basis for an evaluative judgment. Thus Joseph Millichap summarizes, "Rossen changes much of Warren. He centers on the more accessible Willie Stark, though even he is over-simplified into a single-dimensional demagogue" (154). According to these critics, Rossen ignored the major drift of the novel: the question of moral responsibility and human agency in connection to history (cf. Davis 33). In their opinion, he fails to present a convincing cine-matic expression of the novel. What many of Rossen's critics overlook is that film adaptations and remakes rather invite "the viewer to enjoy the *differences* that have been worked, consciously and sometimes uncon-sciously, between the texts," as Andrew Horton and Stuart McDougal have commented (6). Ironically, it was Robert Penn Warren who was one among the first to understood Rossen's film as an autonomous work:

> I think that [*All the King's Men*] is an extraordinarily good movie, with [Rossen's] very special touch. I can praise it, because it seems to me that when a movie is made from a novel the novel is merely raw material, the movie is a new creation, and the novelist can properly attract neither praise nor blame for it. The movie, as a matter of fact, does not "mean" what I think my book meant. It is Bob's movie. (qtd. in Casty 9)

So Warren's statement almost prefigures the debate around adaptation studies that started with George Bluestone's *Novels into Film* (1957) and has lasted up to the present.[3]

The two major changes Rossen brings to the literary text concern transferable information from one medium to another, an aspect that Brian McFarlane notes as one of the reasons for "a complex set of mis-apprehensions about the workings of narrative in the two media" (12). Rossen decided to untie Warren's achronological temporal structure and to de-emphasize the first-person perspective of the film. Although Jack Burden remains in the position of first-person narrator (exempli-fied by several voice-over narrations during the course of the film), he is no longer at the center of the film. Instead, he becomes the feeble bystander, with Willie attracting all the attention. This, of course, is only practical since the presentation of first-person point of view is dif-ficult to portray in film (cf. McFarlane 15). Still, it is important to rec-ognize that Jack's background position supports the general drift of the film. The beginning introduces him as one among several characters, turning him into the main focalizer only in the following scene. Also, the whole of Willie's early career from farmer's son to successful lawyer happens without any connection to (or even mediation from) Jack. As a result, Jack's character recedes to make room for Willie, the actual focus of attention.

Another simplification Rossen opted for with regard to transferable information is a chronological presentation of the events. Part of what makes Warren's novel such an interesting read is its journeys through Jack's mind, his memories, his anxieties, his assessments, and his idiosyncratic narrative tone. The reader follows him through a multi-layered narration, moving through time and space. There are, of course, ways to portray a character's memories and moods in film, but Rossen chose to make his film a straightforward story about the rise and fall of an over-ambitious and naturally depraved man. He ignored a faithful adherence to those literary aspects that are harder to depict and thus strengthened the cinematic enunciation of the film. By moving away from the text both on a thematic and on a formal level, Rossen brought a higher degree of originality to the film. Thematically, his adaptation presents an unambiguous, though one-dimensional portrait of a political leader. Formally, Rossen recognized the two media's difference and adjusted the story. A critical assessment of the film on the sole basis of its fidelity to the novel tends to overlook this.

Instead of complaining about Rossen's deviation from the source text it is more helpful to consider what kind of intertextual relation his film has to the novel. As Christopher Orr remarks: "Within this critical context, the issue is not whether the adapted film is faithful to its source, but rather how the choice of a specific source and how the approach to that source serve the film's ideology" (qtd. in McFarlane 10). Rossen changed the novel's temporal structure and readjusted its focus from Jack to Willie in order to give expression to a political view that differs decidedly from Warren's. Warren emphasizes the interconnectedness of all people, taking great pains to portray the complicated web of mutually dependent causes, and recommends to positively acknowledge the past: "I tried to tell her how if you could not accept the past and its burden there was no future, for without one there cannot be the other, and how if you could accept the past you might hope for the future, for only out of the past can you make the future" (656). In the novel Jack reforms, but in a very different way than in Rossen's film. In the novel, Jack is able to overcome his nihilistic attitude. He and Anne leave Burden's Landing for good, thereby turning their backs on both "Adam Stanton, whom he came to call the man of idea, and Willie Stark, whom he came to call the man of fact" (657). Burden's Landing symbolizes the past that Jack has to accept (and leave behind) to move into the future.

There is nostalgia present in this story—for people loved and lost, for visions and ideas, and for a (particularly Southern) way of life that will never be regained. But by expressing this nostalgia, the characters are also enabled to leave it behind. In contrast to many earlier tales about the South, such as Margaret Mitchell's *Gone with the Wind* (1936), this type of nostalgia does not restrain the novel's characters, but instead offers them a future. In this sense, Warren's text certainly is a novel about politics, but it also goes far beyond that.

Rossen, on the other hand, stresses the merits of idealism and places the weight of moral and political responsibility on an educated elite, represented by Jack and Anne. In this version, Burden's Landing continues to exude its power and influence over state politics. The events of the story are placed not in the South, but in a rather indistinct region somewhere in the US, thereby emphasizing their universal validity. Jack's role in the antecedent events is downplayed (mostly due to his character's background position), and Adam appears as the hero without a fault. As Mike Augspurger put it, "By creating an Adam who has never fallen, Rossen refutes the doctrine of original sin so necessary to Warren's novel. ... Neither the atrocities of World War II nor the political disappointments of the late forties were enough to convince Rossen that a democratic populace was not necessarily a progressive one" (63). Rossen, a member of the Communist Party until 1947 and an avid supporter of the Popular Front (cf. Augspurger 58), used this adaptation (which three years after its publication was still very much present in the minds of the audience) to imbue Warren's story with his own political vision. Arguably, one can disagree with this vision and the overall transformations Rossen brought to the story. From today's point of view, his fast-paced film seems one-dimensional in both political and aesthetic outlook. This vision should not, however, easily be detached from the film's cultural context, a time when the experience of fascism was still vivid, the confrontation with the Soviet Union well underway, and the fight against communism at home a reality.[4] His presentation of an innocent American populace being exploited by a decadent dictator who is counteracted by a morally upright, ideologically unambiguous, and essentially socialist leader figure therefore engages a cultural-political discourse that is specific to its time and place.

Zaillian's lack of a vision

An analysis of Steven Zaillian's *All the King's Men* reveals that Zaillian attempted to stay as close to the novel as possible as regards the story, structure, tone, and message of the film. In contrast to Rossen, he placed the story in a specific setting, 1950s Louisiana, thereby moving it two decades ahead in comparison to the novel. Zaillian also tried to incorporate Jack's perspective into the film by focusing much more on his narrative voice and personal past (via the means of voice-over narration and flashbacks) than Rossen did. In accordance with the novel, Zaillian starts his film with a scene that presents Willie as the already powerful and corrupted governor who is trying to coerce Judge Irwin into submission. Also, right from the beginning, he juxtaposes the rather weak and cynical Jack and the strong and power-thirsty Willie. But his attempt to transfer the novel to the film does not leave room for the development of individual characters, a stable character constellation, or a coherent plot line.

When, after only five minutes, the story moves back in time in order to focus on Willie before he became governor, he does not come across like the naïve country bumpkin which Warren made him out to be. Instead, Willie is presented as a shrewd man whose only fault is that he is not an experienced politician. His political innocence is underlined by his conviction to remain pure at heart. When asked by Jack Burden what he wants to do after having been ousted from his job as county treasurer, he responds: "I wanna keep the faith, Mr Burden." When Tiny Duffy (then tax assessor, later Willie's Lieutenant Governor) comes around to woo him into running for governor in the subsequent scene, Willie's innocence is once more emphasized. The scene implies that Willie only got involved in politics because he was tricked by Duffy. Thus, since the film refrains from emphasizing Willie's naïveté and "hick status," the scene of his political awakening remains rather unimpressive. Zaillian chose to speed up Willie's rise from rags to riches. However, shortening the story time from fifteen to five years (not counting the flashbacks into Jack's youth) necessarily compromised Willie's character development. His attempts at self-improvement through education by earning a law degree, his practical work as an attorney, and his experience of failure at the first state elections, all of which explain his transformation into the man he later becomes, are missing in Zaillian's version. Moreover, the reasons for Willie's impeachment and his subsequent assassination remain ambiguous since the film does not illuminate the dictatorial power he wielded, which brought the impeachment proceedings upon him in the first place.

Although Willie remains morally questionable in this version, Zaillian refrains from exploiting his weaknesses. In contrast to Rossen, he never shows him drunk. In one scene he has his first drink, in the following he is passed out. Sadie gives her powerful speech (which in the novel and in Rossen's version delivers the last straw necessary for Willie's awakening) while he is sleeping off his hangover, thereby forgoing a significant confrontation between her and Willie. Finally, Jack's efforts to raise him from the dead the next morning by giving him the "hair of the dog" (Warren 135) are not included in the 2006 film. Unlike in Rossen's version, Willie's turn to alcohol as a sign of his moral degeneration is thus weakened. As a result, Zaillian's attempt to depict Willie as an ambivalent figure somewhere between "pure at heart" and "recklessly ambitious" fails.

This becomes particularly clear in the scene of Willie's political awakening. Throughout most of the scene the camera stays level with Willie and his audience, alternating between medium shots on Willie and long shots on the people before finally zooming in. There certainly is a build-up, but it is not clear where it is heading. In the beginning of the scene, the focus seems to be on Willie's speech and the message he wants to bring across. Towards the climax, however, the camera zooms in on him and follows his flailing arms and jagged movements in a close-up. The audience is forced to follow Willie's movements, which make him appear rather shifty and out of control. At the same time the music takes on a rather somber note, as if wanting to warn the viewer

Illustration 4.1   Willie Stark (Sean Penn) on the campaign trail for governor of Louisiana in Steven Zaillian's *All the King's Men* (2006)

of the dangerous potential of this man. (And note that the film's beginning has already established Willie as a corrupted and ruthless political power-player.) The next scene, however, opens to a sped-up narration of Willie's election campaign, depicting him in different rural locations where he presents his political agenda to the people. Now the music is sentimental and thus underscores the good in Willie, turning him again into a likeable character. Simultaneously, some of these campaign takes, for instance the swamp scene, turn him into a ridiculous figure, a message that not only contradicts the beginning of the film and the previous scene but also the finale of this one, which ends with a clear political message: "If you don't vote, you don't matter!" The impression resulting from the choice of shots, cuts, and music at the end of this scene is one of celebration. In comparison to the previous scene there is an ambiguity at play which is caused by diverging cinematic characteristics. Consequently, the viewer is at a loss of how to account for Willie's position in the film.

This is also true of Jack's function in the film. Although Zaillian focuses on Jack's depression and his outlook on life, thereby retaining the novel's tone, Jack's struggle is never really resolved. In his last prominent appearance 15 minutes before the film ends, he gives in to a fatalistic acceptance of the events and is subsequently confronted by Anne. Then the film moves on to the assassination scene, which alternates with the scenes of Jack's and Anne's search for Adam. Neither Willie nor Jack is granted final words. Instead, the climax of the assassination is counterbalanced by a depiction of newspaper headlines about Willie's death and a flashback to his initial campaign message: "If you don't vote, you don't matter." What this ending seems to imply is the importance of Willie's political aims. But in contrast to Rossen, Zaillian neither celebrates nor clearly repudiates Willie and his methods to achieve that goal. The message is simply not clear.

This confusion does not only surface at the ending but has been ingrained in the structure of the film all along. The film regularly shifts its focus from one character to the next. It starts out with Jack's principle in life, "What you don't know won't hurt you," which is, in fact, a good way to position him at the center of the story. In the first half of the film the narrative focuses on Jack's and Willie's relationship with sporadic flashbacks into Jack's past. But the second half quickly moves from one scene to the next, always focusing on different plot strands. Many characters disappear during the film or just never fully develop, for example Sadie, who only reappears toward the ending, Willie's wife

Lucy, his son Tom, and, most important of all, Anne and Adam, who are only properly introduced an hour into the film. Furthermore, the scenes now start to move quickly from one to the next. The focus shifts from Sadie's affair with Willie, to Jack's research about the Judge, to Jack's youth in Burden's Landing and his relationship with Adam and Anne, to the impeachment proceedings against Willie, all of which are now and then punctuated by speeches Willie makes in front of the state capitol. These scenes smack of Nazi iconography: the film switches to near black-and-white mode, Willie stands alone and elevated in front of a large crowd, heavily gesticulating and shouting his populist messages. Simultaneously, his overlarge shadow is thrown onto the wall of the capitol. It is, in fact, not clear if he gives only one speech or several speeches because those scenes are presented in fragments. In these speeches Willie restates his willingness to fight for the common people. One might ask what effect the content of Willie's speech is supposed to achieve in regard to the Nazi iconography and his character's development up to this scene. The answer is anything but clear because the visual and verbal tracks of communication seem to clash.

All in all, Zaillian's attempt to remain true to the source text by focusing on the transposition of Warren's first-person perspective, Jack's cynical tone of narration, and a specific philosophical and political worldview result in a gloomy atmosphere which is, however, compromised by the very aspects that are particular to Warren's *literary* narrative and that resist easy transfer into the medium of film. The specifically cinematic aspects that Zaillian can employ—its spatiality, its language and non-linguistic codes, and its presentational aspect—seem to work against the film. For example, almost all reviewers have remarked that few of the main actors seem to master a Southern accent. Furthermore, the score often overdoes or runs against the verbal function of the scene. It seems that Zaillian tried to make up for the fragmentation of the film through the heavy use of symbolism which very often overshadows its function. Repeating shots of crosses on the roadside, the gothic style of some of the night shots of Burden's Landing, Willie's overlarge shadow thrown across the state capitol wall during his speeches, the switches to (near) black-and-white mode, and Willie's and Adam's joining bloodstreams after the assassination are all scenes that not only overplay the underlying issues, but in their metaphorical ambiguity also do not allow for a straightforward interpretation. The film does not offer any significant innovation or originality regarding the reworking of information in a different medium.

Consequently, the political dimension of the 2006 adaptation is not easy to define. The moral of the film seems to be its invocation to go and vote. This is furthermore underlined by the fact that the scene of Willie's campaign trail is used as background for the DVD menu. Another issue that the film foregrounds is Willie's agenda to do good for the people of the state, especially the lower classes. This is congruent with Willie's depiction in Warren's novel. The major difference is, however, that due to the choice of medium Warren has the liberty to explore minutely his characters' strengths and weaknesses, their personal histories, and their inconsistencies. Most filmmakers, in contrast, are bound to a two-hour time frame and thus have to limit themselves. As a solution to this problem, Rossen focused on Willie's development and minimized Jack's role. Zaillian tried to retain both characters as central agents of the story but had to cut down on their depth. As a result the film lacks closure, both with a view to Willie and to Jack. Whereas Warren and Rossen provide Jack with a means to continue his life, Zaillian's Jack is left hanging. After all of the film's efforts to turn Jack into a rounded character, the audience is disappointed in the end. There is no outlook, political or otherwise, and all "agents" involved are literally robbed of their voice. As Ty Burr put it, Zaillian's version of *All the King's Men* just does not have "anything urgent or even interesting to say."

This is particularly remarkable considering the political climate in which this film was produced and the political activism of its leading actor, Sean Penn. At a time when the United States was fighting highly controversial wars in Iraq and Afghanistan, with the country divided along partisan lines and an increasing number of people questioning their president's political abilities, Zaillian's film renders a rather feeble picture of one of the foremost political novels in American literature. With civil rights significantly curtailed by the PATRIOT Act and political opponents accusing neoconservatives of having hijacked the presidency,[5] the audience was surrounded by political narratives that seriously engaged with the themes of power, class, civic responsibility, and political idealism. By refusing to take any stand at all, Zaillian failed to realize "that texts remain alive only to the extent that they can be rewritten" (Leitch 12).

Conclusion

A comparative reading of Warren's novel *All the King's Men*, Rossen's 1949 film adaptation, and Zaillian's 2006 remake-adaptation reveals that Rossen managed what Zaillian could not. Though thematically deviating from Warren's text, the originality of his adaptation is based on two points. First, it had a straightforward message which catered to the zeitgeist of the time, with the depiction of a protofascist dictator at the time of the Red Scare in the US and the inherent warning that something like this could also happen in the States. Second, it focused on transferable elements, thereby creating a film that maintained its coherence. Rossen's originality can thus be understood as thematically innovative and cinematically convincing. Zaillian has seemingly tried to imbue the film with originality *through* fidelity to the source text without acknowledging the 1949 film. In this sense, his film remodels rather than remakes *All the King's Men*. According to the outdated criterion of fidelity it should have been the better and more successful adaptation. By making a film about a novel that had already been adapted to film once before his version automatically became a remake, at least in the eyes of many viewers who knew of the first film. The 2006 version failed, to quote Constantine Verevis, "to satisfy the requirement that Hollywood deliver reliability (repetition) and novelty (innovation) in the same production package" (5). This novelty is missing in Zaillian's version of *All the King's Men*.

The film's relationship to its precursor texts also recalls a question posed at the beginning of this chapter: why does the film try to be faithful to the source text? And to which source text, exactly, should it be faithful? Apart from paying tribute to Warren's truly engaging novel, Zaillian must have found this particular story suitable for this particular time in history. And the relevance of the story for an audience 60 years after its creation must have outweighed the production costs. In contrast to Warren and Rossen, Zaillian established analogies to Governor Huey Long by placing the story in Louisiana and even having Willie sing Long's campaign song "Every Man a King." But this reference seems to stand in opposition to his general approach to the film. As he said in an interview, "One of the reasons that this appealed to me is because there are certain stories that are so basic about human behavior that, even though the arena is politics, it's never not relevant." It is true that the "gray areas" in human behavior that Zaillian tried to portray will "always be worth re-examining." But at the same time even universal assumptions about human behavior need to be updated, specifically because "it's never not relevant." The reference to Huey Long might stir some viewers' memories, but its effect is diminished because of its cursory mention and the story's setting in the fifties. Accordingly, Zaillian's film did not enter into a mature dialogue with its precursor texts.

The 2006 version of *All the King's Men* fails to engage in contemporary political discourses and thus lacks a political vision to which viewers could relate. It almost seems as if Steven Zaillian was reluctant to connect his film to a political statement. Hence, he might have disappointed an audience that at the time was immersed in contested public discourses and therefore primed for political pronouncements. In this sense, the newest film version of *All the King's Men* did not achieve anything new or remarkable by adapting a 60-year-old text. Such a conclusion might be disappointing. But it is important to remember that it was possible to reach it specifically *through* the comparison of the various source text(s). In this way the previous analysis deepened our understanding of the text(s) and transcended an interpretation that an examination of the single text alone could have offered.

Notes

I particularly wish to thank Daniel Stein for his helpful comments, suggestions, and critique.

1. Cf. McFarlane; Horton and McDougal; Naremore; Stam; Leitch; and Verevis.
2. The Great Twitch is an image that Warren constructs to illustrate Jack's nihilistic understanding of life. When Jack returns from his trip to California he meets a man with a facial twitch. He describes the twitch as "simply an independent phenomenon, unrelated to the face or to what was behind the face or to anything in the whole tissue of phenomena which is the world we are lost in" (472).
3. Cf. Albrecht-Crane and Cutchins, and McFarlane.
4. Rossen himself was called before the House Committee on Un-American Activities in the 1950s (cf. Walling 173).
5. Reproaches of this kind did not only come from left-wing commentators, but also from conservatives such as Patrick Buchanan who with his *Where the Right Went Wrong: How Neoconservatives Subverted the Reagan Revolution and Hijacked the Bush Presidency* (2004) gave voice to his criticism of the Bush administration.

Works consulted

Albrecht-Crane, Christa, and Dennis Cutchins, eds. *Adaptations Studies*. Madison, NJ: Fairleigh Dickinson University Press, 2010. Print.
——. "Introduction." Albrecht-Crane and Cutchins 11–22. Print.
All the King's Men. Dir. Robert Rossen. Perf. Broderick Crawford, John Ireland, and Joanne Dru. Columbia, 1949. DVD.
All the King's Men. Dir. Steven Zaillian. Perf. Sean Penn, Jude Law, Kate Winslet, and Mark Ruffalo. Columbia, 2006. DVD.
Augspurger, Mike. "Heading West: *All the King's Men* and Robert Rossen's Search for the Ideal." *The Southern Quarterly: A Journal of the Arts in the South* 39.3 (2001): 51–64. Print.

Bluestone, George. *Novels into Film*. Baltimore, MA: The Johns Hopkins University Press, 1957. Print.

Buchanan, Patrick J. *Where the Right Went Wrong: How Neoconservatives Subverted the Reagan Revolution and Hijacked the Bush Presidency*. New York: Thomas Dunne, 2004. Print.

Burr, Ty. "'All the King's Men' Falls Down: Sean Penn's Overacting Obscures this Retold Tale of Political Corruption." *Boston.com*. NYTimes Co., 22 September 2006. Retrieved on 28 March 2011. www.boston.com/news/globe/living/articles/2006/09/22/all_the_kings_men_falls_down/.

Castille, Philip. "Red Scare and Film Noir: The Hollywood Adaptation of Robert Penn Warren's *All the King's Men*." *The Southern Quarterly: A Journal of the Arts in the South* 33.2–3 (1995): 171–82. Print.

Casty, Alan. "The Films of Robert Rossen." *Film Quarterly* 20.2 (1966–67): 3–12. Print.

Davis, Robert Murray. "'The Whole World... Willie Stark': Novel and Film of *All the King's Men*." *Film and Literature: A Comparative Approach to Adaptation*. Ed. Wendell M. Aycock. Lubbock: Texas Tech University Press, 1988. 33–44. Print.

Halbfinger, David M. "The Soul of Willie Stark, Found in the Cutting Room." *New York Times*. NYTimes Co., 10 September 2006. Retrieved on 24 March 2011. www.nytimes.com/2006/09/10/movies/moviesspecial/10halb.html?scp=1&sq=soul%20of%20willie%20stark&st=cse.

Horton, Andrew, and Stuart Y. McDougal. "Introduction." *Play It Again, Sam: Retakes on Remakes*. Ed. Horton and McDougal. Berkeley: University of California Press, 1998. 1–11. Print.

Kauffmann, Stanley. "Life Forces." *The New Republic* 235.16 (2006): 22–23. Print.

Leitch, Thomas. *Film Adaptation and Its Discontents: From* Gone with the Wind *to* The Passion of the Christ. Baltimore, MA: The Johns Hopkins University Press, 2007. Print.

McFarlane, Brian. *Novel to Film: An Introduction to the Theory of Adaptation*. Oxford: Clarendon Press, 1996. Print.

Millichap, Joseph. "*All the King's Men*, Photography, and Film." *To Love So Well the World: A Festschrift in Honor of Robert Penn Warren*. Ed. Dennis L. Weeks. New York: Peter Lang, 1992. 149–58. Print.

Mitchell, Margaret. *Gone with the Wind*. New York: Scribner, 1964. Print.

Naremore, James, ed. *Film Adaptation*. New Brunswick, NJ: Rutgers University Press, 2000. Print.

Rev. of *All the King's Men*, dir. Steven Zaillian. *Groucho Reviews.com*. Peter Canavese, n.d. Retrieved on 28 March 2011. www.grouchoreviews.com/reviews/2677.

Scholz, Anne-Marie. "Adaptation as Reception: How a Transnational Analysis of Hollywood Films Can Renew the Literature-to-Film Debates." *Amerikastudien/American Studies* 54.4 (2009): 657–82. Print.

Stam, Robert. "Introduction: The Theory and Practice of Adaptation." *Literature and Film: A Guide to the Theory and Practice of Film Adaptation*. Ed. Robert Stam and Allessandra Raengo. Malden, MA: Blackwell, 2005. 1–52. Print.

Turan, Kenneth. Rev. of *All the King's Men*, dir. Steven Zaillian. *Los Angeles Times.com*. Tribune Company. 22 September 2006. Retrieved on 28 March 2011. http://articles.latimes.com/2006/sep/22/entertainment/et-king22.

Verevis, Constantine. *Film Remakes*. Edinburgh: Edinburgh University Press, 2006. Print.

Walling, William. "In Which Humpty Dumpty Becomes King." *The Modern American Novel and the Movies*. Eds. Gerald Peary and Roger Shatzkin. New York: Frederick Ungar, 1978. 168–77. Print.

Warren, Robert Penn. *All the King's Men*. London: Penguin, 2006. Print.

Westbrook, Brett. "Being Adaptation: The Resistance to Theory." Albrecht-Crane and Cutchins 25–45. Print.

Part II

Remake

5
Remaking *The Stepford Wives,* Remodeling Feminism

Kathryn Schweishelm

In 2008, a former acquaintance of Tom Cruise publicly made the scandalous claim that the actor, prior to marrying Katie Holmes, had sought to audition several Hollywood starlets for the "role" of his perfect wife. For the tabloid press, the report was simply confirmation of the label they had branded Holmes with long before: "Stepford wife." In fact, the phrase began to appear almost immediately following the couple's 2006 wedding, in big, bold type in outraged headlines, though rarely with any explanation of its meaning or origin: it seems the yellow press felt safe assuming that the expression's meaning is well understood by its readers. Most people have neither read the original book by Ira Levin, published in 1972, nor seen the first film adaptation, released in 1975, and yet the term has become cemented in popular culture as a way to signify a compliant, passive woman, almost robotic in her subservience to her husband. Indeed, the original book and film touched a nerve in the popular imagination of the 1970s, in part due to the way they addressed the contemporary (and contentious) issue of the women's liberation movement.

The cultural currency the phrase continues to possess is surely something producers were hoping to capitalize on when they released a remake of the film in 2004. But while its predecessor, in keeping with Levin's novel, had used the second wave women's movement as the thematic backdrop for dark, gothic-tinged suspense, the new and improved *Stepford Wives*, detached from this context, metamorphosed into a frothy, kitschy comedy. Discussing the transformation in an interview included on the DVD of the film, the remake's screenwriter, Paul Rudnick, explains:

> Both the [original] novel and the film were a response to kind of a first wave of feminism in America in the '70s. What one of the wives

in the original film does that her husband finds terribly threatening is that she practices photography as a hobby. And the husband really found this quite an assault on his manhood. And I thought, well, we've come a *certain* way since then! So, I was fascinated by the updating we've been able to do.

Leaving aside his serious mischaracterization of the 1960s and 1970s movement as feminism's "first" wave, Rudnick's judgment that significant changes were clearly necessary in order to modernize the story indicates that his 2004 version arguably fits Thomas Leitch's definition of the "update" remake. In Leitch's discussion of the rhetoric of film remakes, he theorizes four different stances a remake may adopt toward its originating text (45). "Update" remakes, he explains,

> are characterized by their overtly revisionary stance toward an original text they treat as classic, even though they transform it in some obvious way, usually by transposing it to a new setting, inverting its system of values, or adopting standards of realism that implicitly criticize the original as outmoded, or irrelevant. (47)

Rudnick's statements would suggest that when it comes to the story of *The Stepford Wives*, gendered power relations have progressed to a point where the original angst-ridden depiction of female struggle is noticeably—even laughably—dated by contemporary viewers' standards, provoking the need for updating.

Of course, Rudnick's comments are not without some basis: in the decades that have passed since the first film's release at the end of the second wave movement, the concept of feminism has become much better established within popular culture and media. Whereas in 1975 Judy Klemesrud remarked that *The Stepford Wives* was "one of the first films to deal with feminism in any manner," by 2004 feminism's precepts could generally be considered familiar to the wider viewing public (29). Gone, we are now regularly assured by the media, is any possible hysteria and anxiety, the silly moral panic over the potential threat that feminism could pose, replaced by a mature and principled acceptance of feminism's claims to legitimacy. As a result, observes Nina K. Martin, the remake's move away from eerie suspense to a loud "campy, farcical tone" can be interpreted as a product of the filmmakers' reasonable assumption "that the dangers inherent in Stepford's sinister imagining are well-past, just as the goals of the '70s women's movement are far behind us."

However, in his discussion of the revisionary aspects of film remakes, Leitch also observes that remakes "establish their value by invoking earlier texts whose potency they simultaneously valorize and deny through a series of rhetorical maneuvers designed at once to reflect their intimacy with these texts and to distance themselves from their flaws" (53). Although Leitch refers specifically to remakes in film, it is noteworthy that for many feminists this rhetoric of disavowal is a significantly more accurate model of the changes that have taken place in terms of feminism's representation within contemporary media as well. Rosalind Gill is representative when she writes: "it would be entirely false to suggest that the media has somehow become feminist and has adopted unproblematically a feminist perspective. Instead, it seems more accurate to argue that the media offers contradictory, but nevertheless patterned, constructions" (161). Gill contends that these patterned contradictions—indeed disavowals—are at the heart of "postfeminism," a widely influential paradigm that arguably informs Rudnick's understanding of contemporary feminism and, by extension, the particular manner in which the story of *The Stepford Wives* is remodeled. In what follows, I perform a close reading of the 2004 filmic adaptation of *The Stepford Wives* against the 1975 version as a means of demonstrating how feminism is "remade" at the same time as the film is remade, reflecting much broader changes in contemporary discourse surrounding the cultural status of the women's movement.

Filmed in 1974 and released in February of 1975, *The Stepford Wives*, directed by Bryan Forbes, is a mostly faithful adaptation of Levin's novel. The story centers on Joanna Eberhart (Katharine Ross), a woman who has just relocated to the suburban town of Stepford from New York City with her husband, Walter (Peter Masterson), and their two young daughters. Although Walter believes Stepford will provide a better place to live and raise their children than the city, Joanna is not convinced, particularly when she begins to notice its residents' odd behavior. Aside from Bobby Markowe (Paula Prentiss)—another newly transplanted New Yorker—all the women Joanna encounters display eerily similar characteristics. These "Stepford wives" are all utterly devoted to their husbands, to the performance of domestic chores, and to the careful maintenance of their immaculate appearances. They obey their husbands' directions with placid and docile submissiveness and seem unwilling or unable to express any thoughts or opinions that diverge from those of the men.

After Charmaine (Tina Louise), the one other woman sympathetic to Joanna and Bobby's complaints, suddenly has a change of personality and adopts the same submissive stance toward her husband as the other women of Stepford, the pair begins to speculate that something is transforming the women into what Bobby describes as "pan-scrubber" zombies. The two convince their husbands of their desperate need to move away; however, before either one of them is able to follow through, Bobby returns from a weekend away with her husband changed into a "Stepford wife" like the rest. Realizing that her friend has been replaced by an inhuman substitute, Joanna decides to take her children and leave town immediately. Her husband tells her that their daughters are at the manor housing the Men's Association—of which all the Stepford men are members—but this is revealed as a trap. When she arrives at the manor, Dale "Diz" Coba (Patrick O'Neal), the association's quietly menacing president, tells Joanna that the men have perfected a technology that enables them to create "ideal" wives. A horrified Joanna flees from Diz, only to stumble across her own android duplicate in one of the maze of rooms. Before the scene closes, the audience witnesses the automaton advance toward Joanna, a taut pair of pantyhose in hand with which to strangle her.

In the final scene of the film, the Stepford wives glide serenely down the pastel aisles of the local supermarket, murmuring banal greetings to one another in tranquil tones. When the audience is finally granted a glimpse of Joanna, it is clear that she did not survive and has in fact suffered the same fate as the other women and been replaced by her own Stepford wife duplicate.

The film is commonly acknowledged, by both the popular and academic press, as having been heavily influenced by the feminist ideas that were prevalent within popular consciousness during its production. Bonnie J. Dow, for example, remarks: "As a film, *The Stepford Wives* both contributed to and drew from popular notions of the purpose and meaning of second-wave feminist ideology and practices" (128). In fact, she affirms that "the second wave of feminism is, in many ways, the subtext required for making complete sense of the film" (127). The film therefore represents a productive artifact through which to discuss the interpretation of second wave feminism within popular culture.

At this point, it is important to clarify that while there is a broad tendency within contemporary popular culture to characterize the women's movement of the 1960s and early 1970s as coherent and unified in its development, politics, and goals, this is of course inaccurate historically. As with any social movement that emerges out of a complex set of historical relations, people came to the issue of "women's oppression" from different backgrounds and experiences, resulting in highly divergent views on what constituted liberation and how that might be achieved. Two major branches were usually acknowledged in the early stages of the movement, generally differentiated by one's focus on "women's rights" and the other's focus on "women's liberation" or, to put it differently, one's "reformist," "liberal" orientation and the other's "radical" orientation (Freeman 51). Jo Freeman, an active participant in the politics of this era, objects to these labels, which are admittedly rather neat; however, given the parameters of this discussion they do prove useful in explaining the movement's origins, as well as the way its range of participants and actions was perceived by the public.

While the different sides of the movement often overlapped in their concerns, there were some fundamental differences in focus and philosophy between the two. While liberal activists, the most visible of whom was perhaps Betty Friedan, co-founder of the National Organization for Women (NOW) and author of *The Feminine Mystique*, tended to push an agenda related to opening space, often via legal reform, for women's equal participation in the public sphere as it already existed, radical feminists typically pushed for the recognition of the ideological significance of behaviors and practices that were until then considered wholly private and personal. Arguably more influenced by writers like Simone de Beauvoir than Friedan, these feminists worked to politicize nearly every aspect of women's private life. The now-familiar slogan "the personal is political" was used to express these activists' realization that dissatisfactions and difficulties in women's individual experience did not in fact represent purely personal problems, but rather were generalizable and therefore indicative of the larger culture's ideology at work. Accordingly, these feminists challenged traditional conventions in a multitude of areas within the so-called private sphere, such as sexuality, reproductive rights, marriage as institution, beauty and fashion regimes, and, in fact, the very notion of gender itself. Throughout these critiques, their focus repeatedly returned to the body as one of the primary sites of women's oppression. The conclusion these activists and authors came to was that the body was fundamentally objectified within normative femininity in myriad ways, whether it be through the medicalization of childbirth, women's lack of knowledge about their own sexuality or the sense of emptiness and deficiency that accompanies women's participation in beauty routines. To endure this objectification ultimately meant existing in a state of alienation, forever cut off from any genuine capacity for agency and self-determination. Sandra Lee Bartky defines this alienation as "a *fragmentation* of the human person and a *prohibition* on the full exercise of capacities, the exercise of which is thought to be necessary to a fully human existence" (323). Further, although these norms had been identified via the close examination of individual women's lives, their transformation could only come about through a radical restructuring of society itself. These feminists argued that societal structures as they stood had been deeply shaped by long-standing traditions of patriarchal dominance, and therefore to try to work for change within their limits would be futile.

These ideas had come to form a recognizable element of popular cultural debate by the time *The Stepford Wives* was published in 1972—significantly, Levin's novel itself opens with an epigraph from de Beauvoir's *The Second Sex*—and are equally reflected within Forbes' filmic adaptation. This perhaps helps to explain as well why Friedan herself walked out on a special screening of the film for feminist "opinionmakers": the themes on which the film draws derive more directly from the radical stream of feminism, focused on "body politics," as these ideas came to be known, rather than legislative reforms.

Indeed, in many ways the Stepford wife forms the perfect symbol for the politics of the second wave as they pertained to the body. Whether it be in relation to her appearance, sexuality, comportment or reproductive ability, the Stepford woman's body is thoroughly homogenized to meet the purported norms of patriarchal femininity. Moreover, the horror within Forbes' film comes precisely from its heroines' eventual submission to these norms, a practice that would otherwise be considered natural and desirable. Like the radical feminists, the film—to use the language of de Beauvoir—depicts normative femininity as requiring woman to exist in a fundamentally disempowered state, one in which her objectified position as other to the essential subject, man, prevents her from ever achieving self-definition or authentic subjectivity. Symbolically, this political stance is rendered within the conventions of the film's genre—which Anna Krugovoy Silver describes as a "feminist, science-fiction allegory" (74)—as a polarized conflict between the men who, as stand-ins for the patriarchy, aggressively reinforce a universal feminine ideal, and the women who desperately try to escape the total annihilation of self that would necessarily accompany their enactment of that same patriarchal ideal.

The influence of these ideas is observable in a variety of ways throughout the film; however, the pivotal issues of sexuality and reproduction provide instructive examples. One of the immediately apparent effects of the women's replacement with automata is the way it ensures the sexual availability of the Stepford wives to the men. In one scene, Joanna and Bobby accidentally overhear one of the Stepford wives having sex with her husband. From upstairs they hear the woman breathlessly enthusing about her husband's performance, calling him the "best" and the "master." In another scene, Joanna witnesses her neighbor obediently enter the house after her husband signals his intentions by slipping his hands over her breasts. These segments make evident that the Stepford wives have been programmed, unsurprisingly, to serve their husbands' desires alone, to affirm their virility and masculinity (admittedly to comically absurd lengths) and to submit to sex whenever their husbands please. Though the wives blandly assert that their sex lives have never been better, it seems clear that they operate as sexual objects rather than sexual subjects (Silver 72). In fact, as "live dolls"—the very same metaphor used by many radical feminists to describe the feminine ideal—the Stepford wives represent little more than sophisticated sex toys. As pure objects, they cannot make any sexual demands of their own. The androids have no independent desire, curiosity or preconditions for reciprocation: they can only reaffirm the competence of the men.

Radical feminists maintained that this type of female sexuality, defined by passivity and a lack of subjective involvement, was widely promoted as ideal within patriarchal culture and therefore was a large source of women's alienation and disempowerment. Similarly, abortion became a major issue for radical feminists because without it, they argued, women would continue to be profoundly objectified by their lack of control over their own reproduction. They reasoned that without the ability to choose whether and with whom to have children, women could never be fully self-determined; the nature of their selves, rather, would be forever determined by the things that "happened to" their bodies. Within the film, the ability of the Stepford women to reproduce is taken entirely from their control. Not only do the men seize absolute power over reproduction by independently creating "manmade" women, but they also foreclose any potential for the women to make autonomous choices regarding their own reproductive ability; after all, the replacements cannot bear children whatsoever because they are not organic beings. For Silver, "the film's emphasis, then, is not on women's choosing *not* to have children, but rather on women's losing the choice to *have* children" (70).

These issues are highlighted during the scene in which Joanna confronts Bobby about her daughters' location. Desperate and frustrated with her inability to focus Bobby's attention, Joanna grabs a large kitchen knife and cuts her own finger, explaining to Bobby: "Look, I bleed. When I cut myself, I bleed. Do you bleed?" When Bobby responds to this action with only mild puzzlement, tutting, "Why, look at your hand," Joanna settles the question herself, growling, "No, you look!" before thrusting the knife into Bobby's abdomen. As anticipated, she does not bleed and therefore is confirmed as inhuman; in addition, the knife's piercing of Bobby's womb reconfirms the women's lack of control over their own reproduction. More significantly, the scene reinforces that the androids represent the patriarchal vision of the ideal feminine body in that the ideal woman does not bleed. Radical feminists often pointed to the ways in which menstruation was viewed as a shameful, dirty, and disturbing occurrence and therefore something to be diligently hidden from public awareness, a burden to be "borne and belied" (Greer 84). A woman, writes Germaine Greer, "hopes she is not sloppy or smelly, and obligingly obliterates all signs of her menstruation in the cause of public decency" (39). Greer and others attributed this belief not to any innate sense of secrecy or shame within menstruating women, but rather to a patriarchal culture that defined woman as other. The penalties that existed for those who did not conform to these expectations "spring from a fear of the 'otherness' of woman," writes Kate Millett (46), resulting in the "poisoning [of] the female's own sense of physical self" (47).

Bobby's lack of blood or pain points again to the dehumanization, objectification, and powerlessness the film suggests are the inevitable consequences of conforming to dominant societal ideals. As Linda Boruszkowski writes of the scene: "The knife wound is traditionally a symbolic castration. Here it can have no effect on Bobby since she's already been castrated/mutilated—she has nothing more to lose" (18). Boruszkowski's analysis also strongly echoes Greer's influential 1970 book, *The Female Eunuch*, wherein she argues that castratedness—that is, inaction and impotence—is the essential quality of the ideal feminine being. Bobby has nothing more to lose because there is nothing left of herself, of her own subjectivity, within the homogenized object that has replaced her: "she no longer possesses a 'self' to defend" (18). The new Bobby perfectly represents the "female impersonator" Greer argued ideal femininity required women to be (61) and exposes the existential impossibility tied to enacting this role.

Viewed from this perspective, the root cause of the Stepford women's disempowerment and suffering in the film was not their personal problems or relationships with individual men, who are overall rather featureless—Bobby's husband, for example, is never even introduced on screen—but rather a much larger set of cultural norms that circumscribed their role and options in life, ultimately denying them the possibility of full control and agency. The homogeneity of the men and their labors to enforce the women's conformity dramatized the operation of asymmetries in gendered power and the impact of this inequality on women's subjectivity. In strong contrast, the 2004 remake depicts the women as being no longer affected by any societal power imbalances whatsoever; in fact, more than anything else they seem to be victims of their own self-directed ambition and extreme success. Each (pre-transformation) female character is portrayed as fully in control, hyper-successful in the public sphere, and victorious in the imagined battle of the sexes. The film's exaggerated reflection of the genuine, but incremental, gains made by women in the public sphere post-second wave is accompanied by the total disappearance of any structural critique of the kind found in the earlier film. This too reflects powerfully popular discourse about the definition and status of the women's movement today.

Within this second film, Joanna (played, fittingly enough, by the wife Tom Cruise left in 2001, Nicole Kidman) is re-imagined as a tightly wound, shrill Manhattan careerist. Walter (Matthew Broderick) is now depicted as Joanna's subordinate at work, and a man who feels outdone by his tremendously successful wife. After her unexpected firing, however, Joanna experiences a nervous breakdown and she and Walter move the family to Stepford as a way to save their marriage, which Joanna blames herself for having neglected. For its part, Stepford is no longer a sedate and traditional New England village, but a wealthy and conservative gated community.

As in the original, Joanna meets and befriends Bobby (Bette Midler)—now a caustic author of bestselling self-help books—soon after her arrival in Stepford. Instead of Charmaine, Joanna is introduced to Roger (Roger Bart), a campy, gregarious gay man who often embarrasses his uptight Republican partner. As expected, Joanna's newfound allies mysteriously begin conforming to the Stepford ideal, including first Roger, whose transformation translates into his becoming more reserved and serious, and then Bobby. Eventually, Joanna is lured to the Men's Association, where her as-yet-lifeless body double is deliberately revealed to her and, in the scene's final shot, she and Walter are lowered into a secret underground room, where we understand he will have her changed. As in the first film, the next time we glimpse Joanna, she is placidly pacing the aisles of the Stepford supermarket, clad in a frilly, pastel dress and high heels, her conversion marked most clearly by the transformation of her previously short, severe dark hair into a long, delicate blonde mane.

Illustration 5.1   Joanna (Nicole Kidman) in Stepford's local supermarket. Unlike the 1975 movie, the 2004 remake of *The Stepford Wives* does not end here

Unlike the original film, however, the story does not end here with Joanna's tragic demise. In the subsequent finale, it is revealed that Mike (Christopher Walken)—the remake's equivalent of Diz—is, in fact, a robot replacement himself, a creation of his jilted and maniacal human wife Claire (Glenn Close), a former neuroscientist and genetic engineer. It is Claire, then, who is ultimately behind all the android replacements populating the town. Further, we learn that Walter had a change of heart and never actually went through with Joanna's transformation; rather, the couple cooperated in faking it so that they could escape and go on to free the others by somehow de-programming them. Finally, in a coda tacked on to the end of the film, the recovered Joanna, Bobby, and Roger giddily recount their ordeal to Larry King on his televised talk show.

Robert Eberwein has observed that "[a] remake is a kind of reading or rereading of the original" that is inflected by the prevalent discourses circulating in a culture at a given point in time (15). In this case, what the distinctive changes in the second film speak to, in part, are the significant shifts in rhetorical strategies between 1975 and 2004 within mediated public discourses about feminism. As mentioned earlier, when it comes to contemporary attitudes surrounding feminism, a number of prominent feminist thinkers have pointed to the rising influence of postfeminism. As a term its definition is still contested;

however, I follow Gill's understanding of it as a "distinctive sensibility" (147). Central to this sensibility is a particular mode of address, one that includes a token acknowledgement of feminism's significance at the same time as it dismisses feminism as no longer necessary or relevant to today's world. In general, Gill's position is shared by other feminist media scholars: Yvonne Tasker and Diane Negra describe this discourse as one of "double address" (108), while Angela McRobbie refers to it as one of "double entanglement" (244). Regardless of the terms used, these theorists could all be said to formulate postfeminism as an increasingly dominant rhetoric of disavowal within mainstream discourse about feminism, one that emphasizes that equality has been achieved and therefore feminism is a "spent force" (255).

This discourse's persuasiveness largely comes from its frequent reference to the well-publicized advances that women have indeed made over the past 35 years, which postfeminism presents as evidence that the ideals of second wave feminism have been progressively adopted by the culture and therefore its goals effectively attained. Importantly, however, the examples to which postfeminism typically refers, such as women's increased participation in work outside the home, are almost exclusively drawn from the goals of the liberal side of second wave feminism. This follows quite naturally from the fact that the mainstream media has long shown a preference for promoting the liberal side over the radical, arguably because it is easiest to incorporate and subsume within the wider culture's existing set of values. Writers such as Dow, Elisabeth A. Van Zoonen and Susan J. Douglas have all noted that from the very beginning of the second wave movement, the popular media only "endorsed a narrow, white, upper-middle-class slice of liberal feminism and cast the rest off as irresponsible, misguided, and deviant" (Douglas 186). Over successive iterations through time, these fabrications concerning what defines the boundaries of legitimate second wave feminism have become instilled within popular culture as a sort of self-evident, received wisdom. This "reformist" feminism which focuses on access to the public sphere rather than private practices is the feminism invoked as having fully achieved its objectives and ensured women's autonomy. Of course, the degree to which even liberal feminism's goals have been attained is debatable; nevertheless, within the basic logic of postfeminism, second wave feminism is equated with liberal feminism, which in turn has been entirely successful in its aims and has at last leveled the playing field, giving rise to its irrelevance. To the extent that women reflect a type of feminist empowerment today, it is expressed through the individual decisions and choices that they make freely now on their own behalf. This emphasis on a finally unburdened female able to make decisions in her own personal best interest, independent of undue outside influence, forms the core of postfeminist rhetoric. "The notion that all our practices are freely chosen," affirms Gill, "is central to postfeminist discourses, which present women as autonomous agents no longer constrained by inequalities or power imbalances whatsoever" (153).

The 2004 remake of *The Stepford Wives* can be seen clearly to reflect the cultural influence of postfeminism in its flattening out of power relations and its corresponding emphasis on individualism. The ultimate challenge for this version's Joanna is not to overcome endemic, structural gender inequality, but to learn to make individual, personal compromises in the interests of romantic love. As director Frank Oz explains: "The movie's about the acceptance of imperfect love. ... The heart of it is about this couple trying to work things out, and I think we can all relate to that" (qtd. in Fine). Conflict or resentment within a marriage or personal relationship, according to both postfeminist logic and the remade film, have nothing to do with larger structural inequalities and expectations, but simply with human flaws, which are universal. Indeed, when Joanna is confronted with Walter's unhappiness, she blames herself for their marital problems and in response makes concerted attempts to fit into Stepford's ideal long before her supposed transformation. The film, Martin observes, repeatedly implies that "gender troubles are to be overcome by personal changes made in order to solidify the institution of marriage—an institution that does not need to be further criticized or questioned." During her interview with King at the film's conclusion, Joanna affirms the lesson she has learned in the importance of acceptance and compromise in marriage. Displaying a short hairstyle once more, though this time of a considerably softer blonde color, Joanna smiles benevolently at her husband standing off camera and explains: "We're doing just great because now we know for sure it's not about perfection. Perfect doesn't work." Thus, within the film relationships of domination are portrayed as isolated, individual occurrences, an interpersonal problem rather than a societal one, solved through flexibility and compromise. In this fashion, notes Martin, what was in the original film a "threat to *all* women" becomes in the remake "a more localized and specific threat toward highly successful *people*, women and men, who overshadow their geeky spouses in both ambition and ability."

This viewpoint is perhaps made most apparent in the inclusion of a gay male couple in the new Stepford. Although the partnership's addition is interesting for its representation of changing social mores, including a "Stepford husband" ultimately works to uphold the atomized notion of power communicated by postfeminist discourse. Within the film's logic, the domination of a stereotypically effeminate gay man by his more butch male partner is functionally equivalent to the domination of a heterosexual woman by her husband, a puzzling suggestion when one considers the larger structures of power supporting each male oppressor's actions. From a greater systemic perspective, both gay men are already oppressed by a still homophobic society; thus the subjugation they are capable of enacting on one another, though real, is significantly different in kind from that which a heterosexual man is able to exploit. Moreover, the reasons why the more "feminine" partner in the gay couple would be singled out for correction are presumed by the film to be self-evident, so that the cultural roots of such an assumption are left completely unexplored.

Hence, the desire for a perfectly subservient mate is presented in the second film not as a product of patriarchal anxiety, but simply the result of an individual spouse feeling stifled, overshadowed or otherwise dissatisfied with a partner. Indeed, the ultimate villain of the remake is not male collective desires at all, but rather a solitary lunatic, a female no less, who reveals—with a further sweep of egalitarianism—that according to her plan even the men would eventually have been replaced by robots too. Such gestures of equivalence indicate especially the lack of political significance the film assigns to the gendered body, in contrast to its predecessor. Indeed, the body is one of the most obvious sites through which gender difference has continuously found expression, and yet the remake avoids this theme entirely. In fact, the second film cannot seem to make up its mind about whether the Stepford wives are robots with transplanted brains, or surgically altered women with nanochipped brains or some other option. This incoherence probably stems from the film's well-publicized production difficulties, which included repeated reshoots after test screenings (Griffin). As a result, however, the film eliminates what was arguably at the heart of the original film's story of human women's replacement by perfect androids: that is, the political significance of the actual *body* of the Stepford wife. Under postfeminism's presumption of fundamental equality, the women's bodies, and their relationships to them, are made once again personal and idiosyncratic, a reflection of individual psychology and not indicative of any wider cultural ideology, or at least not any that does not affect all people equally.

Indeed, the format of the remake in many ways provides the perfect vehicle to investigate the revisionist disavowal that lies at the core of postfeminism. A close comparison of these two versions of *The Stepford Wives* uncovers a significant shift in emphasis from the structural, social level of the first film, to the personal, individual level of the second. The type of interest granted to women's relationships to their bodies and sexuality in the first film does not translate to the second, since these critiques refer to broader sets of cultural limitations that simply do not exist within the context of a postfeminist discourse that sets up liberal feminism as the only feminism and denies structural inequality. Through this comparison the resultant delegitimization and gradual erasure of radical critique from public memory and discussion becomes increasingly apparent.

Thus, in directly comparing these two temporally distant films ostensibly based on the same basic "story," we can begin to grasp some fundamental shifts in popular discourse and to evaluate their roots. Leitch has noted that remakes depend on a "distinction between their story (which links them to some other film) and their discourse (which sets them apart from a re-release of that film)" (46). In effect, this distinction creates a ready-made version of what in semiotics would be termed a commutation test: a form of discourse analysis in which one imagines substituting an alternate signifier for an existing one and then assesses the effect this would have on meaning, thereby gaining insight into how this meaning is created and structured. In the case of *The Stepford Wives*, a careful evaluation of the different signifiers used by each film can reveal some ways in which second wave feminism—our collective cultural understanding of its "meaning" and role—has been itself remade over time within popular discourse, exposing the drift that has occurred in what would otherwise be considered a self-evidently feminist perspective today. For those who study the representation and public perception of a movement like feminism, the comparison of an original film and remake can therefore provide a critical and well-defined illustration of a sea change in public discourse which might otherwise be lost or discounted or, like the significance of the phrase "Stepford wife" itself, simply taken for granted.

Works consulted

Bartky, Sandra Lee. "Body Politics." *A Companion to Feminist Philosophy*. Ed. Alison M. Jaggar and Iris Marion Young. Malden, MA: Blackwell, 1998. 321–29. Print.

Boruszkowski, Lilly Ann. "*The Stepford Wives*: The Re-Created Woman." *Jump Cut* 32 (April 1987): 16–19. Print.

Douglas, Susan J. *Where the Girls Are: Growing Up Female with the Mass Media.* 1994. New York: Times-Random, 1995. Print.

Dow, Bonnie J. "Feminism, Miss America, and Media Mythology." *Rhetoric & Public Affairs* 6.1 (2003): 127–49. Print.

Eberwein, Robert. "Remakes and Cultural Studies." *Play It Again, Sam: Retakes on Remakes.* Ed. Andrew Horton and Stuart Y. McDougal. Berkeley: University of California Press, 1998. 15–33. Print.

Fine, Larry. "*The Stepford Wives* Now a Laughing Matter." *SignOnSanDiego.com.* Union-Tribune Publishing, 10 June 2004. Retrieved on 2 January 2009. http://www.signonsandiego.com/news/features/20040610–0500-leisure-stepford. html.

Freeman, Jo. *The Politics of Women's Liberation.* New York: Longman, 1975. Print.

Gill, Rosalind. "Postfeminist Media Culture: Elements of a Sensibility." *European Journal of Cultural Studies* 10.2 (2007): 147–66. Print.

Greer, Germaine. *The Female Eunuch.* 1970. London: Paladin, 1971. Print.

Griffin, Nancy. "Can This Film Be Fixed?" *New York Times* 6 June 2004: AR13+. Print.

Klemesrud, Judy. "Feminists Recoil at Film Designed to Relate to Them." *New York Times* 26 February 1975: 29. Print.

Leitch, Thomas. "Twice-Told Tales: Disavowal and the Rhetoric of the Remake." *Dead Ringers: The Remake in Theory and Practice.* Ed. Jennifer Forrest and Leonard R. Koos. Albany: State University of New York Press, 2002. 37–62. Print.

Martin, Nina K. "Revisiting Stepford: The House that Postfeminism Built." Society for Cinema and Media Studies Conference, Vancouver. 2–5 March 2006.

McRobbie, Angela. "Post-Feminism and Popular Culture." *Feminist Media Studies* 4.3 (2004): 255–64. Print.

Millett, Kate. *Sexual Politics.* 1969. Urbana: University of Illinois Press, 2000. Print.

Silver, Anna Krugovoy. "The Cyborg Mystique: *The Stepford Wives* and Second Wave Feminism." *Women's Studies Quarterly* 30.1/2 (2002): 60–76. Print.

The Stepford Wives. Screenplay by William Goldman. Dir. Bryan Forbes. Perf. Katharine Ross, Paula Prentiss, and Peter Masterson. 1975. Paramount, 2004. DVD.

The Stepford Wives. Screenplay by Paul Rudnick. Dir. Frank Oz. Perf. Nicole Kidman, Matthew Broderick, and Bette Midler. 2004. Paramount, 2004. DVD.

Tasker, Yvonne, and Diane Negra. "In Focus: Postfeminism and Contemporary Media Studies." *Cinema Journal* 44.2 (2005): 107–10. Print.

Van Zoonen, Elisabeth A. "The Women's Movement and the Media: Constructing a Public Identity." *European Journal of Communication* 7.4 (1992): 453–76. Print.

6
The Return of the Pod People: Remaking Cultural Anxieties in *Invasion of the Body Snatchers*

Kathleen Loock

Don Siegel's *Invasion of the Body Snatchers* (1956), based on a novel by Jack Finney, has become one of the most influential alien invasion films of all time. The film's theme of alien paranoia—the fear that some invisible invaders could replace individual human beings and turn them into a collective of emotionless pod people—resonated with widespread anxieties in 1950s American culture. It has been read as an allegory of the communist threat during the Cold War but also as a commentary on McCarthyism, the alienating effects of capitalism, conformism, postwar radiation anxiety, the return of "brainwashed" soldiers from the Korean War, and masculine fears of "the potential social, political, and personal disenfranchisement of postwar America's hegemonic white patriarchy" (Mann 49).[1]

Engaging with the profound concerns of its time, *Invasion of the Body Snatchers* is widely regarded as a signature film of the 1950s. Yet despite its cultural and historical specificity, the narrative of alien-induced dehumanization has lent itself to reinterpretations and re-imaginations like few others, always shifting with the zeitgeist and replacing former cultural anxieties with more contemporary and urgent ones. Siegel's film has inspired three cinematic remakes over the last 55 years: Philip Kaufman's *Invasion of the Body Snatchers* (1978), Abel Ferrara's *Body Snatchers* (1993), and, most recently, Oliver Hirschbiegel's *The Invasion* (2007). Bits and pieces of the film have also found their way into the American popular imagination, taking the form of intermedial references to *Invasion of the Body Snatchers* in movies, television series, cartoons, and video games.[2] By remodeling the theme, plot, characters, narrative devices, visuals, sound, and special effects of Siegel's film in ever new contexts, the cinematic remakes and pop-cultural citations have decisively influenced the film's cultural currency beyond its immediate 1950s background.

That *Invasion of the Body Snatchers* would become a touchstone of American popular culture was, however, not to be expected when the film was released in 1956. It received little critical attention; many theaters did not even book the movie in its first run. Although it eventually grossed $1,200,000 at the box office at a production cost of only $416,911, the steady increase of the film's popularity and cultural importance both for fans and critics set in after its initial broadcast on television in 1959 (Grant 7). This development reached its climax with the canonization of *Invasion of the Body Snatchers* in 1994, when the film was among the 25 "culturally, historically or aesthetically significant films" that are annually added to the US National Film Registry at the Library of Congress under the terms of the National Film Preservation Act of 1988 ("Key Features"; "25 Films"; Grant 7). While this canonization attests to the (cult) status the film has finally gained as a classic of American cinema, it must also draw our attention to the remakes of *Invasion of the Body Snatchers*. They are one of the reasons why the 1956 B-movie has not been forgotten, why it has remained present in the popular imagination, and why it continues to be an object of scholarly investigation.

In fact, the remakes seem to have spawned academic discussions and re-readings of the 1956 movie: most articles on Siegel's film have been published after the release of Kaufman's highly successful 1978 remake; similarly, Ferrara's 1993 and Hirschbiegel's 2007 remakes were followed by an influx of scholarly writing on the first movie. Academic interest in studying the original apparently correlates with the production of new versions of the same story. More recent publications usually approach Siegel's film within the framework of its cinematic remake(s) in order to foreground changes and/or examine cultural transformations at work.[3] Yet scholars seldom seem to ask why *Invasion of the Body Snatchers* has generated a pattern of repetition and variation that has resulted in the three remakes to date, that is, updated versions every 15 to 20 years or so. Neil Badmington speaks of a "compulsion to revisit the tale" (14). "To tell it anew," he writes, "appears to be motivated in part by a desire to 'get it right,' to settle an old score" (14). Jim Hoberman, in contrast, sees commercial rather than artistic reasons behind the production of so many remakes. After all, he states, "*Invasion of the Body Snatchers* has a title that suggests nothing so much as Hollywood's boundless capacity to feed upon itself" (29), evoking the idea that remakes are in and of themselves a sort of body snatching in the name of box office success. In this chapter, I want to show that the story's particular suitability for cinematic remaking has led to its reinterpretations within the historical and cultural contexts of the respective periods of production. I propose a case study that bestows equal emphasis on all films and analyzes them for patterns and structures that will explain the recurrent interest in the body snatcher story.

In his volume on Siegel's *Invasion of the Body Snatchers*, Barry Keith Grant explains that "the film's enduring popularity derives in large part from a combination of a central metaphor for the monstrous that, like the vampire or zombie, is sufficiently flexible to accommodate multiple interpretations with a style and structure that is admirably economical even as it is highly expressive" (8–9). I shall appropriate Grant's observation about the film's popularity and specify the three elements he mentions—metaphor, style, and structure—for my analysis of the film's suitability for cinematic remaking. Accordingly, Siegel's B-movie offers an "all-purpose metaphor" (Hoberman 29) for dehumanization and the loss of individuality that locates the monstrous in the normal; its style can be described as *film noir* aesthetics[4] somewhere in between the science fiction and horror genres; and it has a historically specific setting, linear plot, simple character constellation, and an arguably ambiguous ending. These basic features have, to return to Grant, ensured the movie's "enduring popularity" and inspired multiple readings of *Invasion of the Body Snatchers* in the past (and will probably continue to do so in the future). More importantly, though, I would suggest that precisely these features of the first movie already invite *repetition, variation*, and *continuation*—in short: they invite film remakes that explore and rethink choices director Don Siegel, screenwriter Daniel Mainwaring, producer Walter Wanger, and—eventually—the Allied Artists film studio had made for the 1956 movie.

Repetition

Film remakes (similar to sequels and series) always contain elements that are not altered or advanced, but reproduced from earlier renditions. This is necessarily so, since by definition, remakes are based on previous works and repeat recognizable textual structures of their models.[5] From the film industry point of view, repetition "[satisfies] the requirement that Hollywood deliver reliability" (Verevis 4) and thus ensures box office success by virtually putting a pre-sold product on the release schedules. Umberto Eco considers the remake (along with the retake, the series, the saga, and intertextuality) as a type of repetition in which "(1) something is offered as original and different (according to the requirements of modern aesthetics); (2) we are aware that this something is repeating something else that we already know; and (3) notwithstanding this—better, just because of it—we like it (and we buy it)" (167). Yet remakes cannot rely on repetition alone; they also require "novelty (innovation) in the same production package" as Constantine Verevis reminds us (4). A derivative copy of an earlier film, produced for purely commercial reasons, rarely wins over audience and critics. Eco suggests that to conform to "a 'modern' conception of aesthetic value," works of art "must achieve a dialectics between order and novelty—in other words, between scheme and innovation" that can be readily perceived by the (knowledgeable) audience (173–74). For my case study of *Invasion of the Body Snatchers* and its remakes, I am interested in those elements that are reproduced in each film and in the choices that introduce innovations. I will further look at instances of continuity that situate the body snatcher films closer to the series or sequels than might generally be expected of cinematic remakes.

In *Invasion of the Body Snatchers*, the central metaphor, linear plot, and basic character constellation remain the same in all its cinematic versions. The four films to date share these three features, resulting in the fact that the basic narrative is always recognizable: parasitic alien life forms (pods) invade earth and assume the shapes and memories of human beings in their sleep. In the process, the humans turn one by one into a collective of seemingly calm but emotionless people. At first, the pod people keep up the pretense of normalcy. But friends and relatives who have not yet been transformed notice that others have somehow changed. As they too are soon taken over, the human façade of the ever growing number of pod people is no longer necessary, and they openly persecute the few people they have not yet absorbed. Among these—and they will eventually be the last ones—are the protagonists who struggle to fight the alien invasion. Even though each remake re-imagines the setting and ending of the first adaptation, casts it in a different style, introduces new themes, and develops earlier ones, all of them repeat essentially the same story about the threat of dehumanization and retain important *narrative elements* and *key scenes*, two of which I will discuss in the following.

The premise that human beings are taken over by the alien invaders in their sleep, for example, is central to all films and provides chilling moments of horror. I am not only referring to the horrifying transformation and subsequent loss of self, here. Still more terrifying is the fact that the alien takeover happens while the victims are asleep, that is, in a temporary state of unconsciousness from which they awake as different persons without even noticing. In the 1956 movie, psychiatrist and spokesperson of the pods, Danny Kaufman (Larry Gates), explains the process to protagonists Miles Bennell (Kevin McCarthy) and Becky Discroll (Dana Wynter): "They're taking you over cell for cell, atom for atom. There's no pain. Suddenly, while you're asleep, they'll absorb your minds, your memories, and you're reborn into an untroubled world." The presumably painless takeover, absorption, and rebirth, as Kaufman promotes the transformation in this scene, leads to only one horrifying conclusion: sleep, a basic human necessity and major requirement for physical and mental health, turns out to be fatal.

In his analysis of Finney's novel and Siegel's movie, Glen M. Johnson relates the threat lurking in a normal, everyday activity like sleeping to "the familiar cold war metaphor of sleep vs. wakefulness" (6) and the paranoid conviction that during the late 1940s and 1950s communists had infiltrated American society (cf. Hoberman 30). As these "traitors" were supposedly hiding their true loyalties and secretly working towards the communist subversion of the United States, American citizens were encouraged to be watchful at all times and to report suspicious behavior of family members, neighbors, or acquaintances, which in turn led to a series of denunciations and investigations (Johnson 6). According to Johnson, it is in this sense that both Finney and Siegel employ the sleep metaphor. In novel and film, he argues, it stands "for lack of vigilance and consequent vulnerability to subversion" (6) and therefore endangers individuals as well as society at large.

While all of the remakes repeat the idea that sleep is required for the aliens to absorb human bodies, the political connotations of this narrative device change over the decades. Particularly after the terrorist attacks of 11 September 2001, sleep has taken on a very different meaning (cf. Ulonska 165). In the aftermath of 9/11, "sleeper" became a well-known term to designate terrorists who lead lives as law-abiding citizens within a given society (that is, they lie dormant) until they are activated to perform a terrorist act against that same society. *The Invasion*, Hirschbiegel's 2007 remake, contains several allusions to the contemporary threat of terrorist sleeper agents or sleeper cells. Tucker Kaufman (Jeremy Northam), director of the Center for Disease Control (CDC) and Dr Carol Bennell's (Nicole Kidman) ex-husband, is summoned to investigate the crash of the space shuttle *Patriot*, which had exploded during an unscheduled landing attempt.[6] An alien life form clings to the shuttle's debris that lies scattered all the way from Washington, DC to Dallas. Like an intelligent virus, this alien life form infects human beings upon entering their blood streams and transforms them into pod people once they enter REM sleep. Tucker is one of the first infected by the virus and subsequently exploits his position and the CDC structures to spread the virus under the disguise of flu inoculations. In other words, he undermines the human life form *from within*: instead of preventing an epidemic he causes it, preparing for a pandemic and the global takeover of the aliens along the way. He acts as if he were activated by the virus to destroy the society he has lived in and whose values he has shared so far. Furthermore, he does not remain alone but forms cells with strangers and holds conspiratorial meetings.[7]

Because he is working for the US government agency CDC, Tucker is also the film's representative of the nation's information policy and handling of the crisis, both of which are severely critiqued in *The Invasion*. At an emergency meeting of the CDC, organized and led by Tucker, for example, transformed waiters spew infectious bile into the coffee pots, further spreading the virus, at an event designed to provide information and a rescue plan for the supposedly impending flu epidemic. The "vaccine" Tucker presents at the meeting is, of course, nothing other than the alien virus that will infect everyone who participates in the large-scale inoculation campaign that follows. Carol, who is told that while in Europe and Japan (where the virus has also spread) scientists are running epidemic protocols, in the US everyone is just talking about the flu, confronts her ex-husband: "What are you really covering up, huh? What is it? You've got people lining up like this is smallpox or something. What are you really inoculating them for, Tucker?" Carol's questions express a sense of betrayal by the government authorities and accuse them not only of providing false information about what is actually going on but also of taking the wrong actions.

In the film, this critique is extended to the management of real crises. At a dinner party, the Russian ambassador Yorish Kaganovich (Roger Rees) asks Carol: "Can you give me a pill? To make me see the world the way you Americans see the world? Can a pill help me understand Iraq or Darfur, or even New Orleans?" Yorish refers to the 2003 US-led invasion of Iraq in the immediate aftermath of 9/11, to the questionable role of the US in the Darfur conflict, and to the US government's failure following Hurricane Katrina's flooding of New Orleans in 2005. His questions imply that in order to grasp the political and military decisions that had shaped these crises, he would have to take psychiatric medication that changes his perception of the world. Yorish's explicit critique of US foreign and domestic politics is, however, muffled because he is Russian and aware of his status as an outsider in the US—"perhaps being a Russian in this country is a kind of pathology"—and because, after raising these provoking questions, his concern is given a more general (and, unfortunately, apologetic) twist: Yorish is convinced that civilization in general is "an illusion, a game of pretend" to "hide our true self-interest" and that a world without violence and atrocities would not be human. "Civilization crumbles whenever we need it most," he concludes. "In the right situation we are all capable of the most terrible crimes." Even though his observations anticipate both the peace accords covered in the television news *and* Carol's killing and injuring numerous pod people in an attempt to rescue and protect her son, they distract from Yorish's underlying critique of government action—a critique that is central to *The Invasion* and much more prominent than in the previous remakes. There, the authorities are generally out of reach or gradually taken over in the course of the alien invasion. At the same time, the protagonists use their professional position to investigate what is happening. For instance, Matthew Bennell (Donald Sutherland) and Elizabeth Driscoll (Brooke Adams), of the 1978 remake, work for the Public Health Department, while Steve Malone (Terry Kinney), in the 1993 *Body Snatchers*, is employed by the US Environment Protection Agency. In *The Invasion*, government agents are involved in the alien takeover from the beginning, acting under the disguise of protecting public health and safety. I will be returning to these observations, but at this point, suffice it to say that even if the same narrative elements are repeated in the cinematic remakes, they carry very different connotations which are closely related to current political events.

In the movies, sleep is associated with the pods, wakefulness with humans struggling for survival, or, as Johnson puts it, "people can be snatched only while they sleep; awake, they recognize subversion and fight it" (6). This is, of course, a recipe for trouble because humans cannot live without sleep. "We'll get him!...He can't stay awake forever," the pods remark about Matthew in the 1978 movie (and they will be right, as the ending reveals). To a certain extent, *Invasion of the Body Snatchers* focuses as much on sleep as on sleep deprivation (rather than wakefulness). In fact, the lack of sleep fulfills a narrative function: the characters become more and more jumpy and panic-stricken; they are also less alert and in constant danger of dozing off. All this increases the sense of paranoia inherent in the body snatcher story, creates suspense, and contributes to the sense of urgency conveyed in the movies. Once the pod people gain the upper hand, there is no remedy except trying to stay awake and alert. But how much longer can they go on without sleep?

Illustration 6.1 "Don't sleep"—Dr Carol Bennell (Nicole Kidman) leaves a message for her son Oliver. Sleep and sleep deprivation are central themes in *Invasion* (2007) and the three earlier body snatcher movies

The protagonists eventually resort to drugs: in the 1956 movie, Miles hands Becky pills ("Here. Take two of these. They'll help you to stay awake."); in the 1978 remake, Elizabeth finds her colleague's supply of speed when she hides with Matthew in the office, and they decide to take five pills instead of the prescribed dose of one. In Abel Ferrara's 1993 remake, which is set on an American army military base, protagonists repeatedly rouse each other from sleep during mid-transformation, which results in scenes that are evidently designed to showcase the film's elaborate special effects. Both the hysterical psychiatrist Major Collins (Forest Whitaker)—who eventually commits suicide when he is cornered by the pod people—and the protagonist's father Steve Malone—who turns into a pod person and is killed by his teenage daughter Marti (Gabrielle Anwar)—take pills, while she and her boyfriend Tim (Billy Wirth) finally survive without consuming any stimulants. The 2007 remake, in contrast, puts much emphasis on staying awake with the help of drugs that Carol finds in the pharmacy section of a small supermarket where she waits for her friend Ben Driscoll (Daniel Craig). In fact, the movie opens with shots of flickering neon lamps, sounds of heavy breathing, and eventually a focus on Carol, nervously foraging pharmacy shelves for drugs. In the voice-over accompanying this scene, we can hear her thoughts: "Adderall gone. Ritalin, gone. Amitryptiline. What is it?...Modifinil, CNS, Dopamine. A stimulant. Clonazepam. Clonazepam, good. That's right. Yes. Good. Citric acid, yes. Oh, sugar, sugar. Fructose. Mountain Dew, Mountain Dew." The fast cuts between close-ups of tablet containers and Carol's desperate face enhance the urgency of this opening scene. As we learn, she is already infected by the alien virus and struggles to stay awake on the drugs she finds and swallows down with Mountain Dew. Later in the movie, she instructs her son Oliver (Jackson Bond) to inject adrenaline, which she also finds in the pharmacy section, directly into her heart in case she falls asleep.

Stimulants, then, are readily available for the doctors in the movies. They find them in places where they hide—be it in their practices, offices or in a supermarket pharmacy—and they know what they need to take. In contrast, the drugs are not available for teenage girl Marti and pilot Tim, which explains why they do not take any. In none of the films, however, are drugs a permanent solution, and the protagonists' desperate overdoses draw attention to the use and abuse of stimulants in our everyday lives. While the surviving humans opt for stimulants, the pod people persecuting them are generally equipped with sedatives to make them sleep. The drugs in their vials and syringes match what Johnson describes as the invaders' "perverse messianic promise: deliverance from anxiety through suppression of emotion" (7). The tranquil state of mind the pod people promote indeed resembles the result of psychiatric treatment with anti-anxiety medication. In all movies, the use of drugs therefore creates a highly symbolic juxtaposition: stimulants stand for the paranoid fear and constant alertness of the protagonists, while sedatives are related to sleep, transformation and the anxiety-free life as a pod person. The great emphasis on psychiatric medication not only sheds light on the psychological effects of external threats (associated with the Cold War, bio-chemical warfare, terrorism, etc.) and on how they can be overcome with tranquilizing drugs. It also puts a main focus on anxieties caused by internal psychological stress. In this respect, the juxtaposition of stimulants and sedatives equals the tension between individuality and conformity that is emblematic for each of the societies these films depict. In fact, the films address trends for coping with individual and societal expectations which suggest that the desire for individual self-actualization might be met by taking stimulants, while the constant pressure to function in both professional and private lives can be relieved with sedatives.

Apart from discussing sleep as a recurrent *narrative element*, I also want to focus on a *key scene* that is repeated in all remakes. It can be found towards the beginning of each film, when suspicious relatives claim that their loved ones are not their loved ones. In fact, the exact phrasing of "my husband is not my husband" or "my father is not my father" has become a familiar line by now and makes the body snatcher movies recognizable as such. The attempted diagnostics, closely related to these scenes, differ slightly and generally refer (albeit hazily) to the cultural context in which the film was produced. Thus, psychiatrist Danny Kaufman of the 1956 movie suspects that "worry about what's going on in the world" has probably caused what he diagnoses as "a strange neurosis, evidently contagious, an epidemic mass hysteria." The openness of Kaufman's medical opinion provides, of course, ample room for interpretations of what these 1950s worries might have been and has therefore encouraged the multiple readings of the film mentioned above. In the 1978 movie, pop-psychiatrist David Kibner (Leonard Nimoy) describes the strange occurrences as a popular way to avoid responsibilities in personal relationships, "an excuse to get out," as he phrases it. "People are stepping in and out of relationships too fast because they don't want the responsibility," he explains to Elizabeth (see Grant 96).

Major Collins, head of the base's medical corps in Ferrara's 1993 remake, thinks that exposure to the toxic chemicals on the military base might have affected brain patterns and interfered with chemo-neurological processes, thereby fostering psychosis, paranoia, and narcophobia among his patients on the base. He does not look for internal but external factors that could have produced the eerie symptoms, introducing environmental concerns and preoccupations with toxic waste into the expanding, and continually updated, fictional universe of the body snatcher movies. Delusions and psychological problems do not necessarily come from within (that is, they are not necessarily caused by anxieties) but from the physical world in which we live. Set in the aftermath of the Gulf War,[8] the movie also raises critical questions about the exposure of American soldiers to toxic chemicals during Operation Desert Storm which caused a chronic illness in veterans that has become known (and recently recognized) as Gulf War syndrome.

Ironically, in the 2007 remake, psychiatrist Carol treats her regular patient Wendy Lenk (Veronica Cartwright), who thinks her husband is not her husband, as in any other session—"I've told you before, nothing you say in this office is stupid or crazy"—and prescribes her an anti-psychotic. Her professional attitude seems rational, cold and emotionless—as if she were a pod already—and Wendy's problem "normal" for our times. In fact, only when Carol steps out of her professional role and worries about her son, when her maternal instincts to protect her child guide her every move, does she google the phrases "My husband is not my husband" and "My son is not my son" (getting 1,188,400 search results) and suddenly knows that something extraordinary is happening. The combination of scenes featuring the symptoms with a subsequent diagnostic is repeated in every movie. Still, as I have attempted to show, each one offers different insights into the cultural context of production with its historically specific preoccupations and anxieties. All movies tell a horror story against a science fiction backdrop that is a timeless metaphor of the threat of dehumanization. The fictitious premise and allegorical value of the body snatcher story turn it into an intellectual playground where pressing concerns can be projected onto different scenarios that are themselves inspired by recent or expected future events. This is possible precisely because the remakes are always set in the immediate present of their respective decades of production. While they are required to repeat certain narrative elements in order to retell the same story, the films can spell them out very differently so as to accommodate these contemporary concerns.

Variation

Film remakes contain elements that are changed or updated and bear little or no resemblance to the original film or earlier remakes. In contrast to repetition, which, in Thomas Leitch's words, serves to "valorize […the] potency" of an earlier film (53), variation generates the distinctive features of the film remake. By rethinking and remodeling certain elements, filmmakers not only try to distance their movie from its models; they also want to reinforce the remake's aesthetic autonomy and work towards its own cultural potency. In this sense, film remakes can certainly be understood as "serial" productions, in Eco's sense, whose aesthetic value derives from the tension between repetition and innovation (173–74). The guiding question for my case study is: which elements invite innovation or variation? I suggest that the style, the setting, and the ending of *Invasion of the Body Snatchers* lend themselves to variation because they belong to the kinds of aesthetic and narrative choices that have no impact on the overall body snatcher premise, the central metaphor, the character constellation, or the way the plot unfolds. In other words, the story remains recognizable as such (and in extension, the film as a remake), even if the style, setting, and ending are changed.

If the 1956 movie is a generic hybrid which oscillates between horror and science fiction, stylistically resembling *film noir* (Grant 50), then its remakes generally exchange *film noir* for action and thriller. Even though Robert Shelton observes for the 1956, 1978, and 1993 movies that "just a slight shift in tone moves us from film noir to science fiction, from science fiction to horror" (71), and Marty Roth even sees a "move ... toward screwball comedy" in Kaufman's version (106),[9] the fights, (car) chases, and explosions as well as the atmosphere of apprehension and alarm in all three remakes hint at a combination of the horror and science fiction genres with action movie and thriller aesthetics. Kaufman's 1978 remake is a horror film in an urban setting with occasional action scenes including car chases and explosions, whereas Ferrara's *Body Snatchers* is more of a "family melodrama" (Shelton 75)[10] turned "tough-talk action flick" (Hoberman 30). The second remake indeed stands out among the body snatcher films as the most radical (or least faithful) reinterpretation of the basic narrative. It introduces the (patchwork) family theme (which will be central in the next remake) with teenage girl Marti Malone. She cannot stand living with her six-year-old brother (Reilly Murphy), father, and stepmother (Meg Tilly), who, she says in the narrative voice-over at the beginning of the movie, has "replaced" her mom. But as the pods take over the military base where the story is set, the family trouble is soon forgotten. Early on, Marti's stepmother transforms into a pod and although the rest of the family tries to flee, Marti eventually shoots her father and later drops her brother from a helicopter in self-defense. *Body Snatchers* eventually turns into a Rambo-style action film with Marti and chopper pilot Tim's "aerial rampage-revenge against the Pod People dressed in Army drab" (Shelton 76). Although Hirschbiegel's 2007 version ends with a similar action-laden showdown, the suspenseful emphasis on conspiracy and paranoia as well as the twists and turns throughout the rest of the movie qualify it as a thriller. Like Siegel's *Invasion of the Body Snatchers*, then, each remake plays with generic conventions, and mixes and blends different looks and styles against the science fiction backdrop of the story, thereby enhancing the aesthetic value and originality of each work.[11]

The most obvious changes, however, concern the spatio-temporal *setting* of each movie. It moves geographically from small-town Santa Mira, California, to San Francisco, to a military base in Alabama, and finally to Washington, DC. The apparent logic behind these choices seems to imply that the pods pose an ever greater threat to humanity while the chances of defeating them decrease exponentially. For instance, in the 1956 movie, the alien attack is locally restricted to one small town, threatening to reach other cities in California by the end of the movie, while in the 1978 remake, the takeover is extended to a densely settled urban center in California and, at the end, pods are shipped to other cities in the US and to some foreign ports. Ferrara's *Body Snatchers* is set on a military base which immediately changes the nature of the threat because now the alien invaders are supported by the armed forces, spread nationally via other military bases, and would not only be capable of a military coup but global attacks as well—even though that thought is not explicitly spelled out in the movie. Finally, set in the capital of the US, Hirschbiegel's *The Invasion* goes a step further by involving government agencies and depicting a global invasion that is already happening. To a certain extent, these changes exemplify a competitive strategy of surpassing or outbidding previous films in an attempt to resolve the tension between repetition and variation.[12] Furthermore, the temporal setting of the films is consistent with their respective decades of production, that is, it shifts from the 1950s, to the 1970s, to the 1990s, and the 2000s. This change is required by the story, which draws its suspense from the fact that it is always set in the present (not in the past or future). It caters to contemporary conspiracy theories and real or imaginary threats lurking outside the movie theater. More importantly, it allows addressing the immediate anxieties of the era in which the film was produced—an aspect that makes the body snatcher films particularly interesting for cultural analysis, as the multiple publications on the subject of past years confirm.

Likewise, the *ending* of each remake changes, seemingly to fulfill current cultural needs, as I will suggest here. Apparently, after the first publication of *The Body Snatchers* as a *Collier's* magazine serial in three installments, back in 1954, Finney already felt the need to retell his story with a variation in the Dell paperback novel of 1955.[13] In other words, the tension between repetition and variation, which characterizes the dynamics of serialization, is already contained in the literary original. Both texts have happy endings in which the alien invaders leave earth and mankind is rescued. In the course of the flight from their hometown Santa Mira, California, Miles and Becky set fire to a field of alien seed pods with three hundred gallons of gasoline—"a final gesture of defiance" as Johnson writes (11). They find themselves immediately surrounded by pod versions of the townspeople, yet nothing happens to them because the pods that have not burned miraculously rise into the sky and the alien force thus withdraws from the planet, leaving the pod people—now without mission and no longer dangerous—behind. The two divorcees, Miles and Becky, marry and live happily ever after. Most townspeople, however, except their friends Jack and Theodora Belicec, who were not snatched during the alien invasion, die within five years, and gradually new families arrive in Santa Mira to replace them.[14]

In the *Collier's* version of Finney's novel, the burning gasoline guides Jack Belicec and the FBI to Miles and Becky. The FBI agents arrive armed with riot and machine guns, and eventually—without any violence—the pods decide to leave the "fierce and inhospitable planet" earth (Finney, "The Body Snatchers: Conclusion" 73). Johnson remarks that "it is no surprise here to find the salvation of humanity resting in the hands of the national police" (11) because in the 1950s so much emphasis was put on "cooperation with the military authorities, as the only guarantee of individuals' safety" (Murphy qtd. in Johnson 12). While the army, the president, and telephone companies can no longer be trusted or counted on for help (and are therefore depicted negatively in the novel), the FBI is never doubted (Johnson 12). In Finney's book version of *The Body Snatchers*, however, the FBI does not intervene. Miles tries in vain to call the federal agents; the phone company has long been taken over by the alien invaders. Miles and Becky's actions alone make the aliens leave. As a consequence, Johnson aptly observes, "the book's ending [is] a testimonial not to para-military authority, but to the indomitability of individual spirit" (12).

In contrast to Finney's novel, the ending of the 1956 movie is much less optimistic, even though it follows the source text(s) very closely. Much has been written about the two endings of Siegel's *Invasion of the Body Snatchers*:[15] The first, intended by director, screenwriter, and producer, shows a disheveled, confused Miles attempting to stop cars on a freeway overpass and warn people about the alien invasion. In the final shot, he turns to the camera and screams frantically, "You're next! You're next!" as it zooms in on his face. Following poor audience reactions after three preview screenings of the film, the Allied Artists studio imposed the addition of a narrative frame and voice-over narration (Grant 14, 37; Shelton 72). Thus, in the second ending we see Miles in an emergency room as a patient (not a doctor). He finishes his flashback narration of the events in Santa Mira—including the frantic freeway scene—and turns to Dr Hill, hoping that he will believe his incredible story. And, indeed, Dr Hill alerts the police and calls the operator to get in touch with the FBI. Intended as an upbeat ending which provides closure, these final scenes do nonetheless little to help the audience get over "the shocking loss of Dr. Bennell's love interest, Becky

Driscoll…, to the alien's synergetic and affectless collective" (Shelton 73)—a narrative twist this movie introduces and that will be taken up in the remakes. The ending imposed by the studio may be less desperate than the original one, yet, as Grant observes: "Siegel may have had the last laugh, for the film's undeniable power derives in large part from the fact that the end remains unsettling despite the apparent closure" (14). Many questions are left unanswered: will they be able to alert the authorities or will the operator divert the call because the phone lines are already taken over by the pod people? Or, even more sinister: is the entire story a product of Miles' own psychosis, a projection of his fears and paranoia?[16]

In the 1978 remake of *Invasion of the Body Snatchers*, the FBI will definitely not come to the rescue. "The CIA? The FBI? They're all pods already" Jack Belicec (Jeff Goldblum) believes. His resignation may be explained by a lack of faith in government authorities that marked the 1970s after the Vietnam War and the Pentagon Papers, the Watergate scandal, and president Richard Nixon's fall. In the end, Matthew fights the pod people all by himself. He sets fire to a warehouse in which alien pods are grown and prepared for delivery, taking up the idea from Finney's novel. He is then, however, betrayed by the pod version of Elizabeth, who alerts other pod people with a horrible shriek, now typical for the alien invaders.[17] Matthew can actually escape and the dramatic scene is followed by a cut, a white screen, and a fade-in onto school buses that bring children to the San Francisco Public Health Department to be transformed. Next, we see Matthew alone on the street in front of his work place, at his desk, and together with colleagues. No one speaks, and it remains unsettlingly unclear if he has turned into a pod person or just pretends to be one of them. The last scene is shot outside, in front of City Hall, where Nancy Belicec (Veronica Cartwright) comes up hesitantly to Matthew and calls his name. In the final shot, Matthew points at Nancy and emits the pod shriek to denounce her, as the camera zooms into his open mouth and fades out. In comparison to Siegel and particularly in comparison to Finney, as Annette Insdorf remarks, "Kaufman…makes a darker, cautionary tale in which the heroic impulse is insufficient." In fact, "the sole survivor here," she further observes, "turns out to be Nancy (as opposed to Matthew), a secondary female character rather than the hero."

While the 1978 remake provides a dreadful closure, the ending of Ferrara's *Body Snatchers* is as ambiguous as the 1956 movie. Marti and Tim can escape in a helicopter and succeed in destroying the military base as well as a convoy of seed pods leaving the camp.[18] When they land on a military airport in Atlanta, we see a low-angle shot of a soldier awaiting them on the ground. This final scene is accompanied by Marti's voice-over narration ("They get you when you sleep. But you can only stay awake so long"), a distorted voice that repeats the words her transformed stepmother had uttered on the Alabama base ("Where're you gonna go? Where're you gonna run? Where're you gonna hide? Nowhere. 'Cause there's no one like you left"), and an uncanny musical score. Unless Marti's voice-over is (another) plot hole, it would imply that Marti survives to tell the story, and, as a consequence, Marti and Tim must have defeated the pods and saved humanity. Yet, the ending as it is cut and edited invites more pessimistic readings in which the Atlanta military base may have already been taken over by the pod people. The ambiguity arises from the film's premise that "military mentality, emphasising collective action and unthinking obedience to orders, makes it impossible to distinguish professional soldiers from those who are pods" (Grant 98).

Interestingly, the last remake to date, Hirschbiegel's *The Invasion*, has a happy ending. Although it depicts the apparently unstoppable global takeover of the alien invaders, eventually a cure is found (from Oliver's blood) by an international team of brilliant scientists working secretly underground. None of the other movies holds the possibility of transforming back from being a duplicate, and in the novel, life as a pod person is even limited to only five years. Inventing a vaccine that can rescue and restore humanity, therefore, is a radical departure which both attests to the belief in scientific and technological solutions and critiques aggressive human behavior because, once healed, "the world is returning to its previously violent state of affairs" (Grant 103). But what does it mean to change the ending like this? Considering Simon McEnteggart's explanation of "the appearance (and recurrence) of superhero films during periods of sociocultural destabilization and unrest" (172) with what he describes as "cultural 'need'" (173), I would argue that something similar applies to the body snatcher movies, and to *The Invasion* in particular. Maybe there is not only a commercial or artistic desire for variation, a competitive strategy of surpassing an earlier film, but a cultural "need" to revive the story and rewrite its ending. In a post-9/11, post-SARS and avian flu context, *The Invasion* allegorically addresses the threat of bioterrorism, and new anxieties concerning the government's capability to deal with these potential crises. However, by opting for the happy ending brought about by scientists and new technologies, the movie restores stability and alleviates fears.

Continuation

In the case of *Invasion of the Body Snatchers*, certain ideas are developed from one film to the next. In these instances, the boundaries between the remake and the sequel seem to blur. According to Carolyn Jess-Cooke and Constantine Verevis, the remake "prioritize[s] repetition of an original," whereas the sequel "rather advances an exploration of alternatives, differences, and reenactments that are discretely charged with the various ways in which we may reread, remember, or return to a source" (5). Leitch writes about the "fundamentally different appeal" of remakes and sequels: "The audience for sequels wants to find out more, to spend more time with characters they are interested in and to find out what happened to them after their story was over. The audience for remakes does not expect to find out anything new in this sense: they want the same story again, though not exactly the same" (44). As I will briefly show in this last part of my analysis, certain elements of the body snatcher remakes match these definitions of the sequel. In fact, Leitch thinks that Kaufman's *Invasion of the Body Snatchers* is one of the "occasional remakes [...that] contain elements of sequels" (44), but he does not provide evidence for his assumption.[19]

First, cameo appearances of actors from earlier films are not only a special reward for knowledgeable viewers,[20] but they also suggest continuity. Kevin McCarthy, who stars as Miles Bennell in the 1956 *Invasion of the Body Snatchers*, reappears in Kaufman's film, still running among cars, warning people, and looking for help. He stops Matthew, who is driving with Elizabeth, and shouts frantically, "Help! You're next! They're already here!" This scene takes up, and thereby pays tribute to, the intended ending of Siegel's film.[21] It also suggests, as Insdorf notes, "that the action of the remake *follows* that of the original film" (emphasis added). Moreover, this is implied by the setting because San Francisco was "one of the major urban destinations of the truckloads of pods on the main highway in the original" (Grant 93). Another cameo appearance is that of actress Veronica Cartwright, who plays Nancy Belicec in Kaufman's *Invasion of the Body Snatchers* and Wendy Lenk in Hirschbiegel's *The Invasion*. As mentioned, she is the last survivor in Kaufman's movie, a narrative stumbling block that leaves many questions unanswered. Now, in Hirschbiegel's remake, she is the first who turns out to be immune against the alien virus. More precisely, her case leads her psychiatrist, Carol, and Ben to the assumption that Carol's son Oliver might be immune as well and that a vaccine could be generated from his blood. This innovation adds retrospective causality to what happened in the earlier movie, proposing that Nancy Belicec might have stayed human because she was immune. In both cases, then, we seemingly learn "what happened to [the characters] after their story was over" (Leitch 44).

Second, the changing of characters' names has become a standard procedure in the production of body snatchers remakes and suggests an interest in playfully continuing a "tradition." Thus, psychiatrist Mannie Kaufman in Finney's novel turns into Danny Kaufman in Siegel's movie and into David Kibner in Kaufman's remake (maybe to avoid confusion with the director's last name [Grant 95]). The name has a comeback as Tucker Kaufman, Carol's ex-husband, CDC official, and, like the other characters, spokesperson of the pod people. Similarly, the first names (and gender) of the protagonists change. Shelton even sees a continuity which includes Ferrara's (in this aspect radically different) *Body Snatchers*, namely, "the M-arc [that] runs from Miles to Matthew to Marti" (75) in the first three films. In *The Invasion*, the female protagonist's first name is Carol—taking up the stepmother's name from Ferrara's movie.[22] Becky, Elizabeth, and Ben Driscoll similarly change their first names (and gender). As a consequence, the characters remain recognizable, yet their new first names mark them as (slightly) different versions (or imperfect duplications) of their former selves: they are embodying their own times. This, in turn, allows for exploring how personal relationships and gender roles change over time. Most obviously, the female characters are advanced and developed, alternatives explored: divorcee Becky, whose "independence and self-assured sexuality" (Grant 80) supposedly threaten Miles, quickly falls back into homemaking and domesticity when preparing breakfast for him, and both return to their conventional gender roles (82). Becky is replaced by Elizabeth, who works at the Public Health Department and eventually leaves the unhappy relationship with her boyfriend to be with her colleague Matthew. Until her transformation, she remains an autonomous and active partner, confirming that gender roles have changed since the 1950s. As if to underline this, the earlier breakfast scene is substituted with a scene in which Matthew is cooking dinner for them. A similar scene in which Ben makes pancakes for Carol can be found in the 2007 remake.[23] Grant observes that "the gender reversal of the roles of the romantic leads, signaled by Carol's and Ben's last names, is an indication of the film's ostensibly progressive gender theme" (102). Carol, a single mother and psychiatrist, describes herself as a "postmodern feminist" in the dinner scene of the movie. With her, the female lead character in the body snatcher movies develops from a romantic interest that will eventually betray the male protagonist into a strong heroine who succeeds in saving herself, her child, and the entire world. In these same circumstances, her male equivalents in the other movies broke down or failed.

Apart from these two examples of continuation, one could also mention the development of special effects for the scenes of transformation or the increasing importance of the disposal of human bodies. Borne out of practical considerations, they take up and advance earlier ideas in an attempt to avoid loop holes and inconsistencies of earlier movies. More could be said about distorted camera angles, for example, or scientific explanations of the invasion, technology used to investigate it, the pod shriek, and so on. At this point, however, it must suffice to end with the observation that the remakes of *Invasion of the Body Snatchers* apparently do not intend to disguise the existence of earlier renditions, nor do they have to come to terms with what Leitch describes as the "fundamental rhetorical problem of remakes ... to mediate between two apparently irreconcilable claims: that the remake is *just like* its model, and that it's *better*" (44). Updating, in this specific case at least, entails repetition, variation, and *continuation* precisely because *Invasion of the Body Snatchers* and its remakes, with their numerous markers of one specific historical period, all pose a question that is rather typical of the sequel and the series: what happens next? In other words, because the films have engaged with the anxieties and profound cultural changes of their respective times of production, they have created a "serial desire" to revisit the story and characters, to see what would become of them in a different spatial setting and in a different historical, cultural, and political context.

Notes

1. For different readings of the film see: Badmington; Booker 59–73; Byers; Grant 63–89; Hendershot; LeGacy; Mann; Müller; Samuels; Sanders; and Seed.
2. For example, *Gremlins* (Joe Dante, 1984) and *The Faculty* (Robert Rodriguez, 1998)—discussed at length in Koch 68–81; episodes of *Mork & Mindy* ("Invasion of the Mork Snatchers," 1980) and *Dharma & Greg* ("Invasion of the Buddy Snatchers," 1998); the *Looney Tunes* cartoon "Invasion of the Bunny Snatchers" which casts Bugs Bunny in the role of Miles Bennell; and the videogame *Metal Gear Solid 3: Snake Eater* (2004). Cf. Grant 8.
3. See, for example, Badmington; Grant 93–104; Higashi; Hoberman; Insdorf; Nelson; Roth; Seed; Shelton; and Ulonska.
4. The film's voice-over narration and flashback structure, the protagonist's impending doom and the cramped, dark spaces (basements, closets,

greenhouses, tunnels) form part of the *film noir* aesthetics of *Invasion of the Body Snatchers*. Nighttime scenes are prevalent and closely linked to the use of chiaroscuro effects. In this context, Grant observes: "The film's multiple shots of headlights, flashlights, matches and lamps as dwindling pools of light in the engulfing darkness are images common to noir, along with the thematic sense of defeat and gloom that they suggest" (52–53). Apart from the lighting, the film's characteristic low angle shots, and recurring contrasts of depth of field are also elements of the film's noir style. See Grant 50–55; Sanders 55, 64; Seed 165–66.

5. On definitions and taxonomies of film remakes see Druxman; Leitch; Manderbach; and Verevis.

6. Later in the film, Ben Driscoll complains about lack of information concerning the real reasons for the crash. "Fifty scientists have resigned over the shuttle debacle," he tells Carol, "They've all signed a letter saying the government's ignoring their findings, because they think the shuttle crashed on purpose."

7. Similar scenes are prevalent in the three other movies where they equally fuel paranoia.

8. Tim tells Marti that he has killed Iraqis during the Gulf War.

9. Roth identifies the telephone activity, the general confusion of identity, and incoherent conversations as typical screwball themes (106). Roth's analysis is problematic because, even if there are comic situations in the 1978 film, all these examples hint at a very different (rather horror than comic) theme paramount to the movie: failed communication.

10. See Koch 62–63.

11. These stylistic changes must also be seen within the film-historical context of the respective decades of production: in the postwar 1940s and 1950s, classic *film noir* was a prominent style of black and white film that created an atmosphere of anxiety and suspicion; the New Hollywood films of the 1970s generally favored experimental filmic devices, deviated from conventional narrative forms, and had no happy endings; high budget action films of the 1990s spent money on spectacular special effects including explosions, shootouts, and car chases (often neglecting the plot and character development); while films produced in the 2000s made use of digital technology and CGI imagery to improve visual effects.

12. Here, I take up the idea of serial contest in American television series that is subject of the larger research project "The Dynamics of Serial Outbidding *(Überbietung)*: Contemporary American Television and the Concept of Quality TV," directed by Frank Kelleter and Andreas Jahn-Sudmann as part of the Research Unit "Popular Seriality: Aesthetics and Practice" at the University of Göttingen (Germany), funded by the German Research Foundation (DFG): see http://popularseriality.uni-goettingen.de

13. In 1978, coinciding with Philip Kaufman's cinematic remake, the novel has again been published under the title *Invasion of the Body Snatchers*. The action is moved from August 1953 to October 1976.

14. Cf. Johnson 11. A decisive difference between the novel and the films is the premise that "duplication *isn't* perfect" (Finney, *Invasion* 183). The aliens plan to use up the human bodies and everything living they occupy on the planet within five years, and will then move on to other planets. This adds

an ecological dimension to the novel that cannot be found in the first movie. Prof. Budlong, already a pod, confronts Miles with the similarities between the human and alien behavior: "Don't look so shocked, Doctor. ... After all, what have you people done—with the forests that covered the continent? And the farm lands you've turned into dust? You, too, have used them up, and then ... moved on" (184).

15. See, for example, Badmington; Booker; Grant; Hoberman; Insdorf; Johnson; LeGacy; Sanders; Shelton.
16. For a reading along these lines, see Sanders 66–70.
17. Hoberman calls it "the capacity for pod-people to transform themselves into banshee alarm systems" (30).
18. Shelton suggests an important narrative lapse here: in the 1956 movie, the pod people let Miles go because he posed no threat to them. They were convinced that no one would believe his story. In Ferrara's movie, General Platt tells his troops to let Tim and Marti go on the same grounds but does not consider the threat they pose—"General Platt has just 'let go' an armed attack helicopter and pilot" (76).
19. In an interview, Kaufman said about his movie: "it is more a sequel done twenty years later than a remake" (qtd. in Badmington 15).
20. Cf. Leitch 42; Verevis speaks of "celebrity intertextuality" in contemporary remakes (20).
21. Don Siegel, too, has a cameo appearance (as a taxi driver) in Kaufman's remake.
22. Carol Bennell's son in the movie is called Oliver, like the director Oliver Hirschbiegel. This might be a playful hint at earlier naming coincidences.
23. With an ironic wink at the breakfast scene in the 1956 movie, Ben's pancakes are all burned.

Works consulted

"25 Films Added to National Registry." *New York Times* 15 November 1994: n. pag. Retrieved on 25 August 2011. www.nytimes.com/1994/11/15/movies/25-films-added-to-national-registry.html.

Badmington, Neil. "Pod Almighty, or, Humanism, Posthumanism, and the Strange Case of *Invasion of the Body Snatchers*." *Textual Practice* 15.1 (Spring 2001): 5–22. Print.

Body Snatchers. Dir. Abel Ferrara. Perf. Gabrielle Anwar, Terry Kinney, and Forest Whitaker. Warner Bros., 1993. DVD.

Booker, Marvin Keith. *Alternate Americas: Science Fiction Film and American Culture*. Westport, CO: Praeger, 2006. Print.

Byers, Thomas. "Kissing Becky: Masculine Fears and Misogynist Moments in Science Fiction Films." *Arizona Quarterly* 45.3 (Autumn 1989): 77–95. Print.

Druxman, Michael B. *Make It Again Sam: A Survey of Movie Remakes*. Cranbury, NJ: A. S. Barnes, 1975. Print.

Eco, Umberto. "Innovation and Repetition: Between Modern and Post-Modern Aesthetics." *Daedalus* 114.4 (Fall 1985): 161–84. Print.

Finney, Jack. "The Body Snatchers: Part One." *Collier's* 26 November 1954: 26–27, 90–94, 96–99. Print.

———. "The Body Snatchers: Part Two." *Collier's* 10 December 1954: 114, 116–25. Print.

———. "The Body Snatchers: Conclusion." *Collier's* 24 December 1954: 62, 64–65, 68–69, 71–73. Print.

———. *The Body Snatchers.* New York: Dell, 1955.

———. *Invasion of the Body Snatchers.* 1978. New York: Scribner Paperback Fiction, 1998. Print.

Georgi, Sonja, and Kathleen Loock, eds. *Of Body Snatchers and Cyberpunks: Student Essays on American Science Fiction Film.* Göttingen: University of Göttingen Press, 2011. Print.

Grant, Barry Keith. *Invasion of the Body Snatchers.* British Film Institute. New York: Palgrave Macmillan, 2010. Print.

Hendershot, Cyndy. "The Invaded Body: Paranoia and Radiation Anxiety in *Invaders from Mars, It Came from Outer Space,* and *Invasion of the Body Snatchers.*" *Extrapolation* 39.1 (Spring 1998): 26–39. Print.

Higashi, Sumiko. "*Invasion of the Body Snatchers*: Pods Then and Now." *Jump Cut* 24.25 (1981): 3–4. Retrieved on 14 July 2010. http:// www.ejumpcut.org/ archive/onlinessays/JC24–25folder/InvasionBodySntch.html.

Hoberman, J. "Paranoia and the Pods." *Sight and Sound* 4.5 (May 1994): 28–31. Print.

Insdorf, Annette. "Seeing Doubles." Museum of the Moving Image, 26 June 2008. Retrieved on 18 August 2011. www.movingimagesource.us/articles/ seeing-doubles-20080626.

Invasion. Dir. Oliver Hirschbiegel. Perf. Nicole Kidman, Daniel Craig, and Jeremy Northam. Warner Bros., 2007. DVD.

Invasion of the Body Snatchers. Dir. Don Siegel. Perf. Kevin McCarthy, Dana Wynter, and Larry Gates. Allied Artists Pictures Corp., 1956. DVD.

Invasion of the Body Snatchers. Dir. Philip Kaufman. Perf. Donald Sutherland, Jeff Goldblum, and Leonard Nimoy. United Artists, 1978. DVD.

Jess-Cooke, Carolyn, and Constantine Verevis, eds. *Second Takes: Critical Approaches to the Film Sequel.* Albany, NY: SUNY Press, 2010. Print.

———. "Introduction." Jess-Cooke and Verevis 1–10. Print.

Johnson, Glen M. "'We'd Fight... We Had To.' *The Body Snatchers* as Novel and Film." *Journal of Popular Culture* 13.1 (Summer 1979): 5–16. Print.

"Key Features of Public Law 109–009." National Film Preservation Board, Library of Congress, 10 August 2011. Retrieved on 25 August 2011. www.loc.gov/film/ filmabou.html#legislative1988.

Koch, Markus. *Alien-Invasionsfilme nach dem Ende des Kalten Krieges.* München: Diskurs Film-Verl. Schaudig & Ledig, 2002. Print.

LeGacy, Arthur. "*The Invasion of the Body Snatchers*: A Metaphor for the Fifties." *Literature/Film Quarterly* 6.3 (1978): 185–92. Print.

Leitch, Thomas. "Twice-Told Tales: Disavowal and the Rhetoric of the Remake." *Dead Ringers: The Remake in Theory and Practice.* Ed. Jennifer Forrest and Leonard R. Koos. Albany, NY: State University of New York Press, 2002. 37–62. Print.

Manderbach, Jochen. *Das Remake: Studien zu seiner Theorie und Praxis.* Medien und Kommunikation 53. Siegen: University of Siegen, 1988. Print.

Mann, Katrina. "You're Next!: Postwar Hegemony Besieged in *Invasion of the Body Snatchers.*" *Cinema Journal* 44.1 (Fall 2004): 49–68. Print.

McEnteggart, Simon. "Sequelizing the Superhero: Postmillennial Anxiety and Cultural 'Need.'" Jess-Cooke and Verevis 171–89. Print.

Müller, Manfred Alexander. "It Used to Be a Man's World: Manhood and Masculinity in Don Siegel's *Invasion of the Body Snatchers.*" Georgi and Loock 87–97. Print.

Nelson, Erika. "*Invasion of the Body Snatchers*: Gender and Sexuality in Four Film Adaptations." *Extrapolation: A Journal of Science Fiction and Fantasy* 52.1 (Spring 2011): 51–74. Print.

Roth, Marty. "Twice Two: *The Fly* and *Invasion of the Body Snatchers.*" *Discourse* 22.1 (Winter 2000): 103–16. Print.

Samuels, Stuart. "The Age of Conspiracy and Conformity: *Invasion of the Body Snatchers* (1956)." *Hollywood's America: Twentieth-Century America Through Film.* 4th ed. Ed. Steven Mintz and Randy W. Roberts. Malden, MA: Wiley-Blackwell, 2010. 198–206. Print.

Sanders, Steven M. "Picturing Paranoia: Interpreting *Invasion of the Body Snatchers.*" *The Philosophy of Science Fiction Film.* Ed. Steven M. Sanders. Lexington, KY: University of Kentucky Press, 2008. 55–72. Print.

Seed, David. "Alien Invasions by Body Snatchers and Related Creatures." *Modern Gothic: A Reader.* Ed. Victor Sage and Allan Lloyd Smith. Manchester: Manchester University Press, 1996. 152–70. Print.

Shelton, Robert. "Genre and Closure in the Seven Versions of *Invasion of the Body Snatchers*: Finney ('54, '55, '78), Siegel ('56, '56), Kaufman ('78) and Ferrara ('93)." *West Virginia University Philological Papers* 49 (2003): 71–77. Print.

Ulonska, Benjamin. "Human Monsters: The Function of the Horror Motif in Don Siegel's *Invasion of the Body Snatchers* and Its Remakes." Georgi and Loock. 161–72. Print.

Verevis, Constantine. *Film Remakes.* Edinburgh: Edinburgh University Press, 2006. Print.

7
Cyber-noia? Remaking *The Manchurian Candidate* in a Global Age

Sonja Georgi

Re-making paranoia

"Imagine not just a corporation, Marco, but a goddamn geopolitical extension of policy for every president since Nixon. Cash is king, Marco, cash is king." These are the words that the underground expert in biotechnological warfare Delp, a character in Jonathan Demme's 2004 remake of *The Manchurian Candidate*, says to Major Bennett Marco when the latter confronts the scientist with extensive research on a corporation with the name of Manchurian Global and a conspiracy theory about the corporation's illegal biotechnological experiments on American soldiers during the Gulf War. Suggesting that the corporate influence goes far beyond a senator's or even president's power as it is deeply rooted within international policies and global economics, Demme's remake of John Frankenheimer's 1962 version, which was adapted from the 1959 novel by Richard Condon, takes up the theme of Cold War paranoia of the earlier film and sets it in a post-9/11 context where the effects of globalization and information technology on the American society and the country's "war on terror" dominate US politics and television news. Reviewed as a "political thriller" (Scott), the remake combines characteristics of cultural anxiety about the "communist other" of the earlier version with what Wendy Chun calls "techno-orientalist" imagery of science fiction (9).

The original film's theme of paranoia makes it part of and sets it towards the end of a larger trend of mid-twentieth-century science fiction films, such as *Invasion of the Body Snatchers* (Don Siegel, 1956) and *Invaders from Mars* (William Cameron Menzies, 1953), which reflect public discourses of cultural anxiety about the political and cultural "other." The threat of atomic weapons as well as a climate of social, political, and consumer culture as expressed in white middle-class, small-town lifestyle, political conformity in light of anticommunist sentiments, and the development of the mass market, found its way into cinemas through science fiction films (Carruthers 77). In these films, the threat has often been posed onto the alien for example in the form of seedpods, or alien creatures which are slowly invading American middle-class suburbia. As Victoria O'Donnell writes:

> by dislocating the narratives to different times and/or different worlds, the science fiction genre catered to public anxiety about the bomb and communism. In most of the films, scientists and the military managed to vanquish the enemy, offering reassurance that these threats could be overcome. (169)

Both versions of *The Manchurian Candidate* offer mixed perspectives on authorities and favor individual actions (of soldiers and FBI agents) over scientists and the military at large. The political climate of the 1950s and 1960s was characterized by anticommunist movements, most prominently subsumed under the "system of political repression," also known as McCarthyism (Carter; see also Carruthers, and Pease). Also, the Korean War between 1950 and 1953 and stories about the "brainwashing" of American prisoners of war by the Korean and Soviet enemies dominated public discourses in the mid-twentieth century (Jacobson and Gonzáles 46).

Frankenheimer's *Manchurian Candidate* tells the story of the brainwashing of a group of American prisoners of war under the command of Major Bennett Marco (Frank Sinatra) by Chinese communist forces who plan to install Senator John Yerkes Iselin (James Gregory) as sleeper president under the spell of his communist wife Eleanor Iselin (Angela Lansbury). A key role in the political complot is played by Eleanor's son, Sergeant Raymond Shaw (Laurence Harvey), who was part of the platoon kidnapped in Korea and secretly trained to assassinate his stepfather's political competitors. Released in 1962, the film falls between the Cuban Missile Crisis in 1962 and the assassination of John F. Kennedy in 1963 and, as Susan Carruthers writes, "has been variously interpreted as both a subversion and an affirmation of certain Cold War conventions by subsequent film critics and cultural historians" (75). Demme's remake of Frankenheimer's film offers many interesting aesthetic and theoretical insights into remake practice, yet I am interested here not so much in the remaking process of the film but in the "adaptation" of cultural discourses in Demme's remake.

About 15 years after the end of the Cold War, American public discourses at the release of the remake revolved around the terrorist attacks of 11 September 2001, the subsequent international invasion of Afghanistan, America's war on Iraq, the possibility of manipulated elections not only in new democracies abroad but also in the United States,[1] and continuing globalization processes. As Roger Ebert writes in his review of the remake, "it's a stretch to imagine a communist takeover of America, but the idea that corporations may be subverting the democratic process is plausible in the age of Enron." Within this context of political upheaval paired with the rise and fall of the New Economy, Matthew Frye Jacobson and Gaspar González observe in their book-length study on both Frankenheimer's and Demme's versions of *The Manchurian Candidate*,

> it is altogether fitting, then, that someone should decide to update and remake *The Manchurian Candidate* for this new era. But Demme rather shunted aside the obvious parallels between the Cold War and the War on Terror, focusing instead on the deeper and less obvious question of corporate power in what is beginning to look like a post-national epoch. (193)

Exploring the effects of globalization processes and the ubiquity of media and information technology paired with a conspiracy story about political and economic domination of a post-9/11 American society as depicted in Demme's 2004 remake, I would like to situate *The Manchurian Candidate* in its contemporary political and cultural contexts and analyze the film as a work of cyberfiction.[2] The remake translates the Cold War anxiety of the earlier film to draw a portrait of a twenty-first century where multinational capitalism and international terrorism have formed a strange liaison. Encapsulating the terrorist attacks on America, the film oscillates between the first Gulf War and a post-9/11 era where the nation is constantly on "terror alert," yet where terrorist forces are from various parties and wear various masks.

Microchips that are secretly inserted into the brains of US army soldiers, high-tech mobile laboratories hidden behind bedroom walls and in train wagon restrooms as well as a glossy presidential election campaign financed by a large corporation position the 2004 version of *The Manchurian Candidate* in a technologically satirized world dominated by political spin doctors, media advertisements, corporate finance, and the abstract but constant fear of terrorist attacks. Here, the remake shares many features with cyberfiction literature and films that depict a technologically saturated future US society, such as William Gibson's novel *Neuromancer* (1984) and Ridley Scott's film *Blade Runner* (1982). However, as will be discussed below, key features of these early literary and cinematic cyberfictions are not only the setting in a dystopian version of a globalized world controlled by multinational corporations, but also the particular rhetorical and visual deployment of the "ethnic other," most prominently of the "Oriental," which serves to criticize global capitalism and to familiarize audiences with the realm of cyberspace, as has been argued by, for example, Wendy Chun and Lisa Nakamura.[3] In this context, cyberspace is thus an imaginary realm for the online world created by computer networks as well as for discourses about the effects of information technology on Western societies in which ethnicity plays a crucial role.

"The revolutionary science of biogenetics"

Demme's remake of *The Manchurian Candidate* tells the story of the war veteran Major Ben Marco (Denzel Washington), who serves as commander during the first Gulf War. Shortly before the Operation Desert Storm his troops are attacked and abducted in Kuwait while on a surveillance mission. The story the soldiers unanimously tell after their successful escape from the enemy forces is that they were led by one of their comrades, Sergeant Raymond Shaw (Liev Schreiber), through enemy terrain into safety. For this deed, Shaw receives the Medal of Honor for bravery in combat upon their return to the United States. Years after the incident and during the early stages of the Second Gulf War, Marco is still in the army and suffering from post-traumatic stress syndrome caused by his experience as prisoner of war in Kuwait. Yet as it turns out, Marco is not the only one haunted by the experience when one day he is contacted by one of his former comrades and asked if he also suffers from nightmares and an uncanny feeling of remembering what happened during the days after the attack but without the feeling of actually having experienced the situation: "I remember that it happened," the soldiers say, "but I don't remember it happening." Although Marco shrugs the confrontation off, suggesting to Al Melvin (Jeffrey Wright) that he should see a psychiatrist, he soon begins to investigate the affair, determined to find out what really happened during the three-day abduction in Kuwait. When he later visits Melvin in his run-down apartment, he finds that countless notebooks as well as the

Illustration 7.1   Major Ben Marco (Denzel Washington) finds out that he is not the only one suffering from disturbing nightmares in *The Manchurian Candidate* (2004)

room's walls are filled with drawings and journal entries about Melvin's memories and nightmares of the event. Gradually, the audience finds out that all soldiers retell the events with the exact same words, suggesting that they were made to memorize the event by heart and introducing the film's theme of brainwashing/mental conditioning, which is also expressed by Marco's remark that "sometimes memories shift." When asked about Shaw, all prisoners answer in a monotonous voice with the same phrasing, "Raymond Shaw is probably the kindest, bravest, and most selfless person I know."

Meanwhile, Shaw has made a career in politics and is nominated as vice-presidential candidate for the upcoming election. Completely controlled by his mother, Senator Eleanor Prentiss Shaw (Meryl Streep), he seems to be a puppet and rather out of place in the political circus around him, and he only becomes active, or animated, on demand for his spellbinding campaign speeches. This impression of Shaw as a politician "on remote control" is strengthened when we see a scene where he first receives a phone call after which he seems to be hypnotized and then walks into a hidden room behind his bedroom where a scientist and his team are waiting to inspect the microchip in his brain, which they had secretly implanted during the three-day abduction. Marco, who now extends his investigation to Shaw, visits him in his New York headquarters and confronts him with the nightmares and the mysteriousness or virtuality of the attack's aftermath. As Marco did with Melvin, Shaw shrugs him off, suggesting that he should seek professional help. Determined to prove his case, Marco attacks Shaw, bites off the microchip from underneath the skin of his shoulder blade and takes it to the underground biotechnology expert Delp (Bruno Ganz), who identifies the chip as the latest invention in computer engineering, a thing "which is not supposed to exist" and which was commissioned by the army and developed by a corporation with the name of Manchurian Global. The cyber-expert carries out a similar operation on Marco as the scientist did on Shaw, yet this surgery does not cause Marco to forget the past events but brings back the "real" memories of the events that happened during the troops' abduction. The audience finds out that the soldiers were not fighting their way home through enemy terrain in the desert but that they were kept in a cyber-laboratory where their brains were technologically and psychologically brainwashed, culminating in the crews' killing of those two comrades who were reported to have died as casualties during the flight, and thereby demonstrating the "successful" treatment of Manchurian Global's scientist. Convincing the female FBI officer Rosie (Kimberly Elise) of the corporate complot that wants to install Shaw as the next vice president and as Manchurian Global's sleeper, Marco and Shaw secretly plan to counteract the corporation's plan for implanting Shaw as president puppet. Instead of assassinating the newly elected President, as he had been "programmed" to do, Marco kills Shaw and his mother thus interrupting, if not ending, the corporate grip on the White House. Rosie in turn shoots Marco and the FBI takes him into their custody and into safety. At the end of the film, we see Marco visiting the small island to which he and his comrades were taken, and the circle of brainwashing and paranoia seems to have come to an, at least temporary, close.

Demme's remake of *The Manchurian Candidate* can be called cyberfiction not only because of its allusion to global capitalism and its depiction of biotechnology, but also because of its rhetorical and visual practices of orientalism, which reflect an underlying discourse in the film that relies on the visual and rhetorical strategy of "ethnic othering" of the corporate enemy. According to Edward Said, orientalism, "the knowledge of the Orient that places things oriental in class, court, prison, or manual for scrutiny, judgment, discipline, or governing" (41), is a cultural discourse that in the public imagery of the West has taken precedence over the presentation of the Orient by itself. With regard to the global age and information technology, Said writes that "one aspect of the electronic...world is that there has been a reinforcement of the stereotypes by which the Orient is viewed. Television, the films, and all the media's resources have forced information into more and more standardized models" (26). Linking cyberfiction to orientalism, Said's words suggest that cyberfiction's deployment of rhetorical and visual practices of orientalism only repeat (old) stories using familiar rhetoric and images by placing them in an allegedly new context.

In popular cyberfiction works such as *Blade Runner* and *Neuromancer*, which thematize increasing processes of globalization, it is a large corporation that is the eerie controller of a whole city/society, or even planet, operating openly and having replaced the nation state and democratic governments. Set in Japan, America, Turkey, cyberspace, and outer space, *Neuromancer* tells the story of the young white American man Case, who used to work as a computer specialist for a multinational corporation buying and selling electronic data in cyberspace. After Case steals information from his employees, they damage his nervous system, making him unable to access cyberspace. In search for a cure, he travels to Japan, as this is the place of neurosurgery and where he hopes to be healed in order to work again as a computer hacker. At first sight, the corporate enemy is presented as a multinational and Asian-dominated threat to American mainstream middle-class society. Yet this "coloring" of the future as Asian by creating rhetorical images such as the "Mitsubishi Bank of America," upon a closer examination reveals a rhetorical strategy that locates Asia in a time that is not the cyber-technological future of the West but a nostalgic version of a pre-digital past that American cyberspace heroes have long left behind (Nakamura 62). Using the city as model for cyberspace, the novel opens with a description of Chiba City, Japan:

> The sky above the port was the color of television, tuned to a dead channel. "It's not like I'm using," Case heard someone say, as he shouldered his way through the crowd around the door of the Chat. "It's like my body's developed this massive drug deficiency." It was a Sprawl voice and a Sprawl joke. The Chatsubo was a bar for professional expatriates; you could drink there for a week and never hear two words in Japanese. Ratz was tending bar, his prosthetic arm jerking monotonously as he filled a tray of glasses with Kirin. He saw Case and smiled, his teeth a webwork of East European steel and brown decay. Case found a place at the bar, between the unlikely tan of one of Lonny's whores and the crisp naval uniform of a tall African whose cheekbones were ridged with precise rows of tribal scars. (Gibson 3)

The professional expatriates are, like Case, former computer specialists addicted to the virtual reality created by computer technology, and who work as hackers dealing with data and drugs. The Sprawl voices indicate that the guests in this bar are mostly from the financial and economic center of the US, as the Sprawl in *Neuromancer* describes a huge urban and industrial area that stretches from Boston via New York City to Atlanta (43). Here, it is the seemingly out of place characters, the African sailor and the East European bartender, who exemplify the orientalist practices at work, because they are not characters but merely stage props for the white male American hero. When read from a postmodern point of view, all characters in the Chatsubo can be seen as freaks, and the white computer hackers, African sailor, Russian bartender and unidentified prostitutes are likewise out of place, or rather in place as their freakishness is taken for granted. Yet when reading this passage from a postcolonial point of view "against the grain" of a postmodern celebration of multicultural eccentrics, it becomes apparent that the "freaks"— the African with tribal scars and the Russian with decaying teeth—are recognized as freaks here because of ethnic markers: the rotting steel situates the bartender in an industrial East Europe (certainly outdated in the digital age of cyberspace) and the African sailor characterized by tribal scars is fixed in a mythic and certainly pre-digital Western version of Africa. In contrast, the references to everyday technologies such as television and the atmosphere of a bar situate the American urban future in a realm familiar and negotiable to its audience. Applying the vocabulary of postcolonial theory to cyberfiction, Wendy Chun terms this rhetoric "techno-orientalist" (9):

> Rather than simply describing the Orient, orientalists have *projected* an Orient that does not easily map onto geographies and cultures deemed oriental. The status of the Orient as fictional yet indexical to an 'other' space parallels the status of cyberspace as science fiction made digital. (9, emphasis in the original)

The "techno-orientalist" rhetorical strategies that *Neuromancer* and subsequent cyberfiction works deploy must be read and analyzed within the context of cultural discourses of globalization. For Manuel Castells, the increasingly integrated global economy is characterized by information technology, which he defines as

> the *converging set* of technologies in micro-electronics, computing (machines and software), telecommunications/broadcasting, and

opto-electronics. ... I also include genetic engineering ... not only because genetic engineering is focused on the decoding, manipulation, and eventual reprogramming of the information codes of living matter, but also because biology, electronics, and informatics seem to be converging and interacting. (29, emphasis in the original)

According to Castells' definition, at the beginning of the twenty-first century we are at the threshold of a new era: a digital revolution brought about by information technology. The development of this new social structure during the last three decades of the twentieth century is, according to Castells, based on three independent processes, which together form "a new social structure predominantly based on networks" (1). The three processes that shape this "network society" take their roots in economy, society, and technology. While the economic sector has demanded flexible managements and the liberalization of financial sectors and trade and labor markets, society has expressed the wish for individual freedom and open communication. Developments in information and communication technologies as the third process in Castells' picture have been able to answer these demands (1).

It is in the analysis of historical, political, and social constellations that the "orientalism" of cyberfiction becomes apparent, as I would like to argue in the close reading of the brainwashing memories of Marco, Melvin, and Shaw in *The Manchurian Candidate*. In the remake, the characters picture the memories of the brainwashing events quite differently than they do in the earlier film. This shift of imageries involves ethnicity and gender and creates a disturbing visual coalition between politics, multinational corporations, and terrorism. While in the 1962 film, Marco pictures the Chinese "brainwasher" Yen Lo (Kigh Dhiegh) as the head of a group of elderly women from a New Jersey garden club, in the remake, the face of the scientist Atticus Noyle blurs into the face of a veiled and henna-tattooed Arab woman holding a large tomato.

In both film versions, the memories of what actually happened during the soldiers' abduction return in the form of an unchanging nightmare. In the earlier film, Marco's brainwashing memories picture him and his comrades sitting hypnotized and under the spell of the Chinese scientist Yen Lo on a stage in an auditorium where Lo presents the results of the brainwashing process to a group of communist army officials who form the clients and potential customers of his practices. Demonstrating the efficiency of the brainwashing, Lo orders Shaw to kill two of his comrades. Both Shaw and the two soldiers to be killed follow Lo's orders without question while the rest of the group watches quietly and looks bored. A close up shot shows Marco yawning while his comrade Ed Mavole is being suffocated by Shaw. As the soldiers are also conditioned to forget the incident by believing that a different event occurred—the meeting of the women's garden club—in the dream the actual happenings are conflated with the cover-up story. As they were told that they were attending a meeting of the New Jersey women's garden club, the auditorium takes the form of a parlor, Lo is replaced by an elderly, teacherly woman, and the Russian and Chinese officials take the shape of the elderly middle-class club members. Memories of the real event blur with the conditioning to create an absurd mix of ridicule and horror. Carruthers points out that this scene addresses "fear of the violation of individual freedom [which] was particularly potent in the 1950s and indeed early 1960s" and was spurred by "the increasing technologised nature of 'mass society,' the spread of communications media and the growth of commercial advertising in particular" (77). The remake resumes and translates the theme of manipulation of the individual through the media coverage of politics when the underground scientist replies, "We have all been brainwashed," to Marco's statement, "My dreams seem more real to me than what I actually remember happening over there."

In Demme's version, the nightmare pictures the abducted soldiers in a field camp laboratory on a small island. We see the scientist Atticus Noyle conditioning the soldiers by showing them an animated video of what they are supposed to believe has happened to them during the abduction. In contrast to the original, here the brainwashing seems only secondary and the primary goal of the abduction must have been the insertion of a microchip into the soldiers' bodies through which Noyle, as member of the Manchurian Corporation, seeks to maintain mental control over Shaw and Marco. While Noyle remains the same person in the nightmare recollections of Marco, the elderly women of the New Jersey garden club are replaced with henna-painted and veiled women holding large tomatoes and what look like brains in their hands. Here, media images contemporaneous to the film's twenty-first-century audience from real-life television news coverage are used to reflect cultural discourses of terrorism and warfare.

"I thought I knew who the enemy was"

The Manchurian Candidate incorporates public discourses of the post-9/11 period in which images of Middle Eastern looking people purport ideas of an immediate danger. Mita Banerjee writes of the history of stereotypical presentations of Arabs in American film: "Hollywood has a long history of stereotyping the Arab. From *The Cafe in Cairo* to *The Siege*, this Arab—invariably male—figures as the religious fundamentalist who sees in terrorism the only way to spread Islam over the entire globe." It is thus not a coincidence or merely owed to the plot that the flashback scenes and the brainwashing memories of Marco visually conflate the white male scientist Atticus Noyle with an Arabian looking woman dressed in a black scarf. Hence, at a first sight this "ethnic coloring" of the communist enemy of the original film has been translated to a common media image of terrorism of the twenty-first century. But upon closer inspection, the woman is not so much the face of the current "enemy" but of the global corporation. In the remake, this corporation media effectively wears the mask of terrorism. In the post-9/11 discourse that the film presents, with Manchurian Global the United States faces an opponent that combines practices of global capitalism and international terrorism.

Manchurian Global's intricately outlined plan is, first, to seize the White House and, second, to commercialize the "war on terror" by selling the biotechnological weapons they produce to the US government, which they have infiltrated with their own executives. As Senator Thomas Jordan says to Shaw after having seen Marco's research on the conspiracy, "You are about to become the first privately owned and operated vice president of the United States." Additionally, by controlling the media, the corporation constantly feeds the American society with news from the front and frequently changes terror alerts. As Jacobson and Gonzáles write:

> Post-Cold War American culture has evidently built us to peaceably accept a "common good" that is increasingly defined by multinational corporate marauders and their willing servants in government. Once the Berlin Wall came down, and the Soviet Union broke apart, all brakes were removed from the operations of "the free market". We reap this whirlwind in the form of the world's many runaway Manchurian Globals. (193)

In the media circus the film presents, one can detect that the visual manipulation of Marco's nightmare influences the viewer as well. Written into the film's criticism of the interrelationship between global capitalism and American politics is the visual conflation of corporate control and terrorism. Manchurian Global is ultimately not represented by the white, male business executives who are simultaneously politicians, such as the managing director who is also the co-chair of the US International Policy Caucus, but by the oriental woman cradling the technologically modified brains of the American soldiers. Conflating the capitalist scientist visually with the female terrorist, the film obfuscates the wirepuller of the intricate link between American economics and politics. Hence, the film suggests that the "real" threat to individual sanity and public security is not, as Jacobson and Gonzáles write, "the spreading tentacles of Halliburton or McDonald's or Wal-Mart" and their gospel of the free market (193), but the fear that it is the public concern with terrorism will disguise global capitalism and brainwash not only American soldiers but also the American public.

To the audience, the veiled woman holding a large tomato in her hands as if offering a treat to the soldiers does not speak of culinary specialties of the Middle East but of hijacked biotechnology, thus making the connection between consumerism and terrorism for the viewer when she mumbles in Marco's dream, "The revolutionary science of biogenetics, which has literally transformed... Yet note the complexities of the frontal lobe." On the one hand, the genetically engineered tomato can be read as the "American" brain technologically and psychologically modified by a global corporation that seeks control over Western democracy, and the oriental woman becomes the "face" of this formerly anonymous global corporation. Thus, in the film, terrorism and corporate control are not only thematically linked but also visually conflated, as Manchurian Global is not represented by white, male business executives as one would expect, but by the oriental female "terrorist." Following the film's visual strategies, more disturbing than US capitalism in the form of Halliburton and Co., then, is global capitalism disguised as terrorism. However, as these images are presented in Marco's dream alongside and alternating with the television news coverage of the presidential election campaign of Shaw, the faces of the Middle Eastern woman and the American corporation might obfuscate the film's underlying discourses on the other hand. In this case, then, the audience does not see the images of the cyber-lab as criticism of the intricate network between American politics and global economics but as a sign of hijacked American technology and democracy by international terrorism.

Because of the troubling image of the woman holding the soldier's brain in Marco's nightmare, the messages the film relates are complex and multilayered. While it is certainly critical of what Gibson calls the "dance of biz" performed by politicians, the media, and large corporations (11), in line with earlier cyberfiction works it obfuscates this criticism by "coloring" the corporate "enemy" oriental. Hence, in the film global capitalism and international terrorism conflate, fighting the democratic ideals of the American public with its own weapons of "mass consumerism" and political media spin. Also, the film's ending is in line with earlier cyberfictions when in the last scenes of the film we see the Manchurian Global executives stunned and speechless as their coup d'état fails, and it is the FBI and brave American individuals such as agent Rosie, Major Marco, and Congressman Shaw who remain as individual forces able to control the corporate-oriental threat after realizing that they in fact "did not know who the enemy was," as Marco says retrospectively about the brainwashing. That in Demme's 2004 remake of *The Manchurian Candidate* these institutions and the individuals that represent them too transgress the borders of integrity, legality, and democracy is the bitter pill we have to swallow if we want to continue shopping safely at the Wal-Marts, McDonald's and Best Buys across the globe.

Notes

1. An example of public debates about tamper-proof elections in the West would be the 2000 presidential election of George Bush, his defeat of Al Gore, and the ensuing debate about the electoral system in the US, caused by Gore's winning of the public votes and Bush's winning of the electoral votes.
2. Mostly considered a sub-genre of science fiction, I use the term "cyberfiction" here to refer to writers and filmmakers who discuss the impact of information technology and globalization on contemporary Western societies.
3. The original film experienced a revival in the 1980s around the time *Blade Runner* was released (for a discussion of *The Manchurian Candidate*'s revival in the 1980s, see Carruthers). Interestingly, the mind control and paranoia theme of Frankenheimer's film can also be found in *Blade Runner*, which deploys the theme of manipulation of memories and identities by a multicultural corporation when a character finds out that she is in fact a cyborg. The film *Blade Runner* also explores the meaning of memory for human identity. The underlying question that occupies all characters in the story—human and cyborg—is whether memories of a "real" personal history define one as human and, if this is the case, what happens to humans when they find out that their memories of an individual past are not real and have been implanted in their minds. In the American future scenario the film portrays, history, collective memory, and individual identity have been reduced to corporate homogeneity while the multicultural cityscape the film features is portrayed as a development resulting from recent processes of globalization with large groups of labor immigrants from so-called third world countries taking over the streets of downtown Los Angeles.

Works consulted

Banerjee, Mita. "Arab Americans in Literature and the Media." *American Studies Journal* 52 (2008): n. pag. Retrieved on 5 May 2011. http://asjournal.zusas. uni-halle.de/archive/52/154.html.

Blade Runner. Dir. Ridley Scott. Perf. Harrison Ford, Rutger Hauer, and Sean Young. Warner Brothers Pictures, 1982. DVD.

Carruthers, Susan L. "*The Manchurian Candidate* (1962) and the Cold War Brainwashing Scare." *Historical Journal of Film, Radio and Television* 18.1 (1998): 75–94. Print.

Carter, James M. "McCarthyism." *Encyclopedia of American Studies.* Ed. Miles Orvell. Baltimore, MA: The Johns Hopkins University Press, 2011. Retrieved on 3 May 2011. http://eas-ref.press.jhu.edu/view?aid=583.

Castells, Manuel. *The Rise of the Network Society.* Vol. 1. 2nd ed. Oxford: Blackwell, 1996. Print.

Chun, Wendy. "Orienting Orientalism, or How to Map Cyberspace." *Asian America.Net: Ethnicity, Nationalism and Cyberspace.* Ed. Rachel Lee and Sau-ling Wong. New York: Routledge, 2003. 3–36. Print.

Condon, Richard. *The Manchurian Candidate.* New York: McGraw-Hill, 1959. Print.

Ebert, Roger. "The Manchurian Candidate." Review. *Sun Times* 30 July 2004. Retrieved on 25 August 2011.http://rogerebert.suntimes.com/apps/pbcs.dll/article?AID=/20040719/REVIEWS/40719005/1023.

Gibson, William. *Neuromancer.* New York: Ace Books, 1984. Print.

Invaders from Mars. Dir. William Cameron Menzies. Perf. Helena Carter, Arthur Franz, and Jimmy Hunt. Twentieth Century Fox, 1953. DVD.

Invasion of the Body Snatchers. Dir. Don Siegel. Perf. Kevin McCarthy, Dana Wynter, and Larry Gates. Allied Artists Pictures, 1952. DVD.

Jacobson, Matthew Frye, and Gaspar Gonzáles. *What have they built you to do? The Manchurian Candidate and Cold War America.* Minneapolis, MN: University of Minnesota Press, 2006. Print.

Nakamura, Lisa. *Cybertypes: Race, Ethnicity, and Identity on the Internet.* New York: Routledge, 2002. Print.

O' Donnell, Victoria. "Science Fiction Films and Cold War Anxiety." *Transforming the Screen, 1950–1959.* Ed. Peter Lev. New York: Scribner, 2003. 169–96. Print.

Pease, Donald E. "Cold War." *Encyclopedia of American Studies.* Ed. Miles Orvell. Baltimore, MA: The Johns Hopkins University Press, 2011. Retrieved on 3 May 2011. http://eas-ref.press.jhu.edu/view?aid=582.

Said, Edward. *Orientalism.* 1979. New York: Vintage Books, 2004. Print.

Scott, A. O. "Remembrance of Things Planted." Review. *New York Times* 30 July 2004. Retrieved on 25 August 2011. http://movies.nytimes.com/movie/review?res=9902EFD9103DF933A05754C0A9629C8B63.

The Manchurian Candidate. Dir. John Frankenheimer. Perf. Frank Sinatra, Laurence Harvey, and Janet Leigh. United Artists, 1962. DVD.

The Manchurian Candidate. Dir. Jonathan Demme. Perf. Denzel Washington, Liev Schreiber, and Meryl Streep. Paramount Pictures, 2004. DVD.

8
A Personal Matter: *H Story*

Constantine Verevis

In the summer of 1963 Nobel Prize winning author, Kenzaburo Oe, visited Hiroshima to write the first of several essays, or "notes," which were published serially in the monthly journal *Sekai* (*World*) and were later collected under the title *Hiroshima Notes* (*Hiroshima Noto*, 1965). Accompanied by illustrations reprinted from a small volume of A-bomb drawings, *Pika-Don* (*Flash-Bang*, 1950), Oe's book is a deeply moving statement about the meaning of Hiroshima, written "on the spot" (in Hiroshima) while Oe's first-born child lay in a Tokyo hospital incubator with an affliction that would leave the child with a permanent intellectual disability. At the same time as putting together his *Hiroshima Notes*, Oe produced a fictional work—a novel entitled *A Personal Matter* (*Kojinteki na Taiken*, 1964)—in which the child of the main character ("Bird") has a monstrous deformity: a massive brain hernia. Briefly stated, the young father, Bird, is a character with anti-social tendencies who, when previously faced with life's difficulties, has typically turned to drink and (sexual) violence. Confronted with the child's deformity, Bird initially considers abandoning the infant—even killing it—before finally resolving to commit himself with "hope" and "forbearance" to its upbringing.[1] As editor David Swain points out in the foreword to the English edition of *Hiroshima Notes*, "it is no secret that [at a time when the nuclear threat to human existence was mounting daily] Oe's own commitment to his afflicted son drew great strength and inspiration from his encounters with the *dignity* of the A-bomb survivors in Hiroshima and with the *authenticity* of those who steadfastly cared for them" (9). The opening lines of Oe's *Hiroshima Notes*—"Perhaps it is improper to begin a book [on Hiroshima] with a reference to one's *personal experience*" (14, emphasis added)—reflect the fact that Oe shares with Hiroshima an encounter with tragedy that is at once unique and intimate yet also banal and universal. This chapter seeks to draw a line from Oe's two books—*Hiroshima Notes* and *A Personal Matter*—through to two films—*Hiroshima mon amour* (Alain Resnais, 1959) and its remake, *H Story* (Nobuhiro Suwa, 2000)—and in doing so encourage reflection not only on the relationship between a personal story and a cultural history, individual trauma and worldwide catastrophe, but also on that between original and remake.

As is widely known, *Hiroshima mon amour* was initially conceived as a documentary film, a Japanese-French co-production—provisionally entitled *Pika-Don* (*Flash-Bang*)—about the atomic devastation of Hiroshima, and its aftermath. Having recently completed a short film about the Holocaust—*Night and Fog* (*Nuit et brouillard*, 1955)—Alain Resnais was secured to direct, but he soon abandoned the idea of another documentary film, deciding instead that *Pika-Don* should be a fiction film, and that the impact of Hiroshima would be refracted through the personal viewpoint of a foreign woman (see Davies, Jones, Wilson). Resnais subsequently took the project to novelist Marguerite Duras who—in close collaboration with director Resnais and literary consultant (and then lover) Gérard Jarlot—produced a "new generic hybrid": the novella-screenplay, *Hiroshima mon amour* (Pauly 257; see also Davies, Wilson). As Rebecca Pauly describes it, "Duras translated the atomization and devastation of the nuclear firestorm into [a] fragmented modernist narrative of two searingly destructive passions": specifically, the tragic account of a French woman twice driven "mad" by impossible love, first with a German soldier in wartime Nevers (in France) and later with a Japanese man in post-war Hiroshima (257). Like Oe's comment on the mild impropriety of framing his *Hiroshima Notes* as a "personal matter," Duras called *Hiroshima mon amour* a "sacrilege" for its invocation of the atomic devastation through the banal and melodramatic device of a casual, if intensely felt, affair between a French woman and Japanese man: "One can talk about Hiroshima anywhere, even in a hotel bed, during a chance [encounter], an adulterous love affair."[2] But, Duras immediately adds, "What is really sacrilegious, if anything is, is Hiroshima itself" (9).

In *Hiroshima mon amour*, Resnais and Duras created, "with the greatest delicacy and emotional and physical precision,...an anxious aesthetic object, as unsettled over its own identity and sense of direction as the world was unsettled over how to go about its business after the cataclysmic horror of World War II" (Jones, n. pag.). As a key precursor to the French new wave, *Hiroshima mon amour* "heralded a new kind of...cinematic modernism, foregrounding cinema's conventional codes

by *exploding* them, opening them to *contamination* by [poetic] literature on the one hand and [documentary] realism on the other" (Lupton
59, emphasis added). Nobuhiro Suwa's relatively unknown *Hiroshima
mon amour* remake—*H Story*—is a film that confirms the continuing
relevance of Resnais' modernist take on the ambiguities of historical
representation, but is also a film that *challenges* its (cultural) authority,
registering that much has changed in historical context in the 40 years
that separate the two films.[3] Moreover—and again, as in the case of the
author, Oe—Suwa replays his experience of Hiroshima as "a personal
matter." Interviewed at the time of *H Story*'s Cannes Film Festival pre-
miere, Suwa said:

> Having been born in Hiroshima ... I asked myself one question: "How
> would it be possible to express both *my own feelings* about the city
> and the *historical facts?*" ... My thoughts about this challenge always
> led back to the film *Hiroshima mon amour*. Of course, numerous
> Japanese films have been shot in Hiroshima. But I feel the Resnais
> film is the only one that succeeds in depicting Hiroshima for what it
> really is. The film courageously opened the window between history
> and cinema. ... The introduction to the Marguerite Duras synopsis
> recognizes that, "it is impossible to speak of Hiroshima. All one can
> do is to speak of the impossibility of speaking about Hiroshima." The
> scenario of the film was crystallized by this observation: [it is impos-
> sible to speak of Hiroshima]. (Suwa, n. pag., emphasis added)

In her "synopsis" to the published screenplay for *Hiroshima mon amour*,
Duras alludes to the production history of the film, saying that the
"personal story [of two lovers], however brief it may be, always domi-
nates Hiroshima. If this premise were not adhered to, this [film] would
be just one more made-to-order picture, of no more interest than any
fictionalized documentary. If it is adhered to, we'll end up with *a sort of
false documentary* that will probe the lesson of Hiroshima more deeply
than any made-to-order documentary" (10, emphasis added). Resnais'
strategy is to include "real documentary" material—archival and recon-
structed evidence that displays and memorializes the devastation of
Hiroshima and its people—but incorporate this into a love story in
which the personal traumas of the characters are so entangled with
the social history of Hiroshima that the experience of the war will be
(actively) re-produced rather than simply re-presented. Understood as
"a sort of false documentary," *Hiroshima mon amour* is a work, then, that
reflects on its uneasy relationship to the past, and in doing so not only

destabilizes and problematizes cinema as a documentary mode, but more generally interrogates cinema as a *representational* mode, specifically through its staging of the production of a documentary—a film about the peace movement in which the Frenchwoman plays a nurse—within the frame narrative of the Resnais film (Varsava 119).

Suwa embraces the *mise en abyme* structure of *Hiroshima mon amour*, beginning *H Story* with an inscription that reads—"With reference to the motion picture 'Hiroshima mon amour,' produced by Argos Films, directed by Alain Resnais, based upon Marguerite Duras' screenplay and dialogue, published by Editions Gallimard"—before undertaking not simply to remake *Hiroshima mon amour* but to replay, or remodel, it as a sort of (meta-) false documentary: a film *about* the remaking of *Hiroshima mon amour*. That is, if *Hiroshima mon amour* tells the story of a French actress "Elle/She" (played by Emmanuelle Riva) who has come to Hiroshima 14 years after the war to make a peace film about Hiroshima then *H Story* tells the story, 40 years later, of a French actress, Béatrice (played by Béatrice Dalle), who comes to Hiroshima to make a film, in this case a *remake* of *Hiroshima mon amour*. Or, in other words, *H Story* adopts and amplifies the *mise en abyme* structure to tell the story of a French actress who comes to Hiroshima to make a film about a French actress who comes to Hiroshima to make a film about Hiroshima. As the story unfolds it becomes evident that Suwa, the director of the remake (played by Nobuhiro Suwa), has determined to follow closely Duras' original screenplay/novella—line by line, scene by scene—but finds himself increasingly frustrated by the undertaking and ultimately elects to close down the production. Contributing to this decision is the fact that Béatrice begins to struggle with the impossibility of having to reproduce exactly the dialogue and motivations of the character (Elle) that she is replaying from *Hiroshima mon amour*. Béatrice experiences her own breakdown or "madness" and finds refuge (in the frame story) in and through a relationship she (a French woman who has come to Hiroshima to make a film about Hiroshima) establishes with another Japanese man, the writer Machida (played by Kou Machida) who has come to Hiroshima to undertake research for a future novel about Hiroshima. Accordingly, *H Story* does not simply adopt the double narrative of *Hiroshima mon amour*—one that links the personal trauma of a Frenchwoman with the appalling events in Japan's wartime past—but *multiplies* the transgressive achievement of the earlier film through its inscription of a cinematic text "which simultaneously tells an easily understandable story [that is, a film crew undertakes to remake *Hiroshima mon amour*] and interposes between that story and its perception a screen of multiple signs resistant to narrativity" (Ropars-Wuilleumier, "How History Begets Meaning" 173).

As described by several commentators, a pivotal scene in *Hiroshima mon amour*—one in which many of the film's central concerns and questions are foregrounded—takes place at the beginning of Part II,[4] the section immediately following the film's 15-minute long documentary-like prologue in which the French actress' words invoke commemorative images of the city and its tragedy on the screen while the Japanese man's responses ("You saw nothing in Hiroshima") question the ability of the subject to know, to re-produce, the experience of Hiroshima (Craig 28–29; Wilson 49–53). At the start of Part II, the female protagonist (Elle) is awake in the early morning after her first night with her Japanese lover. Dressed in a yukata she stands on the terrace of her hotel room looking out over (new) Hiroshima city. The Frenchwoman moves inside and looks at the twitching, outstretched hand and arm of her sleeping lover, "Lui/He" (played by Eiji Okada). Almost immediately, Elle's brow furrows and the quiet image in present-day Hiroshima is supplanted for a few seconds by a glimpse of another man's hand (later recognized as the hand of Elle's wartime lover), blood stained and twitching in pain. The flashback is lost almost as soon as it appears and Lui awakens and pursues a conversation with Elle (she asks what he has been dreaming about), but from this moment onward temporal linearity and spatial unity are no longer operative: like a dream-image, "time has become a fluid category: 'past' and 'present' [now] intermingle freely and unpredictably" (Craig 28). Equally important, writes Siobhan Craig, the sequence draws attention to the artificiality—or the "artifactuality"— of the diegetic universe of the film, reminding the viewer that "there is no possibility of direct 'knowledge,' and that anything that [the viewer] might be tempted to take as 'truth' is in fact delivered...through the complex mediating processes of the film [medium...]. All we can ultimately 'know' is that we are watching a film" (29).

H Story begins with (a rendering of) a film still—Elle dressed in yukata on the hotel terrace—taken from the beginning of Part II of *Hiroshima mon amour* before cutting to a silent establishing shot in which lead actress Béatrice is discussing the staging of the (same) early hotel room scene with director Suwa: "His arm reminds her of something...buried in her memory. This shaking hand reminds you of the past," Suwa tells Béatrice.[5] The ambiguity of (cinematic) language and (cross-cultural) translation is foretold almost immediately when—once sound is introduced after a few seconds of screen time—it becomes evident that the image presenting the (apparent) mutual understanding between actress and director is mediated by the voice of an off-screen translator (played by cinematographer Caroline Champetier) and the presence of a second actor, Umano (Hiroaki Umano in the role of Eiji Okada), waiting for direction nearby. Catherine Lupton's comments about *Hiroshima mon amour* point to the way that *H Story*'s pre-text dismantles the conventional order of cinematic representation: "*Hiroshima mon amour* achieves a narrative—[that is] the causal and logical explanation by the actress ... of what happened to her in Nevers during the war—but only through the mobilization of traces (disconnected image-fragments) that point towards what they cannot represent" (60). In a similar way, the cinematic construction of *H Story* rests on techniques that signify rupture and intransitivity—*mise en abyme* structure, elliptical and fragmented editing, separation of sound and image, suspended takes and unmotivated inserts, failure to distinguish between the recreations and the frame story, the open ending, and absence of a meta-narrative—to foreground the fact (to paraphrase Duras) that it is impossible to *re*-make *Hiroshima mon amour*. All one can do is to present the impossibility of remaking *Hiroshima mon amour*.

H Story carries out its "explosion" and "contamination" of cinema's (and the cinematic remake's) material and conventions, in part, through its close—though often *non-chronological* and *incomplete*—adaptation (and restaging) of 12 segments from (the Duras screenplay for) *Hiroshima mon amour*:

H Story	*Hiroshima mon amour* screenplay
1. INT. HOTEL ROOM. DAY. ELLE: Do you want some coffee?	Part II, p. 29.
2. INT. HOTEL BEDROOM. DAY LUI: You are like a thousand women ...	Part I, pp. 27–28.
3. INT. HOTEL BATHROOM. DAY. LUI: You're a beautiful woman ...	Part II, p. 32.
4. INT. HOTEL ROOM. DAY. ELLE: To-meet-in-Hiroshima.	Part II, p. 33.
5. EXT. RIVER BANK. NIGHT. ELLE: It's sometimes necessary ...	Part IV, p. 70.
6. INT. HOTEL ROOM. DAY. LUI: I'd like to see you again ...	Part II, pp. 34–36.

7. INT. HOTEL CORRIDOR. DAY.
LUI: Where are you going in France?   Part II, pp. 36–38.
8. INT. HOUSE BEDROOM. DAY.
LUI: Was he French, the man ...   Part III, pp. 47–48.
9. INT. CAFÉ. NIGHT.
LUI: Nevers doesn't mean anything ...   Part IV, pp. 53–55,
                                                  57 & 64–65.
10. INT. BAR. NIGHT.
STRANGER: Are you alone?   Part V, p. 81.
11. INT. HOUSE. DAY.
ELLE: You're alone in Hiroshima?   Part III, pp. 45–46.
12. INT. HOUSE BEDROOM. DAY.
LUI: All we can do now is ...   Part III, p. 52.

H Story follows *Hiroshima mon* amour to develop its own textual strategies of resistance and multiplicity. The second segment (taken from slightly earlier in the *Hiroshima mon amour* screenplay than that which opens *H Story*) begins with four silent, stuttering medium close-ups of the lovers in bed (presented as test shots to establish lighting levels) before (in the fifth shot) the introduction of sound plays out the dialogue in its entirety. Segment three—the shower sequence—follows directly but only as a fragment, a short sequence of two shots without sound. Segment four also begins in silence, but then unfolds as a conversation between the two lovers on the meaning of Hiroshima before being interrupted by a cut to black and the director's call of "Good. That's good, Okay, Good." The fifth segment is more elaborate, commencing with an extended conversation between the actors Béatrice and Umano on the foreshore of the River Ota as they wait for the crew to set up the next shot. "Mr Suwa told me earlier," says Umano, "that this is the river where a lot of people who were burned by the atomic bomb came to drink the water. And they died because of that." The conversation turns to a scene (segment nine) shot earlier that day, but not presented until later in the film. Umano asks: "The scene we filmed earlier on, in the café. What was bothering you?" Béatrice's reply speaks directly to the frustration of attempting a precise reconstruction of *Hiroshima mon amour*: "I'm tired of doing the same thing. I wanted to do things a bit differently ... When we started this film I thought we'd do *more personal things.*" The conversation is dropped as Béatrice and Umano set out their marks and proceed to act a scene from Part IV of *Hiroshima mon amour*.

The film's next sequence—heralded by an archival black-and-white pan shot across the bomb-devastated city of Hiroshima—continues to weave its (two) stories of Hiroshima (past and present, personal and universal) in and through the film's increasingly uncomfortable proximity to the emotional state of the actor, Béatrice. A clapper board announces another take, a medium close-up of Elle/Béatrice, seated at a window, perhaps in a café. An off-screen voice asks her, "Where have you been in Hiroshima?" Her reply—"The museum. That's all so far. I never go out when I'm working... I saw the museum, that's all"—initially suggests that Béatrice is reciting lines from Part I of *Hiroshima mon amour*, but it soon becomes apparent that the conversation is with Béatrice (not Elle). Asked what she thought of the Peace Memorial Museum, Béatrice replies that while the exhibits—a wrist watch frozen at the minute of the blast, a person's shadow etched on a granite door step—are "terrible" and go some way toward representing what happened, she adds that the museum inevitably falls short of re-producing the *experience* of Hiroshima: she says, "But the [exhibits at the] museum... You see, they explain this and that... It's not a criticism, but it's not emotionally... [her words trail away]." Later in the film, the gap between reality and its re-presentation ("original" and remake) is replayed during a visit Béatrice and Machida make to an exclusive gallery of modern art where personal expressions of the tragedy have been transformed into commissioned works—large abstract sculptures—memorializing the theme of the destruction of Hiroshima: "On the 50th anniversary of the atomic bomb," gallery owner Suhama tells Machida, "we commissioned work on Hiroshima from 50 artists." The untranslatability of the tragedy once again finds expression through Béatrice, her restlessness and anomie causing her again to (literally) trail away: leaving Machida behind she wanders outside and away from the gallery.

What becomes evident—beyond the comparative narrative units of *Hiroshima mon amour* and its *H Story* remake—is the latter's interest not only in breaching diegetic levels and generic boundaries, but also in interrogating the proprieties governing the representation of the historical events to provide a layered reflection of a younger generation's sense of an incomplete and disconnected history (Lupton 59). Most obviously, the problem of representation—and the shift in the burden of remembrance from (the experience of) survivors to (the re-presentations of) public institutions—finds expression (in the frame story) in two long exchanges between writer Machida and director Suwa. In the first of these, Machida explains that he has come to Hiroshima to write a book about deceased Hiroshima-born artist Kobori Rintaro: "I've read his book and seen his work...and I felt that it was very personal, based on his experience of the bombing. I thought that by going to Hiroshima, *I could perhaps feel for myself certain things.*" Suwa is asked in turn by Machida, "Why did you want to do it [remake *Hiroshima mon amour*] at this moment in time?" In a reply that suggests the inseparability of memory from forgetting that characterizes *Hiroshima mon amour,* Suwa says:

> When I thought about making a film here, I had a lot of trouble finding a way in... There was this *Hiroshima Mon Amour*... that had been written 40 years ago. It was a text for the cinema, a real screenplay that was used to make the film. But in actual fact, from the moment I encountered this work, I couldn't get it out of my head. Every time I searched for new ideas, I couldn't remove it from inside myself. So, I am so steeped in this film and this text...that as soon as I try to express Hiroshima, I can't avoid them.

Continuing the line of questioning into their second conversation, Machida inquires again, this time more directly: "Tell me...Do you really think...Is it possible to feel the feelings of people who lived 40 years ago?...I think it must be impossible...to feel the things they felt." Suwa's reply—"I know it's unreasonable...After all, the characters lived through the war whereas we have no experience of it. It's only natural that we don't understand what it's like. We cannot feel it physically. Maybe that's the reason why I wanted to *experience* it in the film"— provides a partial answer, but the more compelling response is that provided by Béatrice.

The abandoned café scene (referred to by Umano at the earlier set-up by the edge of the River Ota) is a restaging of the long sequence (Part IV) from *Hiroshima mon amour* in which Elle finally recounts the story of her dead German lover and her incarceration in the family cellar—her "madness" in Nevers—to Lui. The passage is remembered not only for the way it links the lovers through their mutual traumatic experiences of the war, but formally for the way the café sequence extends the shifting relations that characterize the overall structure of *Hiroshima mon amour* through a destabilization of identities, specifically Lui starting to speak to Elle from the subject position of the dead German. *H Story* recreates the segment, beginning with the opening question—LUI: "Doesn't Nevers mean anything in French?"—which prompts Elle to commence her story: "The town is on a river called the Loire. ... Nevers: 40,000 inhabitants. Built as a cathedral. A child can walk around it. I was born there, I grew up there, I learned to read, and had my 20th birthday there ... ." The set-up (a single shot) and dialogue continues until a call from the director ("Good") prompts Béatrice to say, "I'm hot, I'm hot." There follows a cut to a reverse angle shot of Béatrice that picks up the same scene (though some pages later in the script) with Elle's line—"It's awful I can't remember you"—to which Lui responds by holding up a glass and instructing her, "Drink." Elle continues her story—"I'm forgetting you. I tremble at forgetting such love. We were to meet by the Loire at noon. I was leaving with him. When I reached the Loire ... when I reached the Loire ... he wasn't quite dead"—but when she reaches the lines describing her lover's slow demise she exclaims: "I forget exactly when he died. I was lying on him ... And I forget, screw this!" Frustrated, Béatrice reaches for her script and says, "Let's start again." Suwa's words, heard off-screen, and repeated in translation by Champetier, instruct Béatrice to repeat the scene, to do it again "with feeling." Béatrice's response, not just the words—"What feeling? I don't know what I'm saying"—but a characteristic gesture—with a sigh, she blows her fringe from her forehead—recalls not only the "madness" of actor Dalle's enduring screen image—her character Betty, from *Betty Blue* (*37°2 le matin*, Jean-Jacques Beineix, 1986)—but also announces Béatrice's own descent into "madness."

Illustration 8.1   Elle (Emmanuelle Riva) and Lui (Eiji Okada) in the café sequence of *Hiroshima mon amour* (1959)

Béatrice again consults the script and the filming continues ("from the top") with the line "It's awful, I'm unable to remember you..." but within a few sentences Béatrice breaks off once again, saying: "This is pissing me off. It's no fun. I'm sick of this! We've got to stop this." There is a cut to black before the same set-up continues with another attempt (take 3), but the result is much the same: "No," she says, "let's stop, this sucks." There is by this time an extended consultation between Béatrice and Suwa who asks (via translator Champetier): "If she can't do it now will she be able to continue?" However, as the segment unfolds, it becomes evident that Béatrice's words—"It's awful, I've forgotten everything. It's awful, I'm starting to forget you. It's not that, either, I don't know...It's awful, what? It's awful, what, where, why?"—have drifted from the filmic world of *Hiroshima mon amour* to the pro-filmic of Suwa's production. In a similar way to that in which Lui/He verbally assumes the identity of the dead German lover, speaking in his voice, Béatrice appears to assume the voice of Elle/She both in the story space and also in that of the frame narrative. Mirroring the dissolution of epistemological categories (undercut in Part IV and elsewhere in *Hiroshima mon amour*), it becomes increasingly unclear whether the lines belong to the character Elle or the (frame narrative) character Béatrice. In this way—through this visceral type of forgetting—Béatrice provides her own answer to the problem of representing the *experience* of past. That is, the replaying of the exact lines—the tale of Elle's impossible first love with an occupying German soldier—serves as a catalyst of transference, leaving Béatrice to struggle physically and emotionally with the inevitable distance between past and present, experience and documentation. Béatrice's candid exhibition of *personal* grief seems to be designed to draw sympathy and understanding toward Hiroshima's past. It demonstrates the "uniqueness and incommensurability" of the event and its representation (history and story, original and remake), and through the "illicit conjunction of banality and tragedy signal[s] contemporary anxieties about the place and significance of historical memory in [contemporary Japanese] culture" (Lupton 60).

A little later in the film, Béatrice is seen in conversation with Suwa. They are setting up the "stranger" scene from Part V of *Hiroshima mon amour* in which Elle is approached by a second Japanese man in the "Casablanca" night club "at the end of the night which marks the beginning of their [Elle and Lui's] eternal separation" (Duras 80). Suwa tells Béatrice: "We must talk about the café scene from the other day. We couldn't finish that scene. I think we really need to do it again. ... We have to talk it over... and find out what the problem was." Béatrice says that the problem is not, exactly speaking, hers: "We've gone over the problem so much…I didn't want to make a carbon copy of *Hiroshima mon amour*. Was that your idea?…Doing the same thing as *Hiroshima mon amour*, redoing exactly the same thing…There'd be too much missing." These words articulate—more clearly than anywhere in the film—a problem of (close) cinematic remaking: specifically the idea that an irreducible difference plays simultaneously between the most mechanical of repetitions.[6] Otherwise stated, this passage from *H Story* seems to recognize that the closer the remake draws to the original screenplay—Duras' dialogue, Riva's gestures, Resnais' *mise-en-scène*—the wider the gap between the two productions. As Champetier puts it: "She can't accept it [that is, a replica of *Hiroshima mon amour*]. [There'd be] *too much missing…*" In this passage Béatrice's comments seem to echo those of Marie-Claire Ropars-Wuilleumier who writes: "To film Hiroshima…means to show in what way the event *exceeds* the possibility of fixing it within filmic representations" ("How History Begets Meaning" 179, emphasis added). Similarly, Greg Hainge (invoking Gilles Deleuze) writes that if the structural principle of *Hiroshima mon amour* is "atomic," one of differential forces—personal and universal, fictional and documentary—held in tension, then in adapting this formal method, but abandoning any attempt to reproduce its content exactly, *H Story* is not its predecessor's double, but rather its *plural* (165): "*H Story* is not an exact copy of *Hiroshima mon amour*…Rather, it is one of the possible expressions produced by *Hiroshima mon amour* when the latter is apprehended as an abstract diagram, as an individuated entity which is built according to a principle of immanent multiplicity" (166).

One of the strategies adopted by *H Story* is to revisit the textual ambiguity of *Hiroshima mon amour* "by switching the threads of its double narrative" (161), allowing dialogue and events to proliferate, in this case to drift from filmic to pro-filmic, from text to context. Only a small number of remakes—notably Shunichi Nagasaki's 2005 *Heart, Beating in the Dark* (*Yami utsu shinzo*) remake of his earlier 8mm film (*Heart, Beating in the Dark*, 1982), which follows the progress, 20 years later, of the character-actor couple of the original and brings them together with their remake pair—seek to engage actively with the idea of remaking the context (production, reception) of an earlier film property.[7] As Hainge points out, from its beginning, *H Story* is a work that blurs the distinction between genres (documentary and fiction) and diegetic levels (remake and frame story), but the greatest degree of "incommensurability" comes as elements from the reconstructions of *Hiroshima mon amour* (text) pass into frame narrative (context) of its remaking

(152). The transgression of boundaries occurs (as described above) when Elle's madness-inducing trauma migrates from the staging of the café scene to become Béatrice's "madness" as she recoils from the idea of a close remake of *Hiroshima mon amour.* Immediately following Béatrice's breakdown at the (discontinued) café sequence, she takes a stroll with the writer Machida, and (later) Machida is asked (as a favor to Suwa) to occupy the role of "the stranger"—the other Japanese man—in the "Casablanca" night club sequence. Béatrice and Machida are together, too, standing at the estuary to the River Ota, when the latter receives a call from Suwa who tells him: "Thank you for agreeing to help. With the film, I mean. But I can't just carry on with this shoot. Personally, I very much regret it....I intend to break off the shoot." These words effect the final movement of the film, the last segments from *Hiroshima mon amour* (Part V) realized not as recreations of the intimate exchanges between Elle and Lui (from the actress' final night in Hiroshima), but in the wanderings of the players, Béatrice and Machida, through the streets of present-day Hiroshima.

H Story pointedly "traces" the exact scenario of *Hiroshima mon amour,* but in order to demonstrate the impossibility of re-presenting (the *difference* that inheres in) the past. In one telling example (already mentioned above) there is inserted in *H Story* some US military footage—specifically, a black-and-white pan across A-bomb-devastated Hiroshima—which is later "replayed," but as a (re-filmed) color pan shot across the rebuilt (remade) skyline of present-day Hiroshima. This pair of shots not only demonstrates the (historical) distance between shots that cover the "same" terrain, but the way in which the structures that have been built out of the literal (and metaphorical) rubble of Hiroshima are no more than provisional constructions that will never claim the authority or permanence of their predecessors. The pairing of these shots of the Hiroshima skyline suggests—beyond the unfounding of notions of original and remake—that in *H Story* (as in *Hiroshima mon amour* before it) all "epistemological certainties, those proud edifices that once dominated the landscape, [now] lie in ruins" (Craig 26). In this manner, *H Story* confronts the gap in time (and provisionality of knowledge), releasing Béatrice and Machida (Dalle and Machida) to the new city, allowing them to re-trace the nocturnal steps of Elle and Lui (Riva and Okada) as they walk along a Hiroshima city shopping arcade, past the same "Fukuya" (department store) roller shutter sign seen in *Hiroshima mon amour.*[8] Significantly, these scenes, played out in French and Japanese (without a translator), create an understanding of the original relationship that—like the technique of a Situationist *dérive* or drift—is intuitive (emotional) rather than representative (cognitive). The echoes and shadows enable Béatrice and Machida to find—to feel— their own stories in Hiroshima. If *Hiroshima mon amour* can be understood as an "urban film," one in which Elle's perambulation through the city enables her to experience her trauma and history of the city *differently,* then *H Story* "expands the notion of place [of Hiroshima city] from [its] initial meaning as literal geographical locale to a wider metaphorical *topos,* at once spatial, rhetorical and political" (Higgins qtd. in Wilson 59).

For Hainge, the intensity and sentiment of the closing segments of *H Story* re-create *Hiroshima mon amour* anew, coming "far closer to the intensity, spirit and emotion of the original ... than the attempted close reconstructions" seen earlier in the film (154). Hainge argues that *H Story*'s final sequence—Béatrice and Machida wandering around ruins that closely resemble those in which Elle and her German lover are seen to meet in Nevers—is an "exact structural analog" of *Hiroshima mon amour,* one that provides "a commentary not only on the ending of Resnais' film but also on some of its referential network of paratexts" (155). That is, if the ending of *Hiroshima mon amour* is marked by the impossibility of knowing whether Elle stays with her Japanese lover or returns to her family in France then *H Story* not only engages with this idea by interrogating (and contesting) Resnais' anecdote—that Elle *did* indeed stay with Lui—but also by deliberately amplifying the ambiguity of the original ending. The final sequence begins (with sound, but without any dialogue) with a long in duration, extreme long shot of Béatrice and Machida seated on the ground, framed in a large doorway of the brick walled ruins, creepers growing in the rubble-strewn foreground. There is a fade to ten seconds of black before cutting to the next shot, a tighter extreme long shot of the same scene, Béatrice now standing. Béatrice begins to move through the opening, and the camera pans with her (right to left) as she passes (unseen) behind the wall and then past two window openings. When Béatrice traverses a third window opening, the camera stops, stubbornly awaiting Machida to follow, but before he is seen a hand twice obscures the image, and the film ends with a white flare: "an atomic inversion of cinema's fade to black" (155). In one final anamorphic gesture, "the enigmatic language of untold stories—of experience not yet completely grasped—that resonates throughout the film [*Hiroshima mon amour*]" is embraced in *H Story,* to provide "a new mode of seeing and of listening—a seeing and a listening from the site of trauma" (Caruth qtd. in Davies 152).

In one of the best pieces of writing devoted to *Hiroshima mon amour,* Ropars-Wuilleumier predicts the "impossibility" of remaking Duras' text and Resnais' film: *"Hiroshima [mon amour]*'s legacy is substantial; yet the film, unmakable and never remade, remains without an heir, and in that respect it is unique in so far as it defies that very law of succession which it created. At the precise moments when lines of meaning converge they disappear or disperse..." ("How History Begets Meaning" 173). Just as *Hiroshima mon amour* delivers its cinematic shock "through a forceful cinematographic *écriture* [which] dismantles the conventional order of cinema" (173), *H Story* offers a *re*-writing of *Hiroshima mon amour* by enacting the tensions within the text (personal story–cultural history, individual trauma–worldwide catastrophe), and defining the tension in the remake (repetition–difference, original–copy) that is essential for its cultural transformation. In closing, Suwa's comment—that his own feelings and historical facts about Hiroshima always led him back to the film *Hiroshima mon amour*—suggests that the introduction of personal recollection into the encounter of history and representation enables both films to be created anew: not simply as films about the impossibility of representing the past, but of restoring the transformative work of memory and forgetting to the concept of the remake.

Notes

1. These exact words—"hope" and "forbearance"—conclude the novel: "On the inside cover [of the dictionary], Mr Delchef had written the word *hope.* Bird intended to look up *forbearance*" (Oe, *A Personal Matter* 214).
2. Wilson comments on the opposition this aroused in Japan: "Hiroshima survivors felt that its [the film's] sensuality was an insult to the A-bomb dead" (47).
3. Lupton makes a similar point but with reference to Chris Marker's film of the Battle of Okinawa, *Level Five* (1997).
4. Following the breakdown of Duras' screenplay, the film is typically divided into five parts.
5. All (English subtitled) dialogue from the film is taken from the *H Story* screenplay at Database of Movie Dialogs.
6. This point is made with reference to *Psycho* (Alfred Hitchcock, 1960; Gus Van Sant, 1998) in Verevis 75. Jorge Luis Borges' "Pierre Menard, Author of the Quixote" is frequently invoked as a canonical case of meta-remaking and of the play of "irreducible difference" (see Braudy 327).
7. Other examples include: *Shadow of the Vampire* (E. Elias Merhige, 2000) and *Nosferatu: A Symphony of Horror* (F. W. Murnau, 1922); *Rumour Has It* (Rob Reiner, 2005) and *The Graduate* (Mike Nichols, 1967), and *Irma Vep* (Olivier Assayas, 1996) and *Les vampires* (Louis Feuillade, 1915).

8. These ambulatory tracings are perhaps those, too, of director Resnais: "When I got to Hiroshima for the first time, I left the hotel at three in the morning and went wandering through the city. I tried to identify myself with the heroine of the film. I wandered like her through the streets, letting myself be guided by the lights, and like her I ended up at the station" (qtd. in Wilson 58, n.24).

Works consulted

Braudy, Leo. "Afterword: Rethinking Remakes." *Play It Again, Sam: Retakes on Remakes*. Ed. Andrew Horton and Stuart Y. McDougal. Berkeley: University of California Press, 1998. 327–34. Print.

Craig, Siobhan S. "*Tu n'as rien vu à Hiroshima*: Desire, Spectatorship and the Vaporized Subject in *Hiroshima Mon Amour*." *Quarterly Review of Film and Video* 22 (2005): 25–35. Print.

Davies, Rosamund. "Screenwriting Strategies in Marguerite Duras's Script for *Hiroshima, Mon Amour* (1960)." *Journal of Screenwriting* 1.1 (2010): 149–73. Print.

Deleuze, Gilles. *Cinema 2: The Time-Image*. Trans. Hugh Tomlinson and Robert Galeta. Minneapolis, MN: University of Minnesota Press, 1989. Print.

Duras, Marguerite. *Hiroshima mon amour*. Trans. Richard Seaver. New York: Grove Press, 1961. Print.

Hainge, Greg. "A Tale of (at least) Two Hiroshimas: Nobuhiro Suwa's *H Story* and Alain Resnais's *Hiroshima mon amour*." *Contemporary French Civilization* 322 (1980): 147–73. Print.

Hiroshima mon amour. Dir. Alain Resnais. Perf. Emmanuelle Riva, Eiji Okada. Argos Films, 1959.

H Story. Dir. Nobuhiro Suwa. Perf. Béatrice Dalle, Hiroaki Umano, Kou Machida. Dentsu, 2000.

H Story. Screenplay. Database of Movie Dialogs. n.d. Retrieved 28 May 2011. http://movie.subtitlr.com/subtitle/show/110458.

Jones, Kent. "*Hiroshima mon amour*: Time Indefinite." *The Criterion Collection*. n.d. Retrieved on 28 May 2011. http://www.criterion.com/current/posts/291-hiroshima-mon-amour-time-indefinite.

Lupton, Catherine. "Terminal Replay: Resnais Revisited in Chris Marker's *Level Five*." *Screen* 44.1 (Spring 2003): 58–70. Print.

Oe, Kenzaburo. *Hiroshima Notes*. Ed. David L. Swain. Trans. Toshi Yonezawa. Tokyo: YMCA Press, 1981. Print.

——. *A Personal Matter*. Trans. John Nathan. Tokyo: Tuttle, 1981. Print.

Pauly, Rebecca M. "From Shoah to Holocaust: Image and Ideology in Alain Resnais's *Nuit et brouillard* and *Hiroshima mon amour*." *French Cultural Studies* 3 (1992): 253–61. Print.

Ropars-Wuilleumier Marie-Claire. "Film Reader of the Text." *Diacritics* 15.1 (1985): 18–30. Print.

——. "How History Begets Meaning: Alain Resnais' *Hiroshima mon amour* (1959)." *French Film: Texts and Contexts*. Ed. Susan Hayward and Ginette Vincendeau. London: Routledge, 1990. 173–85. Print.

Suwa, Nobuhiro. Interview. n.d. Retrieved on 28 May 2011. www.filmfestivals. com/cgi-bin/cannes/film.pl?id=3013&site=us.

Swain, David L. "Foreword." *A Personal Matter* by Kenzaburo Oe. Trans. John Nathan. Tokyo: Tuttle, 1981. Print.

Varsava, Nina. "Processions of Trauma in *Hiroshima mon amour*: Towards an Ethics of Representation." *Studies in French Cinema* 11.2 (2011): 111–23. Print.

Verevis, Constantine. *Film Remakes*. Edinburgh: Edinburgh University Press, 2006. Print.

Wilson, Emma. *Alain Resnais*. Manchester: Manchester University Press, 2006. Print.

Part III
Remodel

9
Remaking Texts, Remodeling Scholarship

Robin Anne Reid

This chapter argues that scholars who are doing academic research in traditional humanities fields such as film, media, and cultural studies need to become more conscious of the possibilities of the remixing and remodeling that occur in the amateur settings of science fiction and fantasy media fandoms.[1] As Henry Jenkins argues in *Convergence Culture: Where Old and New Media Collide,* one of the most important elements of the contemporary state of converging cultures is people taking "media into their own hands" (17). Humanities scholars who ignore the existence of creative and critical works circulating on the internet that use approaches and tools generated outside academic spaces are limiting themselves to an outdated cultural focus. While interdisciplinary scholarship already performs a kind of remixing and remodeling, by drawing on methodologies and theories from multiple academic disciplines, the sources drawn upon remain academic. With the blurring of boundaries between the "academic" publication "industry" and commercial spaces, and "fan" publications and spaces that is facilitated by the internet, there is good reason for acknowledging relevant work produced by fan scholars. Such acknowledgement includes citation by academics. I am not arguing for replacing academic scholarship with fan scholarship, but for adding fan scholarship, especially when fan scholarship addresses significant gaps in the academic body of work of new and emerging fields of study.

Matt Hills defines a fan scholar as a fan who uses similar research tools and methods as academics in order to create scholarship for a fan audience (16–20). To complicate the binary of academic scholars and fan scholars, there are also academic fans, known as "aca-fans," who participate in fandom and academia and who produce work for both audiences.[2] "Aca-fan" is the term used to identify people who are actively participating in fandom activities while also doing academic research on fandom, as opposed to those fans who may work as academics but do not do scholarship on fandom or those academics who do research in fan studies but do not identify as a fan. Aca-fans are, I argue, the best placed for knowing the scope of fan scholarly discourses and acknowledging the value of such work.

The processes known as remixing and remodeling can be applied to any number of types of text, in multiple media, for any number of audiences and purposes; my focus in this chapter is the necessity of drawing on fan productions that do critical race work in the context of a gap in fan studies. One reason for using fan productions is that work created by the members of the community often deals with topics that have not yet appeared in the academic scholarship. A historical example of how fans addressed topics not found in academic scholarship is the extent to which feminist fans in science fiction fandom were active years before academic scholarship on feminism and science fiction appeared. Monographs by Helen Merrick and Justine Larbalestier show how feminist work by women fans and male allies on gender, sexuality, and feminism in science fiction was part of the public discourses of fandom, appearing in letter columns of professional magazines and fanzines, and in convention programming before the first scholarship appeared in academic publications. WisCon (the only feminist science fiction convention) began in 1977; the earliest academic scholarship (defined as that written by professional academics and printed in peer-reviewed journals and scholarly monographs) began appearing in the 1980s (for example, Marleen Barr's *Future Females* in 1981, Natalie Rosinsky's *Feminist Figures* in 1984). Larbalestier and Merrick's work emphasizes the interlaced and interactive nature of feminist practices in science fiction fandom, analyzing both science fiction texts and fandom practices. However, the academic feminist work published in the United States, the United Kingdom, and Australia focuses primarily on science fiction texts through the lens of gender analysis, focusing on work done by white women in these English speaking cultures.[3]

Merrick's work ends with a chapter titled "Beyond Gender? Twenty-first Century SF Feminisms" which argues that critical race and social justice work in online fandom is a contemporary example of how activist work is being done in the fan communities before academic scholars engage with it. During the 1990s and the 2000s, a great deal of activist and critical work drawing on critical race and intersectional theories has been done in science fiction fandom, including the creation of the Carl Brandon Society in 1999 "to increase racial and ethnic diversity in the production of and audience for speculative fiction" ("About the Carl Brandon Society") and the creation of blogs and communities on a variety of social networking sites to critique and change the lack of racial and ethnic diversity in mainstream media as well as to provide spaces for fans of color to work together. Additional spaces and discussions concern the question of if or how white allies can support anti-racist efforts.

Before discussing the specific elements of race discussions in online fandom, I must note my whiteness and a family history that benefited from the historical oppressions and marginalizations of some immigrants in the US. Four generations (on my mother's side) and six or seven on my father's originate most immediately in the Welsh, Scottish, and German immigrants who came to Virginia and West Virginia, then later applied for and received land grants in the Washington territory before statehood (these were grants that came from lands removed from the Spokane nation by the US government through political and military force).

I present this brief autobiographical information for several reasons: I need to acknowledge that my own whiteness is inescapably a part of my academic work. I always have an ethical and professional responsibility to fandom as a member of the community, as well as an academic, to avoid harming anyone: a very real concern given that my academic work includes essays on Real People Fiction, slash fiction, and dark/torment fic in the Lord of the Rings online fandom. In this case, I have the additional compelling responsibility to attempt to avoid harming or further oppressing people of color. Fans of color are marginalized in fandom(s), and part of that process involves demands that they do not speak about their experiences or their perceptions of racist elements of the source texts, fan fiction, or fandom itself. I would not wish to participate in further silencing through this project, and, by talking about myself, I wish to undercut the idea of a unbodied and unraced or objective scholarship and to draw attention to the marginalization and invisibility of men and women of color in academic discourse in general, not only in areas of fan and audience studies, although as a white woman doing the scholarship, I am unavoidably participating in a history of appropriation and centering myself due to white privilege.

While fan studies has been immediately and centrally concerned with questions of gender from its very beginnings, constructions of sexuality, race and ethnicity, and class have not yet become as important a focus. The primary scholars whose monographs established fan studies as a discipline in humanities areas in the 1980s and early 1990s

(Henry Jenkins, Camille Paglia, Camille Bacon-Smith) are white, and their work does not question how constructions of race might operate in fandom (specifically, convention fandoms). Convention fandom was, arguably, made up of white fans during the 1970s–80s and into the 1990s. An important element of media and some humanities scholarship is analyzing social constructions of race in the media productions which are the canonic texts for fandom, but that scholarship has not been extended to fan studies except for a few cases, such as those of Sarah L. Gatson and Abigail Derechio.[4] I do not expect this chapter to be the definitive or final word on the topic(s); rather, I am hoping to encourage more scholarship by beginning a dialogue in academic spaces about the work already being done in fan spaces.

As an active fan in online media fandom since 2003, as well as having been active in fandom during the 1970s, I have long been immersed in some fan cultures. The debates that began to be widely held on the social networking LiveJournal site during 2006 and 2007 took place in a variety of media fandom communities: StarGate: Atlantis, Dr Who, Life On Mars, Harry Potter, and even multi-communities community. Debates over racial and class stereotypes in fan fiction, as well as racial and class stereotypes in the canon texts of the fandom (including racist terminology used by fans that embodied histories and etymology not widely known outside the US, and ignorance of Jewish religious practices), were hotly debated. Additional levels of conflict occurred because of the international demographic of online fandom, with debates over the history and contemporary racial attitudes in the primarily English speaking fandoms of the US, UK, Canada, and Australia. Other disagreements concerning anti-racist strategies and rhetoric, including the issue of what "tone" can or should be taken when noting the existence of racist language, imagery, or characterizations, reflect different activist theories and practices. The issue of intersectionality (that is, questioning the single focus on "race" or "gender" while ignoring class, sexuality, or ability status) has also affected the nature of the debates in online (and, increasingly, offline) fandom cultures.

An example of such a community and project that directly affected media coverage and reviews of a major film is the Aang Ain't White/ Racebending communities which formed in 2009 to protest M. Night Shymalan's whitewashing of the characters in his adaptation of *Avatar: The Last Airbender* ("Fans Condemn"). The original animated series aired on *Nickelodeon* from 2005 to 2008 and was acclaimed for its setting in an Asian world and its incorporation of a number of religious, historical, cultural, and material elements from the cultures of China and India. The plot of the series involved young protagonists who have to save the world by defeating an evil Fire Lord (the different nations are named after the natural elements of Water, Earth, Fire, and Air). A casting call issued in 2007 which called for "Caucasian or any other ethnicities" was widely interpreted by the fandom to call for whitewashing of the production ("The Last Airbender Primer"). Later casting calls also made a number of blunders in the area of cultural literacies (for example, asking Korean applicants to wear kimonos); additionally, the later calls made it clear that Asian actors would be cast only in minor and supporting roles. Then, for a fantasy world which had neither European nor African settings, the director cast African American extras, setting up a pattern where darker-skinned actors played the villains while the world-saving heroes were white. Fans called for a boycott. The film was released in 2010. While it is difficult to know what financial impact the boycott had, the grassroots organizing on the Aang Ain't White and Racebending sites brought the issues of whitewashing and the need to "advocate for underrepresented groups in entertainment media" ("About Us") into public venues including mainstream media outlets.

Another example of how the anti-racist issues are being publicly discussed in online fandom is "Racefail '09," a wide-ranging discussion of the construction of characters of color in print science fiction and fantasy, cultural appropriation, and the institutionalized racisms in the science fiction community that took place in LiveJournal and on a number of science fiction blogs. The debate that took place during the first three months of 2009 was far from the first discussion of racisms in science fiction and online media fandoms, but it differed from earlier ones in its extent (over 1000 posts linked and identified as part of the debate) and the fact that a number of professional writers and editors participated rather than only fans. As an aca-fan, I can point to numerous posts, challenges, fiction writing festivals, and carnivals that do anti-racist work. The lack of intersectional scholarship that moves beyond the default "white" fan or, in some cases, "the woman fan" to consider multiple axes of identities in fan studies is clear.

There is a growing body of work drawing on critical race and intersectional theories developed in the US used in internet studies, a much broader field of studies than "fan studies." Much of that work is produced by academics in the social sciences and computer science, different disciplines than the majority of fan studies scholars. However, Lisa Nakamura (Director of the Asian American Studies Program, Professor in the Institute of Communications Research and Media and Cinema Studies Department, and Professor of Asian American Studies at the

University of Illinois, Urbana-Champaign) is working in one of the primary disciplines that incorporates fan studies; Wendy Chun (Professor of Modern Culture and Media, Brown University) is another academic in the field of cultural and media studies dealing with critical race theories and the internet. Despite the impressive academic credentials and relevant publications of both scholars, their work is rarely, if ever cited in fan studies scholarship.

Fan studies is a relatively new subject of academic scholarship, with the first publications in the mid-1980s and with major growth since the early 1990s. The first published work included two essays, by Joanna Russ (1985) and Patricia Frazier Lamb and Diane Veith (1986), and the first monographs, by Camille Bacon-Smith (1992), Henry Jenkins (1992), and Constance Penley (1997), appeared in the 1990s. Jenkins and Bacon-Smith's work included a chapter on fan music videos, and Penley analyzes a range of cultural stories around outer space, comparing NASA's visions with the Trek fandom visions while arguing for the value of fandom approaches for academics doing critical studies, much as I am doing here. The concept of academics learning from methodologies created, transformed, or adapted by fans is clearly not a popular one. Despite these early models, much of the scholarship on fan productions that has followed tends to focus on fan fiction rather than other fan creative productions (such as vidding, filking, costuming, and cosplay), although in recent years that is beginning to change. Since the field of fan studies is relatively new, there are bound to be many gaps. However, the creation of more online, peer-reviewed journals means, among other things, that direct links to videos and other graphic media can be embedded in the published scholarship. Online journals also provide open access, meaning that the work is not locked away behind university and academic publishing's economic and technological barriers; fans can access and read such scholarship much more easily than is possible for scholarship published in academic journals which are electronically available only through expensive subscription databases to fans who have access to university libraries or those public libraries which subscribe to the databases.

Recently, more scholarly work began to focus on videos created by fans, known as "vids." A fan video is basically a mix of images from a media text (which can be static screen shots or even images of publicity photographs, or can be whole scenes from the original) combined with music (and, at times, voice-overs or other commentary). A number of the academics doing this work identify as aca-fans. The earliest known vids originated with women in the Star Trek fandom, as Francesca

Coppa argues in her ground-breaking essay, "Women, *Star Trek*, and the Early Development of Fannish Vidding." Coppa began writing on the history and origins of fan videos for several reasons: she was, and is, a fan who creates her own videos, and although fan productions were not her original area of scholarship, she became concerned when she saw presentations at an academic conference on remix culture that placed the origins of remakes, mashups, and remixes with the start of YouTube, or the men creating Machinima, locating the practice solely in post-internet days (about 1996 and thereafter). Yet, as Coppa notes, women were remixing Star Trek since 1975. Since none of the presenters were giving credit to these women, she began to research the topic, a process which resulted not only in her essay but also in efforts to preserve the history and culture of female vidders so their contributions are not lost. The historical parallel she makes is how women's contributions to the genre of the novel were lost as the form became more respected and more men began writing novels. Feminist scholarship had to recover women's novels, and Coppa does not wish to see the same thing happen with regard to vids. Her goal is to document the work that has been done and is currently being done so that it is not so easily lost, or suppressed, or marginalized, at least not to any greater extent than it already is. Her work involves academic publication, but also efforts with the Organization for Transformative Works (OTW), a non-profit organization which was "established by fans to serve the interests of fans by providing access to and preserving the history of fanworks and fan culture in its myriad forms" ("What We Believe"). The OTW supports a fan archive, a wiki, and an online peer-reviewed journal as well as hosting projects to archive older, pre-internet, fan productions.

Coppa's essay provides a number of useful tools for scholars wishing to build on her work about fan videos. Coppa distinguishes fan vids from song or music vids (created to illustrate songs, usually by the corporate or copyright owners). She shows how female fans, using slide shows, even before the existence of VCRs, let alone the internet, created vids and established a convention dedicated to vidding (VividCon) over thirty years ago. While vidding has expanded and changed greatly with new digital technologies and the internet, Coppa argues that despite these changes the vids "share an aesthetic tradition and an analytical impulse not immediately obvious to the outsider" ("Women").

As well as the overview of Star Trek fandom and the different schools of vidding that developed, Coppa also provides a close reading of Kandy Fong's work. Fong, arguably the first vidder, created her productions by blending slide shows of images from the cutting room floor with music. Fong videotaped some of her presentations, and some of the tapes were preserved and are now available on the internet, including the one Coppa analyzes in this paper, "Both Sides Now." This video uses Leonard Nimoy (Spock's) recorded version of the popular song "Both Sides Now" along with clips from the original series, including ones from the "Mirror, Mirror" universe (a canonical alternative universe which is presented as totalitarian and sadistic). In her Curator's Note at the MediaCommons site, Coppa notes the extent of "gender slippage" Fong created, since "Both Sides Now" was written by Joni Mitchell and recorded by Judy Collins before Nimoy recorded it for his album: "By staging the contrast between Nimoy's external appearance and inner voice, Fong foregrounds various kinds of 'bothness': human and alien, public and private, male and female, mainstream and resistant reader" ("Women"). Coppa's conclusion in her essay is that:

> Vidding is a form of collaborative critical thinking. While videos make an infinite variety of arguments about the television shows and films they love—theorizing about characters, fleshing out relationships, emphasizing homoerotics, picking apart nuances of plot and theme—these arguments frequently articulate alternative perspectives, particularly in terms of gender and sexuality. ... To be a vidder is to work to reunite the disembodied voice and the desiring body, and to embark on this project is to be part of a distinctive and important tradition of female art. ("Women")

Coppa's work is important because of its originary nature; as feminist scholarship has shown, not only do creative works by women disappear from cultural memory and production, so too is scholarship by women ignored. But her work in focusing primarily on gender has the potential to erase the presence and productions of women of color.

Inspired by (and featuring) Coppa's work, a special section in the Summer 2009 issue of *Cinema Journal* featured a number of articles on fan videos, primarily through a feminist and gender studies lens.[5] The fact that I know (or met) most of the authors in LiveJournal's online media fandom and in some cases from academic conferences and the Organization for Transformative Works says something about the extent to which members of the aca-fan community made themselves at home in LiveJournal.[6] These scholars (ranging from independent scholars, to graduate students, to junior faculty) are trained in a variety of disciplines, and are somewhat more diverse than found in academia in general: they are all women; de Kosnik has a Filipino background and works on issues of race and fandom through her work on hip-hop and media fandom's comparative remix cultures; both Levin Russo and Lothian locate themselves academically within queer studies. Russo's dissertation was on lesbian fandom and incorporated sections on different vidding communities; Lothian's dissertation is on queer temporality and will have a chapter looking at the temporal politics of vidding from that perspective, including her efforts to use vidding as a tool to engage in scholarly explorations of queer temporality.

From Coppa's single article in 2008 to a theme section in a major academic journal in 2009 is light speed in terms of academic time, and I think this is due at least in part to the community and communications to be found on LiveJournal and other fandom spaces. However, there is a gap in these originary works that I see paralleling the larger body of fan fiction scholarship, whether on fan fiction, fan culture, or fan vidding. Scholarship that does such an excellent job of remixing and remodeling work through a focus on fan productions by academics, who are also identifying as fans, still ignores critical race questions. In Luckett's Console-ing Passions Conference report, she notes two points about the conference that she does not connect but which I see as strongly associated: first, the absence of international media in scholarship in film, television, and new media scholarship at the conference; and second, in another paragraph, she observes, "much of the work presented at the conference, while thoughtful and engaging, did not take the opportunity to interrogate, develop, and pursue new lines of thought about gender" (101). As a feminist scholar who has been working with critical race theory developed by women of color in the 1980s in the context of feminist literary studies, I am aware of the body of work that critiques the whiteness of the second wave feminist movement in the US. Many of these scholars, theorists, and activists have been working offline and online to create global, intersectional, and internationalist work in multiple academic and activist discourses and spaces. Thus, I would argue that it is impossible to say anything "new and engaging" about gender unless the focus moves from a monist approach to intersectional work, combining considerations of race, ethnicity, class, and sexualities with gender.[7] In contrast to academic spaces which are still dominated by white men and women, anti-racist, social justice, activist groups, even if numerical minorities in online media fandom, are engaged in creating a rich and complex body of intersectional work which has so far been largely ignored by academic scholarship. This work of course includes vids, but also includes meta: that is, analytical essays written by fans about fan productions (and canon sources).

An example of such meta is Deepa D.'s "Three Blocks in the Vidding Quilt," an essay that makes a multi-layered analysis of three vids. Her work crosses academic and fan boundaries: an early version, a conference paper, was presented to an audience she describes as consisting of "bemused" academics; her original argument was that "the product and the process [of vids] were infused with a grassroots feminism in which a female gaze was quilted together through communal crafting." The later essay, posted online, expands on that earlier work. She deals with the conflict between readers, including Henry Jenkins, who argue that the best fan vids are accessible to all, with layers that more experienced fans (experienced in the show that is) can tease out, and between those readers who work to privilege a more coded, less accessible female gaze. Deepa D. argues that the female gaze exists in "opposition to the public, universal, essentializing nature of the male gaze ... the female gaze speaks in code and rewards intimacy with knowledge," and she uses three videos to "show how both their creation and consumption manifests as a collectively quilted female gaze—not a homogeneous ideology but a pieced together alliance of creative opinions and critical lenses" ("Three Blocks"). One of the three vidders whose work she analyzes is a male who Deepa D. argues has internalized the female gaze and codes just as women directors can internalize and create the male gaze.

I would assign Deepa D.'s essay to be read alongside the scholarly essays I assign in upper level or graduate courses in new media literacies, especially to illustrate how the dialogic nature of discourse can work: Deepa D. presents a counter argument to Henry Jenkins' argument about the definition of the "best" type of vid and incorporates appropriate scholarly attribution (citing Coppa's work and referencing Judith Butler's gender theories). As an additional note on fan culture, the essay was written for another fan, Sartorias, who won it during the "Con or Bust" auction. The "Con or Bust" auction was created by fans in the wake of "Racefail '09" as a way of raising funds to support fans of color who wished to attend WisCon. As fans have often done, they came together to raise funds for a social-justice issue deemed important to the fandom.[8]

What I am calling social-justice videos are only one type of fan vid, and not necessarily the largest category. Fan videos include a wide range of genres and purposes, just as fan fiction does. In this chapter, I highlight two vids that make critical race and intersectional arguments within the context of the anti-racist and social-justice work that is being done in fandom. These two vids were on a long list of videos recommended to me as ones dealing especially with race issues; I chose them because I am familiar with the text they deal with, the television show *Firefly* (2002) and a later film, *Serenity* (2005), both directed and overseen by Joss Whedon. The short-lived television show (Fox canceled the show due to low Nielson ratings after 11 of 14 episodes aired) created a strong fandom, leading to enough support that Whedon was able to expand the franchise to a film, and to other media (see Hark). The show blends elements of space opera and American westerns, so that the same shot can show characters riding horses and then leaving in their Firefly spaceship. The back-story includes a war which resulted in a centralized government attempting to control various colonies, with parallels to the post-Civil war era in the American west, but with a strong implication of a Chinese dominated government and culture. The show is set in 2517 in a different star system which was colonized in the past; in the present of the show, the outlying colonies on planets and moons are poor and lacking in the technologies of the central planets where the Alliance government, a blend of the Chinese and American superpowers, is more established. Six of the nine characters are white; three are played by actors of color. Zoe Washburn, the second in command on the ship and ex-military, is played by Gina Torres (a New York actor of Afro-Cuban descent), and Inara Serra, a Companion (equivalent to a courtesan), is played by Morena Baccarin (an Italian-Brazilian). Derrial Book, a Shepherd (equivalent to a pastor), is played by Ronald Glass (an African American actor).

The series and film show a future in which Chinese culture is dominant and a large part of the central power, including the use of Mandarin (badly) spoken by the actors. However, most of the main characters were coded as white, and few Asians appeared in any but the most minimal of non-speaking and background roles. The historical parallels with white resettlement out of the South after the Civil War evokes but fails to undercut the actuality of systematic oppression and marginalization of Chinese immigrants to the US in the nineteenth century. During that time, men were imported from China to work as cheap labor on the railroads and in the mines, especially during the gold rush; they faced discrimination, including federal laws passed to restrict their access to citizenship, prevent marriage to white women, and prevent immigrants bringing their families to the US.

The two vids foreground and comment on the racism and oppression in the history that Whedon draws on for his space western. Shati's

"Secret Asian Man" came about when she wondered about vidding a negative: "'Huh,' I said to myself. 'I wonder how you would do a vid about the *lack* of a character. It would be kind of hard to find shots of them. Kind of'" (Shati). This video blends scenes from the series with a song that is itself a parody: Da Vinci's Notebook's "Secret Asian Man" parodies Johnny Rivers' 1966 hit, "Secret Agent Man," a song about the James Bond kind of secret agent who is always at risk of being killed and/or tempted by a beautiful woman who is working for the enemy. Rivers' song came out during the Cold War, and the parody by Da Vinci's Notebook references Russia ironically while shifting the focus to the conflict between China, led by Chairman Mao, and the US. Los Alamos is mentioned, but even more at risk are America's "Cheetos, Birkenstocks, and Wal-Mart."

Shati does not use the whole song, probably because of intellectual property issues, but has enough to convey the main message, with accompanying images that focus on the "background" characters and public setting more than the main characters, although there are several shots of Mal, Jayne, River, and Inara. The parts of the video that show the "secret" Asian culture include quick shots of a Buddha, fight scenes, street scenes with a group of Asian men who could be either police, a gang, or military, and a shot of a street market where vendors are barbecuing meat, in which the camera zooms back to show dogs in a cage with a sign in English, "Good Dogs." This video emphasizes more public shots and more male characters than Lierdumoa's "How Much is That Geisha in the Window?," a vid which is set to instrumental music rather than a song, and has some voice-overs (from a DVD extra), as well as the vidder commenting explicitly at the end. This vid focuses much more on women characters and interior scenes, intercut three times with the "Good Dogs" scene in the public market. The notable lack of Asian characters in the series is highlighted by how many of the same clips are used by these two short videos. Text in a red font is added: "There is only one Asian Actor with English Dialogue in all of Firefly. She plays a whore." Lierdumoa does an excellent job of finding multiple but short scenes with nameless women characters from the show's background shots, set mostly in bar or brothel settings: a fan dancer, a belly dancer, and a number of shots of Inara that focus on her body, cutting off most of her face. In addition to the critiques of the racialized and gendered aspect of the courtesan/geisha/whore elements of the show, the video also shows nameless, anonymous characters panning for gold and additional images from other films that evoke not only the American west but the Civil War (including a number of battle shots of the losing "Browncoats" and a shot of the Confederate flag). The voice-over elements in an excerpt from the DVD which has the actors singing "How Much Is That geisha in the Window" to the music of "Doggie in the Window" (a jingle performed with revised lyrics by Adam Baldwin, Nathan Fillion, and Gina Torres in the Firefly Extended Gag Reel) and, finally, the vidder saying: "Fuck you Joss, you racist asshole."[9]

"How Much is That Geisha in the Window?" was cited by Rebecca Tushnet, a professor of law, who publishes on the legal issues relating to fan fiction and fan productions, in her testimony at the "Copyright Office DMCA Hearings: Noncommercial Remix." The purpose of citing this particular video as one example is that remix artists need high quality source materials to work with rather than the lower quality in the context of determining what fair use might be in regard to transformative works:

> One random example of how quality is important to show you things that aren't easy to see in the original: a video called "How Much Is That Geisha in the Window?"—a critique of a science fiction series, *Firefly*, by Joss Whedon. *Firefly* is supposedly set in a future where Chinese and American influences are about equal. Low-quality doesn't let you see what you need to see, which is the details of the Asian setting, the constant references to Asian cultures, and the fact that nonetheless there aren't any Asian characters except in deep background—the critique is meaningless if you can't tell why the artist is complaining because one pixilated person looks pretty much like another. (Tushnet)

Both Shati's and Lierdumoa's videos embody the elements of transformative works: although there are scenes from Whedon's shows (and some others), the videos transform the scenes to make a point, by focusing what was not foregrounded, what was not spoken, what was not the center of Whedon's stories: the Asian men and women.

While it is important to see how a legal scholar can cite videos for her rhetorical purposes, what is lacking in the current humanities, cultural, and media scholarship about fandom is awareness of the importance of critical race and intersectional work. This critical work is being done in fandom, and in the social sciences and, increasingly, in literary studies as well. White women scholars have brought a strong awareness of the issues of gender to the scholarship on fan studies, but even the most recent fan scholarship, focusing on new areas of fan production, is so

far ignoring questions of race and intersectional theories and methodologies. The fact that this gap exists, in contrast to the growing body of
work on critical race and intersectional analysis in literary studies in the
US, deserves much greater consideration than it has received. During the
summer of 2007, Henry Jenkins hosted a discussion between a number
of men and women working in the field of fan studies; the discussion
appeared in his blog, and was mirrored in a LiveJournal community.
The mirroring in the community was at the insistence of those women
scholars, including myself, who found their primary online home in
LiveJournal rather than in individual blogs (Jenkins, "Gender and Fan
Studies").

In the summer of 2011, another discussion was hosted on "Coming
Soon: Acafandom and Beyond," which focused on the "Acafan and the
kinds of work this term has done for helping us sort through our complex emotional and intellectual relationships to our object of study and
the equally complicated relationships between our professional lives as
fans and who we are in our personal lives" (Jenkins, "Coming Soon").
One of the disciplines identified in the original blog entry was Race
Theory, and some of the discussions (many of the participants originally listed as hoping to participate were not able to do so) did start
to deal with more intersectional issues than had the previous discussions on gender, although arguably there was a much greater focus on
issues of sexuality and queerness than there was on race and ethnicity,
no doubt reflecting the still largely white bodies and cultures of the
aca-fans.

In November 2011, the *Journal of Transformative Works and Cultures*
featured a double "themed" issue, half of which focused on "Textual
Echoes," and the other half focused on "Race and Ethnicity in Fandom."
As the co-editor with Sarah Gatson of the "Race and Ethnicity" special
issue, I hope that this issue will challenge academics working in fan
studies to consider the rich and complex history of textual analysis of
both print and visual texts incorporating critical race and intersectional
theories that have been circulating in fan spaces and other academic
spaces for decades. They need not only consider their lived experiences
and multiple identities in the context of "fandom" and "academia," and
as "aca-fans," but as members of a profession still largely dominated by
white men and women and to acknowledge the ground-breaking work
of the fan artists and scholars who are taking "media into their own
hands" (Jenkins, *Convergence Culture* 17) to critique the institutionalized and aversive racisms of the twenty-first century.

Notes

I am grateful to the American Studies Division of the English Department at the University of Göttingen and the US Consulate General in Hamburg for their invitation and support for my travel to the 2010 Remake | Remodel Conference. Special thanks go to Kathleen Loock and Dorothea Schuller.

1. While scholarship on sports, celebrity, music, romance, and soap opera fandom exists, it is outside the scope of this project. The extent to which the scholarship works with different types of fandom is something that needs to be questioned, for example, in the creation of a new interdisciplinary and multi-fandom journal, *The Journal of Fandom Studies*, by editors Katherine Larsen and John Walliss, to be published by Intellect Press in 2013.
2. The abbreviation "aca-fan" for "academic fan" has become fairly widely used since the 1980s when an email list called ACAFEN-L: "The Academic Study of Fandom" was started by Patricia Gillikin ("Aca-Fan"). Hills is credited with popularizing the term, and Jenkins has used it in the title of his blog, *Confessions of an Aca/Fan*.
3. Scholarship on national fandoms, especially fandoms in languages other than English-language fandoms, does exist, but is not well known among the English-language scholars: I am aware of work on Finnish science fiction fandom by Irma Hirsjärvi; other scholars I know of who work with Japanese and Korean fandoms in those languages (as compared to the North American fans of translated or dubbed works sold outside the countries of origin) are working in different areas, with publications in English, on a variety of fandoms, but I have seen no indication of work being done that is parallel to or deals with issues of critical race debates in English speaking fandoms.
4. Some scholarship on race and the internet/online communities does exist, primarily from sociological, psychological, and media studies. Lena Karlsson published "Desperately Seeking Sameness: The Processes and Pleasures of Identification in Women's Diary Blog Reading" in *Feminist Media Studies*. Two articles on "nerdness" and race are of interest because of the extent to which fans self-identify as nerds (with gender differences acknowledged between male and female nerds): "Race, Sex and Nerds: From Black Geeks to Asian-American Hipsters" by Ron Eglash in *Social Text* analyzes the cultural intersections of race and "nerd," to critique "reversing" stereotypes. Eglash incorporates gender analysis. Mary Bucholtz, a linguistic anthropologist, presents patterns of self-identification around race and language among self-identified nerds in one high school: "The Whiteness of Nerds: Superstandard English and Racial Markedness" in *Journal of Linguistic Anthropology*.
5. The contributors are: Moya Luckett, who wrote a "Conference Report" on "Console-ing Passions," and half a dozen essays in a section titled "Fandom and Feminism: Gender and the Politics of Fan Production": Introduction by Kristina Busse; "A Fannish Taxonomy of Hotness" by Francesca Coppa; "A Fannish Field of Value: Online Fan Gift Culture" by Karen Hellekson; "Should Fan Fiction Be Free?" by Abigail De Kosnik; "User-Penetrated Content: Fan Video in the Age of Convergence" by Julie Levin Russo; and "Living in a Den of Thieves: Fan Video and Digital Challenges to Ownership" by Alexis Lothian.

6. In recent years, people active in LiveJournal fandom have often moved to other journaling sites, including Dreamwidth, or are active on other social networking sites such as Tumblr.
7. The term "intersectionality" was first coined by Kimberlé W. Crenshaw, Professor of Law at UCLA, in 1989. Critical race theory and intersectional theory are used to refer to a number of methodologies which seek to engage with more than one social construction of identity. The theories are used in a variety of social science, legal, and humanities scholarly fields.
8. Deepa D. was nominated for the British Science Fiction Association's Non Fiction award for her essay "I Didn't Dream of Dragons" which was one of the multiple posts about the issue of cultural appropriation in science fiction that became part of "Racefail '09."
9. The vidder gives the following attributions for her visual sources: "Video: Firefly (2002), with additional source from Serenity (2005), Memoirs of a Geisha (2005), 3:10 to Yuma (2007) and Gone with the Wind (1939)." Additional information on the translation and language issues is in her Author's Note: "A/N: This was made for the 2008 Vividcon challenge. Any Chinese audio not taken from Firefly was recorded by the editor and translated from English by Angela Bai. Special thanks to Emily C. and Adrienne H."

Works consulted

"About the Carl Brandon Society." *Carlbrandon.org*. The Carl Brandon Society, n.d. Retrieved on 27 October 2011. www.carlbrandon.org/about.html.
"About Us." *Racebending.com*. Racebending.com, n.d. Retrieved on 27 October 2011. www.racebending.com/v4/about/.
"Aca-Fan." *fanlore.org*. Fanlore, 21 September 2011. Retrieved on 27 October 2011. http://fanlore.org/wiki/Aca-Fan.
Bacon-Smith, Camille. *Enterprising Women: Television Fandom and the Creation of Popular Myth*. Philadelphia, PA: University of Pennsylvania Press. 1992. Print.
Bucholtz, Mary. "The Whiteness of Nerds: Superstandard English and Racial Markedness." *Journal of Linguistic Anthropology* 11.1 (2001): 84–100. Print.
Busse, Kristina. "Introduction." *Cinema Journal* 48.4 (2009): 104–7. Print.
Chun, WendyHui Kyong. *Control and Freedom: Power and Paranoia in the Age of Fiber Optics*. Cambridge, MA: MIT Press. 2006. Print.
Coppa, Francesca. "A Fannish Taxonomy of Hotness." *Cinema Journal* 48.4 (2009): 107–13. Print.
———. "Women, *Star Trek*, and the Early Development of Fannish Vidding." *Transformative Works and Cultures* 1 (2008): n. pag. Retrieved on 27 October 2011. http://journal.transformativeworks.org/index.php/twc/article/view/44/64.
D., Deepa. "Three Blocks in the Vidding Quilt." *Dreamwidth*. Deepad's journal, 14 April 2010. Retrieved on 27 October 2011. http://deepad.dreamwidth.org/50236.html.
———. "I Didn't Dream of Dragons." *Dreamwidth*. Deepad's journal, 13 January 2009. Retrieved on 27 October 2011. http://deepad.dreamwidth.org/29371.html.
De Kosnik, Abigail. "Should Fan Fiction Be Free?" *Cinema Journal* 48.4 (2009): 118–24. Print.

Eglash, Ron. "Race, Sex and Nerds: From Black Geeks to Asian-American Hipsters." *Social Text* 20.2 (Summer 2002): 49–64. Print.

"Fans Condemn Racial Bias in 'Yellowface' Casting of 'The Last Airbender.'" *Racebending.com*. Racebending.com, n.d. Retrieved on 27 October 2011. www. racebending.com/avatarpr.php.

"Gender and Fan Studies: A Summer Conversation." *LiveJournal*. LiveJournal, 11 June 2007–18 April 2008. Retrieved on 3 November 2011. http://fandebate. livejournal.com/.

Hark, Ina Rae. "Decent Burial or Miraculous Resurrection: *Serenity*, Mourning, and Sequels to Dead Television Shows." *Second Takes: Critical Approaches to the Film Sequel*. Ed. Carolyn Jess-Cooke and Constantine Verevis. Albany: State University of New York Press, 2010. 121–37. Print.

Hellekson, Karen. "A Fannish Field of Value: Online Fan Gift Culture." *Cinema Journal* 48.4 (2009): 113–18. Print.

Hills, Matt. *Fan Cultures*. London: Routledge, 2002. Print.

"Issuefic." *fanlore.org*. Fanlore, 7 April 2011. Retrieved on 27 October 2011. http://fanlore.org/wiki/Issuefic.

Jenkins, Henry. *Textual Poachers: Television Fans and Participatory Culture*. New York: Routledge. 1992. Print.

——. *Convergence Culture: Where Old and New Media Collide*. New York: New York University Press, 2006. Print.

——. "Gender and Fan Studies: Join the Party." *Confessions of an Aca/Fan: The Official Weblog of Henry Jenkins*. 12 June 2007. Retrieved on 3 November 2011. http://henryjenkins.org/2007/06/gender_and_fan_studies_join_th.html.

——. "Coming Soon: Acafandom and Beyond." *Confessions of an Aca/Fan: The Official Weblog of Henry Jenkins*. 3 June 2011. Retrieved on 3 November 2011. http://henryjenkins.org/2011/06/coming_soon_acafandom_and_beyo.html.

Karlsson, Lena. "Desperately Seeking Sameness: The Processes and Pleasures of Identification in Women's Diary Blog Reading." *Feminist Media Studies* 7.2 (2007): 137–53. Print.

Kolko, Beth E., Lisa Nakamura, and Gilbert B. Rodman. *Race in Cyberspace*. New York: Routledge, 2000. Print.

Lamb, Patricia Frazer, and Diane Veith. "Romantic Myth, Transcendence, and Star Trek Zines." *Erotic Universe: Sexuality and Fantastic Literature*. Ed. Donald Palumbo. Westport, CT: Greenwood Press, 1986. 236–55. Print.

Larbalestier, Justine. *The Battle of the Sexes in Science Fiction*. Middletown, CT: Wesleyan University Press, 2002. Print.

——. "The Last Airbender Primer." *Racebending.com*. Racebending.com, 21 October 2009. Retrieved on 27 October 2011. www.racebending.com/v3/background/the-last-airbender-primer/.

Lierdumoa. "How Much Is That Geisha in the Window?" 2008. Retrieved on 27 October 2011. http://mcposse.com/hmitgitw/.

Lothian, Alexis. "Living in a Den of Thieves: Fan Video and Digital Challenges to Ownership." *Cinema Journal* 48.4 (2009): 130–36. Print.

Luckett, Moya. "Conference Report: Console-ing Passions." *Cinema Journal* 48.4 (2009): 99–103. Print.

Merrick, Helen. *The Secret Feminist Cabal: A Cultural History of Science Fiction Feminisms*. Seattle, WA: Aqueduct Press, 2009. Print.

Nakamura, Lisa. *Cybertypes: Race, Ethnicity, and Identity on the Internet*. New York: Routledge, 2002.

——. *Digitizing Race: Visual Cultures of the Internet*. Minneapolis, MN: University of Minnesota Press. 2008. Print.

Penley, Constance. *NASA/Trek: Popular Science and Sex in America*. New York: Verso. 1997. Print.

"RaceFail '09." *Dreamwidth*. rydra_wong's journal, 4 February 2002. Retrieved on 27 October 2011. http://rydra-wong.dreamwidth.org/148996.html.

Russ, Joanna. "Pornography by Women, for Women, with Love." *Magic Mommas, Trembling Sisters, Puritans and Perverts: Feminist Essays*. Trumansburg, NY: The Crossing Press, 1985. 79–99. Print.

Russo, Julie Levin. "User-Penetrated Content: Fan Video in the Age of Convergence." *Cinema Journal* 48.4 (2009): 125–30. Print.

Shati. "New Vid—Firefly—Secret Asian Man." *LiveJournal*. LiveJournal, 9 August 2008. Retrieved on 27 October 2011. http://shati.livejournal.com/230374. html.

Tushnet, Rebecca. "Copyright Office DMCA Hearings: Noncommercial Remix." *Rebecca Tushnet's 43 (B)log*. Blogspot, 7 May 2009. Retrieved on 27 October 2011. http://tushnet.blogspot.com/2009/05/copyright-office-dmca-hearings_7679. html.

"What We Believe: Our Mission." *Transformativeworks.org*. Organization for Transformative Works, n.d. Retrieved on 27 October 2011. http://transformativeworks.org/about/believe.

10

"Prince Arthur Spotted Exiting Buckingham Palace!": The Re-Imagined Worlds of Fanfic Trailers

Sibylle Machat

Fanfic (or fanfiction) are stories written by fans for other fans. They use a source text as their point of origin and then explore or alter character relationships, settings or other ingredients of the original work in different and varied ways, with different degrees of divergence from the source becoming readily apparent to the source-knowledgeable reader. Initially, fanfiction stories were mostly shared in print form (in so-called zines or fanzines), but with the rise of the internet they, like so many other fan productions, have moved on into the digital medium, and large online collections of fanfiction can now be readily found online.[1]

In a 2008 interview on the vidding underground with Jesse Walker from *Reason* magazine, Francesca Coppa argues that the primary aim of fan-made videos is "trying to make an argument about the source text," and that they are therefore close to "political remix videos." The transformative aspect is fore-grounded in both vidding and in political remix videos: "In a vid, instead of writing an essay about your show, you make a visual essay about your show," Coppa explains (Walker). Fanfic trailers emerged from the practice of fan vidding and can be described as follows: instead of writing an advertisement for a fanfiction story, a short video trailer is created by using visual and auditory materials that might or might not be related to the story world in which the fanfiction story is set.

Fanlore.org defines a fanfic trailer simply as "[a] vid designed to advertise or promote a fanfiction story" ("Fic Trailer"). However, stricter definitions and rules also exist, not unlike the ones described by Valentin Seiwald in his article on Sweded Films, another recent online movie development, and thus interesting to study in relation to the fanfic trailer.[2] The rules for fanfic trailers are defined in the artword community on LiveJournal, a group that runs "a monthly Stargate Atlantis and Stargate SG-1 multimedia challenge" made up of "teams of a fanartist and a fanwriter" each (newkidfan, "Artword"). There, the following rules—made by newkidfan, founder and moderator of artword, and posted on LiveJournal in January 2006—are used to classify fanfic trailers:

1. Length: from 30 seconds to 1:30 min. Not more.
2. Format: has to be structured as an actual trailer: video, text, music, even bits of dialogs, credits, etc.
3. Music: unless the music is imposed in the challenge, you can choose your own music (with or without lyrics). (newkidfan, "Guidelines")

This is a rather strict frame within which fanfic trailers have to fit, and even in the artword community these rules were being discussed controversially. Newkidfan replied to the question "Is there any possibility for movement on the rules for video?" by member lim on 1 June 2008 as follows:

I don't know if it's noticeable yet, but I'm remodeling the community from the inside out, my objective being a major loosening of the rules. ... I just haven't rewritten this page yet ... So, pretend I've rewritten the FAQ already, and that there are no rules. (lim and newkidfan)

And while no such remodeling has—as of 1 June 2011—taken place, it can be seen here that a discussion as to the appropriate length, content, and style of fanfic trailers was going on in the community (and indeed, still is). This chapter will not follow the—now somewhat obsolete— definitions of the artword community as to what qualifies as a fanfic trailer, but rather the more pragmatic and organic definition that a fanfic trailer is—as fanlore.org writes—"A vid designed to advertise or promote a fanfiction story."

The definition this chapter will be using is that format and length are *not* reasons for inclusion or exclusion of particular videos into the following analysis,[3] but rather the pragmatic goal and reason for the creation of a fanfic trailer (to advertise and promote a particular piece of fan writing) is the defining criterion of what constitutes a fanfic trailer. Based on this definition, the chapter will introduce the phenomenon of the fanfic trailer in general, before moving on to analyze four typical examples in detail. These analyses provide a close look at the tools and materials used, and at how they are employed to (re-)create the fictional world of the story that is being advertised in the trailers in question.[4]

In this chapter, I will limit my analysis to fanfic trailers that advertise stories connected to fictional universes of either a television show or a movie.[5] Trailers for stories set in written universes are a far rarer phenomenon and involve a different classification scheme from the one I will be introducing here, since they cannot fall back on motion sequences from the canon source. While the practice of fan vidding— "the act or process of creating a fan-oriented vid or fanvid using live action TV or movie footage set to music (or other audio)" ("Vidding")— has been around since the 1970s (cf. Walker), the practice of creating and distributing fanfic trailers is of far more recent origin, coming to prominence with the rise of video sharing websites like YouTube, vidders.net, and BAM.

At the time of writing this chapter, the use of the YouTube search function provides "about 11,200 results" for videos with "fanfic trailer" and "about 11,700 results" for videos with "fanfiction trailer" in the description (multiple matches possible), which is more than double the number that YouTube featured 12 months earlier (on 11 June 2010 YouTube found "about 5,070 results" when searching for "fanfic trailer"). This shows the phenomenon of fanfic trailers to be a rapidly growing field of fan activity. Of these, however, only about three-quarters actually fall within the scope of this chapter,[6] the rest dividing themselves between "regular" fan videos that are mislabeled as fanfic trailers (per fanlore.org definition), or, more frequently, trailers for fanfictions the author has not yet written, but created to explicate an idea and to gauge possible interest for the fic within the community, with requests for feedback.

In the following pages, I will analyze four different types of fanfic trailers in order to demonstrate the different ways in which they construct the story worlds that can be found in the fanfictions they advertise. I will then link my findings back to the different ways in which fans creatively remake and remodel existing canons and materials in their works in order to stress the transformative aspect this remodeling gives their new creations. More precisely, I will first introduce the practice of fanfic trailer creation. Second, I will show the ways in which fanfic trailers construct the internal, fictional world of the story they are advertising. The creation of these worlds differs from trailer to trailer, largely depending on the nature of the material they reflect. Yet the goals of all these different acts of remodeling commercial productions and creating a world for fanfiction stories are the same. Finally, I will argue that, while the internal means by which fanfic trailers construct the fictional world of the story they advertise might differ from each other on a number of levels, they all follow certain narrative conventions in the end. All fanfic trailers face *the problem of needing to defamiliarize viewers from familiar material*, rather than introducing viewers to unfamiliar material. This is the cardinal difference between the movie trailer and the fanfic trailer.

Categorization

Depending on the nature and setting of the story that is advertised, fanfic trailers tend to draw from a number of different sources and work in a number of different ways. Accordingly, they can be separated into two basic categories, taking into account the ways in which they use their source materials. Subcategories exist for both of these basic categories. The most straightforward of possible cases is the one that will also provide my first example later on: a story set within the universe of one television show, the trailer for which uses only visual materials from said show. However, complexity arrives in the form both of the source material of the story as well as in the materials used for the fanfic trailer created for the story in question, in the following two ways.

First, on the side of the source material, writing both crossover or alternate universe stories is a practice common to fanfiction. A crossover is a story in which two (or more) fictional universes are combined in some way, in its most "common form, characters from Fandom A may meet characters from Fandom B" ("Crossover") within the fictional universe of either fandom. Alternate universe stories change one or more elements from the source work's canon—from small changes (Character A's father did not die at the same time as he did in the universe canon, Character B's secret was found out sooner than it was on the television show itself, and so on) and a look at the consequences this entails— to works where a drastic divergence is taken from the source material, by transplanting the characters into entirely different timelines, settings or lives. Fanfic trailers for crossover and alternate universe stories are frequently found amongst the material available, and executed in a number of different ways, which complicates the question of the source materials, since the new reality needs to be constructed in some way in the trailer, and the divergence from the familiar needs to be made explicit to the viewer. This leads to complexity number two: that is, complexities on the side of the source material used in the story world construction.

Second, to depict the story worlds of a fanfiction story, a fanfic trailer can make use of a variety of different sources in different combinations. This ranges from the "simplest" permutation given above (one universe story world, materials taken only from self-same universe's source material) to trailers making use of materials from other film or television sources and materials filmed by the vidders themselves. Add to this the complexity that not all fanfiction stories are based on fandoms that have filmed materials available, or that crossovers frequently combine fictional universes of which only one provides the vidder with visual material (in the case of a novel universe being crossed with a television show universe), and it is easy to see that both the complexities the vidder has to deal with, and the reinterpretatory effort the viewer is asked to make, can be profound.

The more divergent the fictional story world is from the one depicted in the source material, the more complex and diverse the sources used in the fanfic trailer become. Consequently, examples for trailers advertising stories that take place within the universe of one television show and where the trailers only use materials from that show are easily found. Yet the same does decidedly *not* hold true for alternate universe stories for which the trailers use only materials from one television show. These occur but rarely, because in these cases the divergence between the canon the viewers of the show are familiar with and the newly created universe is far greater. Accordingly, a greater variety of sources must be utilized in more complex ways in order both to establish the new story world and to showcase the divergence from what the reader is already familiar with, or, in other words, to defamiliarize and re-contextualize the familiar material.

The following diagram visualizes some of these differences, and shows on which intersections the trailers I will analyze can be found:

The story the trailer is based on is... / The trailer uses...	...set in the universe of a film/TV show	...a crossover between two universes	...set in an alternate universe
...visual material only from said film or television show	"Trust"	–	–
...visual material from the film and television show as well as from unrelated film(s)/ show(s)	"Tintagel"	"Crown of the Summer Court"	"Drastically Redefining Protocol"

Due to the need for brevity, an analysis of examples from all individual sub-types is beyond the scope this chapter. Instead, I have opted for an initial example of a story set within one fictional universe: the "Trust" trailer, which uses only visual materials from the canon source. After that, I will look at world constructions that take a greater divergence from the main source canon by adding materials from other sources. These are sorted by increasing complexity and variety of sources, to lead the reader on a path from story world construction in close relation to the main canon material to ever greater divergence, and to show the construction complexities and challenges this adds for the creator of the fanfic trailer.

Fanfic trailers exist for stories set within the universes of a great number of television shows and movies.[7] At the time of writing, the two trailers with the highest view counts on YouTube are both for *High School Musical* (Kenny Ortega, 2006) fanfiction stories. The first one has an impressive four million views, although this number is probably inflated by viewers looking for the actual movie trailer, as comments on the page suggest (Peaches 0042). This is followed by a trailer with 1.5 million views (MineyMouse00), with third place held by a trailer for a *Twilight* fanfiction story with just over half a million views (littlestaceySAVAGE). Rather than looking at the most popular trailer on YouTube and introducing different fictional universes in this chapter, I will instead concentrate on four typical trailers that all advertise stories from the same fictional universe. In his analysis of fairy tales, Vladimir Propp states that a selection is representative if results do not change when one leaves out examples or adds more of them (34).

The four trailers to be analyzed advertise stories that are set in the universe of and/or use the characters of the BBC television series *Merlin*, which premiered in 2008 and of which three seasons have been aired so far, with a fourth one scheduled to start in the fall of 2011, and an overall production plan for five seasons. The series is based on the Arthurian legends but differs from them in many ways, especially in its interpretation and use of the characters it takes from the legends. The show itself is set during the reign of King Uther Pendragon—Arthur's father—and tells stories about life in Camelot before Arthur ascends to the throne. In the show, the four main characters—Arthur, Merlin, Morgana, and Gwen (Guinevere)—are approximately the same age, Morgana and Arthur are initially portrayed as not being related to each other (Morgana is set up as King Uther's ward, rather than Arthur's half-sister, and it is only in season three that she is revealed to be Uther's illegitimate daughter),[8] and Gwen is not a princess from another land, but instead the handmaiden of Lady Morgana. Magic is forbidden in Camelot (being suspected of sorcery means immediate execution), and thus Merlin, who serves Prince Arthur as his personal manservant, constantly has to struggle to keep his magic hidden from everyone in the castle[9] while continually saving the Prince from mortal danger in particular and the kingdom in general with said magic. The show itself is episodic in nature, with most of the episodes following a "monster of the week" plot, although some overarching storylines also appear. At the end of season three, despite having saved the kingdom and Arthur from danger numerous times and being afflicted with eyes that glow golden whenever he does magic, Merlin has still not been discovered by anyone in Camelot.

"Trust"

My first example is the trailer for the fanfiction "Trust," written by xxDibDabxx and published on fanfiction.net in March 2009. "Trust" picks up on the major tension that runs throughout the whole show: what will happen when someone (especially Prince Arthur, who is set up as Merlin's slightly obnoxious master yet closest friend) finds out about Merlin's magic? The trailer for the story was also created by xxDibDabxx (who recently renamed her YouTube account into DibDab25) and was uploaded to YouTube on 29 March 2009. It is 1:24 minutes long and has had 1613 views at the time of writing this chapter.

"Trust" uses the instrumental "Requiem for a Tower" from the *The Lord of the Rings: The Two Towers* (Peter Jackson, 2002) trailer as its background music,[10] and aside from two intertitles towards the beginning of the trailer, "Trust" exclusively uses material taken from episodes of the television show *Merlin*, selecting, re-cutting and re-ordering them to form the narrative thrust of the trailer. Reminiscences and flashbacks to moments explicating the relationship between the two main characters of Merlin and Arthur are indicated by the use of greyscale (viewers of the video who are familiar with the *Merlin* canon will immediately recognize these scenes, as they constitute some of the most significant moments in the changing dynamics and growing friendship between Arthur and Merlin in the show), whereas the main storyline (which follows Merlin being thrown into the dungeon and Arthur's decision whether or not to have Merlin sentenced to death) is depicted in color, also using a variety of scenes from the show.

In his book *Verführung zum Film: Der amerikanische Kinotrailer seit 1912*, Vinzenz Hediger asks the following two questions of a movie trailer: "1. How is the plot structured, and how much of the story of the movie does it relate to the viewer? 2. Which stylistic and which linguistic-rhetorical means does the trailer use, to recreate the plot?" (32).[11] In his analysis of movie trailers created since 1912, Hediger comes to the conclusion that there exist two basic forms of the movie trailer plot, which I shall paraphrase here:

1. The mystery plot (*Rätselplot*), which presents a number of questions but does not answer any of them, and which mainly appeared before 1960—"Who was the mysterious woman behind the curtain? Why did she reveal the secret of xy to him?" (39).
2. After 1960 the mystery plot gives way more and more to a plot of suspense (*Spannungsplot*), which recreates the three-act formula of exposition, problem, and confrontation and does no longer ask questions but rather makes the viewer wonder about the solution to the problem, and is mostly concerned with building suspense in the viewer (39).

"Trust" follows the second plot scheme, building up to the final (and in the trailer, unanswered) question of whether or not Merlin will be sentenced to death. To build said suspense, xxDibDabxx makes pointed use of three auditory elements from the television show, while also relying on the heavy drive of the music that was used for the trailer. The three elements are: first, at 0:20, Morgana waking up from a prophetic dream (here foreshadowing Merlin's possible execution); second, at 0:31, Arthur stating, "It's my duty" (here re-cast to mean exposing Merlin as a sorcerer, thus pointing towards the central conflict inherent in the story); and third, at the end of the trailer, at 1:16, overlaying the end titles, the gasps of shock of the crowd at an execution, intentionally leaving the question of whether or not Merlin survives open.

Contrary to the three following trailers that I will analyze, the fictional universe of the story "Trust" is created within the trailer "Trust" solely by use of material found within the primary source. To do this, the primary source material is adapted and edited in a number of ways to fit in with the fictional universe created within the fanfiction story. xxDibDabxx uses what film criticism calls the "grid" pattern (following Christian Metz, Lisa Kernan calls these "bracket syntagma" [Kernan 12]) to structure her trailer, interspersing the linear story-time of the main storyline with diverse scenes to illustrate said main storyline, and to illustrate previous events that tell the viewer about both the origins of the present conflict and the relationship between the two main characters. The three trailers I will analyze on the following pages differ fundamentally from "Trust" in their usage of material from outside the primary source, but remain similar in their structuring and intent.

"Tintagel"

The next trailer—Algine2006's trailer for Seperis' story "Tintagel"—was posted on LiveJournal in three installments in April 2009 (Seperis).[12] Merlin and Arthur travel to Tintagel and learn the truth about Arthur's birth, and about the relationships between Arthur, Igraine, and Nimueh (the latter an "evil" sorceress from season one of the BBC show who, in this story, is court sorceress to King Uther and Queen Igraine). The trailer for "Tintagel" was subsequently posted on YouTube (on 25 August 2010), and has received 1586 views since then. It is 1:47 minutes long. The "Tintagel" trailer differs from "Trust" in a number of ways, the most significant of which is that, while "Tintagel" uses no sound elements from the television show, the auditory component of the trailer is made up by the instrumental "The Crossing" by Two Steps From Hell. It uses visual materials not only from the television show *Merlin*, but also from the 2001 TNT television mini-series *The Mists of Avalon* (Uli Edel), re-casting characters and scenes from that source as the ghosts of Igraine and Nimueh in "Tintagel." "Tintagel" also differs from "Trust" in that it uses captions rather than intertitles to contextualize individual scenes for the viewer, although those are used sparingly. Aside from giving publication and creation details about the story and the vid, the captions run to three words only: namely "Love," "Happiness," and "Hate."

   Contrary to the "Trust" trailer, "Tintagel" is closer to the mystery plot than the suspense plot: no overarching suspense is built within the trailer, there is no clear question asked, and the three captions give only a vague idea as to what the story might be about, rather than revealing a central point of suspense. Here, "Tintagel" is closest to what Hediger calls the lists and formula element of trailer that mostly existed before 1960, and in which information about the story is related in phrases such as "a story of love and passion," or "James Stewart in a riveting adventure" (39).

"The Crown of the Summer Court"

The third example is not for a story that merges two universes and for which the trailer uses visual material from both of these universes, although stories (and trailers) like that do exist. Rather, I skip directly to a more complex example of merged universes portrayed in a trailer, via the example of a story (and thus trailer) called "The Crown of the Summer Court," which was written by Astolat and published in February 2009. The story itself is a crossover between the *Merlin* television series and the *Merry Gentry* novels by Laurell K. Hamilton. However, the crossover part is not widely advertised: the author makes no reference to the novels by Hamilton on her website, but only locates the stories in the *Merlin* fandom.

No knowledge of the *Merry Gentry* books is necessary to understand the story. Bookmarkers of the story on the link-sharing website Delicious.com label it as an "alternate universe" rather than a crossover story. Indeed, some readers reacted with surprise when finding out that the story was a crossover at all. The basic outline of the plot is that the (*Merry Gentry*) elves of the Summer Court need to choose a new king, and Merlin (due to being an illegitimate child of the former elven king in this story) is one of the candidates for the throne.

The trailer for "The Crown of the Summer Court" is 2:41 minutes long and was created by the Russian vidder XnerjaveikaX and uploaded to YouTube on 1 January 2010. So far, it has had 11,345 views. Since "The Crown of the Summer Court" is a story that draws on material from two disparate media sources (a television show and a book series) and merges them into a crossover story, a trailer for that fanfiction story needs to find a creative solution to integrate the *Merry Gentry* world into the *Merlin* universe. The trailer can eventually achieve this by using additional material and creating a universe that reflects the merged story world.

The trailer for "The Crown of the Summer Court" solves the problem of adding the *Merry Gentry* elves into the *Merlin* world by drawing on an entirely different source, one disconnected both from the *Merlin* universe itself, the *Merry Gentry* novels *and* the fanfiction story "The Crown of the Summer Court," for which it is a trailer. Nowhere in the *story* "The Crown of the Summer Court" is there even a hint to the *Lord of the Rings* universe, yet the trailer for "The Crown of the Summer Court" casts the elves of *Lord of the Rings* as the *Merry Gentry* elves.

To make this re-casting of the *Lord of the Rings* elves as the *Merry-Gentry*-elves-as-depicted-in-"The Crown of the Summer Court"-story work, the trailer XnerjaveikaX created for this story re-contextualizes them right from the beginning of the trailer. It does this by telling the viewer how to reinterpret the scene when Arwen imagines standing at Aragorn's grave in *Lord of the Rings: The Two Towers* into an unknown elf

(Arwen) mourning the death of the elven king (in this case, the marble statue of Aragorn). To do this, the trailer makes continuous use of captions throughout its first half, providing the viewer with a preferred reading of the images he or she is being shown and thus grounding the individual sequences within the universe constructed by the storyline of "The Crown of the Summer Court" for the reader, as well as making the characters seemingly interact with each other in dialogue form.

In total, the captions throughout the trailer read as follows (and provide a good summary of the basic plot setup of the story):

0:06 The Great Elf King died

0:20 Now they need to choose a new ONE

0:30 The place, where heir will be named

0:32 is CAMELOT

0:43 the best will compete for the Crown

0:51 But why Camelot was chosen?

0:56 It has to be Camelot because...

1:00 ...one more pretendant is here

1:19 I don't want to be your King (Merlin)

1:22 You can't refuse (Merry Gentry elf)

1:26 ONE has to be chosen to fight with you

1:34 He chooses me (Arthur)

1:39 The Crown of the Summer Court by astolat.

Auditory elements, aside from the music used (Two Steps From Hell's instrumental "Legend"), are taken from both *Merlin* and *Lord of the Rings* but are scarce within the trailer. Only three occurrences can be found: first, at 0:23, "Our time here in ending" from *Lord of the Rings: The Two Towers*, there referring to the elves leaving Middle Earth behind, but here used to introduce the reader to the change that is necessary within the elven court; second, at 0:58, Galadriel speaking elvish (here interpreted by the captions as meaning "It has to be Camelot because...one more pretendant is here"); and third, at 1:09, a close-up of Galadriel's mouth over which sound from the show Merlin was edited, namely the voice of the dragon Kilgarrah (who, in the television show, foretells Merlin his destiny) saying "Merlin."

Though the trailer for "The Crown of the Summer Court" is 2:41 minutes long, the use of both captions and auditory elements ends at 1:39

with the depiction of the title and the author of the story, and the trailer in general consists of two different parts: the first 100 seconds in which the general problem of the plot is set up, and the later 60 seconds, in which clips from the television show as well as a brief scene from *The Da Vinci Code* (Ron Howard, 2006) are used to almost summarize the plot of the story, depicting the different challenges Merlin has to undergo in order to be eligible for the crown, including a hint at the resolution of the story. Thus, the first 100 seconds of "The Crown of the Summer Court" are an example of a plot of suspense, whereas the second half is closer to a mystery plot.

The difference between the prominent use and recontextualization of the *Lord of the Rings* elves and the scene from *The Da Vinci Code* is that the reaction viewers have to *The Da Vinci Code* scene is mostly a query about the source of the material, as it is a fairly non-descriptive scene of someone's backside and a whip, whereas none of the commentators wonder where the elves came from. Instead, references to *Lord of the Rings* are common in the comments. Reactions to the trailer do not problematize the merging of these disparate film materials, however, but rather show that while viewers are aware of the original source context of the sequences chosen, they can easily decipher both the original context as well as the new usage the material has been put to, without anyone actually assuming that the story is a crossover between *Lord of the Rings* and *Merlin* (XnerjaveikaX). Thus, the recontextualization and defamiliarization XnerjaveikaX engaged in apparently worked, setting the familiar images up successfully in a new interpretative context.

"Drastically Redefining Protocol"

The final example, and the one which gives this chapter its title, "Drastically Redefining Protocol," is a fanfiction story that was written by rageprufrock and published on LiveJournal over a duration of two months, starting in December 2008. It can now also be found on the Archive of our Own, where it has been housed since February 2009, and where the whole "Drastically Redefining Protocol" series can be found. This fanfiction story spawned eight sequels, not all of them written by rageprufrock herself, as well as a number of fake newspaper articles and websites, including a six-page fictive *Vanity Fair* article. The trailer for "Drastically Redefining Protocol" was created by zoetrope and added to YouTube on 29 January 2009, where it has had 2240 views. The basic premise of the story is a transfer of some of the characters from the BBC *Merlin* universe into modern times. The story features Uther Pendragon as the reigning monarch, Arthur as the Prince of Wales, and Merlin as a medical student whom Arthur encounters upon escaping a press event in a children's cancer ward in a London hospital, and it is thus a modern alternate universe story.

In order to relocate the *Merlin* characters within this modern world, the trailer uses a number of different devices and draws on a wide range of disparate sources, including, amongst others: (1) filmic material used in the television show *Merlin*; (2) material used in "Making Of" and "Behind the Scenes" *Merlin* specials; (3) "Behind the Scenes" material into which rageprufrock edited a camera zoom to portray the point of view of a reporter; (4) material she filmed herself; (5) material she filmed herself and into which she edited text and/or images to fit the premise of the story; (6) material taken from news programs into which she edited text and/or images to fit the premise of the story; (7) said material, which she saved, ran on a television and then filmed running on television; and (8) material from other movies, such as *Notting Hill* (Roger Michell, 1999).

Auditory material from the show is absent within the trailer. The trailer relies instead—and this is a marked difference to the three trailers previously discussed—not on an instrumental piece of music (usually music taken from a film soundtrack) to underscore it, but on a song with lyrics. Thus part of the total narration and all of the auditory narration within the "Drastically Redefining Protocol" trailer relies on the lyrics used within the song, namely Badly Drawn Boy's "Once around the Block." Significantly, the song is not simply used to play along with the images, but also edited to fit in with the overall trailer for the story, with parts of it deleted and others re-cut to form the auditory narration of the trailer.

Furthermore, the trailer for "Drastically Redefining Protocol" not only uses captions to introduce the familiar characters into their new setting, but also relies on a visualization of newspaper headlines and television news mentioned within the story-universe of "Drastically Redefining Protocol" to introduce the premise of the story and thus to carry part of the narration of the trailer. Indeed, the captions of the "Drastically Redefining Protocol" trailer are playful and generic, stating only: "London 2008—when an immovable object meets an irresistible force, things will have to change," while the more specific introduction of the story world via narration is undertaken by the headlines depicted, as well as by the song lyrics.

The visual world constructed in "Drastically Redefining Protocol" functions on a number of different levels, which sometimes involve as many as four levels of shooting and editing to create the universe depicted in the story by rageprufrock, for example in a scene where a television is seen on which a news item about an event from the story is running. To create this scene, vidder zoetrope followed a number of steps: first, she took the "Breaking News" footage from a television show and edited in the news that is breaking in the "Drastically Redefining Protocol" story world in lieu of the actual news item placed there originally; second, she converted this remodeled news item into a video that could be reproduced on a television screen; third, she filmed a television showing the fictitious news item; and fourth, she used the material thus obtained and edited it into the "Drastically Redefining Protocol" trailer. Following these steps, she aims to create a fictive universe that is two levels deep and puts the whole story *mise en abyme* (and thus one level deeper than encountered in the other trailers analyzed).

Structurally, "Drastically Redefining Protocol" is another example of a plot of suspense. The trailer sets up the place and time (London 2008) and the different characters (Arthur is clearly identifiable as the Prince of Wales), and hints at their roles, but leaves open what it is that will have to change, when said immovable force meets said irresistible object.

Conclusion

In the four examples used here, as in other fanfic trailers, one encounters *practices* and *structures* that are also common for the mainstream movie trailer, but that fulfill a different function from their usage in the general movie trailer, due to the different functions that fanfic trailers and movie trailers need to fulfill. Visual and auditory narrative elements are key to the production of meaning in trailers, and while early movie trailers relied solely on intertitles and captions,[13] these elements are still frequently found in movie trailers today. Both intertitles and captions are widely used throughout fanfic trailers to explicate the premise of the story that is advertised and to explain how it diverges from the canon. Thus, while one might say that intertitles and captions link fanfic trailers to movie trailers in their *optics*, their *function* is a profoundly different one: they are not there to introduce viewers to characters they are seeing for the first time, but rather, as I have shown, to *defamiliarize* the familiar images viewers already know from the source canon, to set up the new angle the fanfic is going to take, and to locate the familiar material in a new context.

The same can be said, of course, of segments taken from the source canon. Whereas the traditional movie trailer usually uses scenes from the forthcoming movie as an advertisement for that same movie, the fanfic trailer remakes and remodels scenes from a variety of different sources to construct a world that is *separate* from the direct universe it relates to in one of two ways: either in its plot alone, if the story advertised uses materials viewers are already familiar with from the canon source (see the "Trust" trailer); or in its plot as well as in the source materials used for the fanfic trailer, if the trailer uses materials from a wider array of sources. Thus, what all fanfic trailers have in common is that they use a variety of tools (intertexts, captions, music, speech clips, scenes from different sources) to create a story world that is set apart from all the sources they use in their construction, and that they need to defamiliarize all these sources in order to re-imagine a separate story world. By using these varieties of tools and by creating these story worlds, fanfic trailers thus consistently re-interpret and re-contextualize the source material from which they draw, infer new preferred readings into already familiar material, and transform the disparate sources they use into a new whole.

Notes

1. See, for example, fanfiction.net, or the archiveofourown.org.
2. Sweded Films are a byproduct of Michel Gondry's 2008 Hollywood movie *Be Kind Rewind*. A Sweded Film is a film that re-shoots a well-known movie with a low budget, usually to parody the original movie. Amongst the rules for them are items like "must be based on an existing movie"; "must be between 2 and 8 minutes in length"; "no special effects"; and so on (Seiwald 121–22).
3. The strict definition followed in the original artword rules would disqualify a substantial amount of material that: (1) is identified as a fanfic trailer by its respective creator; and (2) falls within the fanlore definition of a fanfic trailer.
4. Regarding my sources it has to be said that the majority of both primary as well as secondary sources regarding this field of study are located online, and thus unfortunately of a somewhat transitory nature.
5. In the case of crossover stories (a meshing of two different [fictional] universes) at least one of them will have to be from a movie or a television show.
6. This number was arrived at by checking through the first 200 videos that come up when one searches for "fanfic trailer" on YouTube in June 2010 as well as in May 2011. Should there be a different distribution as to the labeling accuracy prevailing in videos that were not amongst these 200 most recent videos in these two months, my numbers might well be off.

7. As well as for other material outside the purview of this chapter, most significantly, of course, fanfiction based on printed materials.
8. Originally a character mentioned only in passing in Arthurian literature (she is first named [as Morgen] in Geoffrey of Monmouth's *Vita Merlini* around 1150 AD), her role is expanded in the thirteenth-century Vulgate Cycle (a major source of Arthurian Literature, written in French), where she is the youngest daughter of Igraine (Arthur's mother) and her first husband Gorlois (who was killed by Uther Pendragon, Igraine's second husband), instead of Uther's daughter. Thus, while Morgan le Fay and Arthur have been sharing a mother since the Vulgate Cycle, in the BBC series *Merlin* they share a father instead (that is, Uther).
9. Except the physician Gaius. He found out in the pilot episode and promised to help protect Merlin.
10. Which is itself a more dramatic rendition of the "Requiem for a Dream" theme from the movie of the same name.
11. Translation by the author. All other quotations from *Verführung zum Film: Der amerikanische Kinotrailer seit 1912* will be translations from the original German (by the author of this chapter). The original quotation reads: "1. Wie ist der Plot strukturiert, und was und wieviel von der Story des zugehörigen Films teilt er mit? 2. Welche stilistischen und sprachlich-rhetorischen Mittel verwendet der Trailer, um den Plot umzusetzen?" (32).
12. Due to the transitory nature of some of my sources, in addition to giving the details of all the materials in the list of References I have set up a page with resources and links, where I will attempt to track all of my online sources, should their location change, or to substitute them with close alternatives should they be deleted forever. This website can be found at www.sibyllemachat.de.
13. Beginning in the 1930s intertitles and captions started to be used in conjunction with voice-over narration. Voice-over narration is not something that I have yet encountered in a fanfic trailer (which is not to say that none that use it exist, but certainly that, if they do, they are scarce).

Works consulted

Algine2006. "Merlin: 'Tintagel,' Arthur/Merlin, Igraine/Nimueh, PG." *Online Posting.* YouTube, 25 August 2010. Retrieved on 10 June 2011. http://www.youtube.com/watch?v=onSfCOr_lO8.

Astolat. "Merlin." *Fanfic by Astolat.* Intimations.org, n.d. Retrieved on 10 June 2011. www.intimations.org/fanfic/#Merlin.

———. "The Crown of the Summer Court." *Online Posting.* Archive of Our Own, 16 February 2009. Retrieved on 10 June 2011. http://archiveofourown.org/works/40561.

"Crossover." *fanlore.org.* Fanlore, 30 September 2010. Retrieved on 31 October 2011. http://fanlore.org/wiki/Crossover.

The Da Vinci Code. Dir. Ron Howard. Perf. Tom Hanks, Audrey Tautou, and Ian McKellen. Columbia Pictures, 2006.

DibDab25. "Trust." *Online Posting.* YouTube, 29 March 2009. Retrieved on 10 June 2011. www.youtube.com/watch?v=_qosDLnYZ5Q.

"Fic Trailer." *fanlore.org*. Fanlore, 23 October 2010. Retrieved on 10 June 2011. http://fanlore.org/wiki/Fic_Trailer.

Hediger, Vinzenz. *Verführung zum Film: Der amerikanische Kinotrailer seit 1912*. Marburg: Schüren, 2001. Print.

High School Musical. Dir. Kenny Ortega. Perf. Zac Efron, Vannessa Anne Hudgens, and Ashley Tiesdale. Walt Disney Company, 2006.

Kernan, Lisa. *Coming Attractions: Reading American Movie Trailers*. Austin, TX: University of Texas Press, 2004. Print.

lim and newkidfan. "Guidelines and Definitions: Discussion." *Online Posting*. LiveJournal, 1 June 2008. Retrieved on 10 June 2011. http://artword.livejournal.com/471.html?thread=316887#t316887.

littlestaceySAVAGE. "Renesmee and Jacob Movie Trailer." *Online Posting*. YouTube, 04 April 2009. Retrieved on 10 June 2011. www.youtube.com/watch?v=v9jbPErT6-8.

The Lord of the Rings: The Two Towers. Dir. Peter Jackson. Perf. Elijah Wood, et al. New Line Cinema, 2002.

Merlin. Prod. Julie Gardner and Bethan Jones. Perf. Colin Morgan, Bradley James, and Angel Coulby. Shine Televisions. BBC, 20 September 2008–present.

MineyMouse00. "'Somewhere A Clock Is Ticking' Video (fanfic)." *Online Posting*. YouTube, 11 May 2008. Retrieved on 10 June 2011. http://youtu.be/6mCVQMg7OtU.

The Mists of Avalon. Dir. Uli Edel. Prod. Gideon Amir and Bernd Eichinger. Perf. Anjelica Huston, Julianna Margulies, and Joan Allen. TNT et al. TNT, 2001.

newkidfan. "Artword." *Online Posting*. LiveJournal, 5 January 2006. Retrieved on 10 June 2011. http://artword.livejournal.com/profile.

——. "Guidelines and Definitions." *Online Posting*. LiveJournal, 6 January 2006. Retrieved on 10 June 2011. http://artword.livejournal.com/471.html.

Notting Hill. Dir. Roger Michell. Perf. Hugh Grant and Julia Roberts. Working Title Films, 1999.

Peaches 0042. "High School Musical 2 Trailer." *Online Posting*. YouTube, 18 January 2007. Retrieved on 10 June 2011. http://youtu.be/8-tOHTDNDB0.

Propp, Vladimir. *Die historischen Wurzeln des Zaubermärchens*. 1928. München: Hanser, 1987. Print.

rageprufrock. "Drastically Redefining Protocol." *Online Posting*. Archive of Our Own, 22 February 2009. Retrieved on 10 June 2011. http://archiveofourown.org/works/3189.

Seiwald, Valentin. "Sweded Films." *Prosumenten-Kulturen*. Ed. Sebastian Abresch, Benjamin Beil, and Anja Griesbach. Massenmedien und Kommunikation 172/173. Siegen: University of Siegen, 2009. 119–32. Print.

Seperis. "Merlinfic: Tintagel, 1/3." *Online Posting*. LiveJournal, 6 April 2009. Retrieved on 10 June 2011. http://seperis.livejournal.com/722590.html.

shadowcat102. "When You Are King." *Online Posting*. YouTube, 9 October 2009. Retrieved on 10 June 2011. http://youtu.be/GNCT76HOtVQ.

"Vidding." *fanlore.org*. Fanlore, 26 June 2011. Retrieved on 27 June 2011. http://fanlore.org/wiki/Vidding.

Walker, Jesse. "Remixing Television: Francesca Coppa on the Vidding Underground." *Reason.com* (August/September 2008): n. pag. Retrieved on 10 June 2011. http://reason.com/archives/2008/07/18/remixing-television.

XnerjaveikaX. "Merlin/Arthur: The Crown of the Summer Court." *Online Posting*. YouTube, 1 January 2010. Retrieved 10 June 2011. www.youtube.com/watch?v=bfWE4XzL1d8.

xxDibDabxx. "Trust." *Online Posting*. Fanfiction.net, 2 March 2009. Retrieved on 10 June 2011. www.fanfiction.net/s/4897627/1/Trust.

Zoetrope. "Trailer for Drastically Redefining Protocol." *Online Posting*. YouTube, 29 January 2009. Retrieved on 10 June 2011. www.youtube.com/watch?v=es9EEaB0h4s.

11
You'll Never See This on the Silver Screen: The Film Trailer as a Template for the Appropriation and Transformation of Hollywood Movies

Lili Hartwig

In September 2005, the New-York based editing assistant Robert Ryang had recently participated in an editing competition run by the Association of Independent Creative Editors. The annual Trailer Park Competition, first held in 2001, had the objective to re-edit a well-known movie into a trailer, advertising the same film, but with a change in genre. Ryang chose to transform Stanley Kubrick's horror classic *The Shining* (1980) into the family-friendly comedy "Shining" and won the first prize, a new Avid Editing Suite and a little trophy, shaped like a travel trailer.

Wanting to show his film to friends, Ryang uploaded a copy on to the webserver of the post-production company he was working for. He sent out the link to the hidden website to two friends, one of whom posted it on his personal blog. Less than ten days later, "Shining" had made internet history by becoming one of the first so-called viral videos. What had happened? Originating from that little-read blog, the link rapidly spread throughout the internet. For a few days it was the most shared link in the blogsphere. Ryang's company server counted more than 12,000 hits a day. The *New York Times* published an article about the video. Copies of the film started to pop up on several online platforms, including the still infant YouTube. Ryang was contacted by major Hollywood studios. "Shining" had hit the nerve of popular internet culture. Matt, the author of the now inactive blog *The Tattered*

Illustration 11.1   The trailer "Shining" re-edits scenes from Stanley Kubrick's horror classic *The Shining* (1980) to advertise a family friendly comedy

Coat, who had followed the film's evolution online, comments: "What's amazing to me, at least, is how quickly this moved—it all happened in a matter of hours after Waxy [a popular blog] picked up on it. That's a testament to both the quality of Robert's trailer and the speed with which information moves today."

It is not just the initial success of "Shining" and its clever re-use of the found material that is worth examining, but also the resulting discussions and debates constituting the video's larger discourse. The video's popularity signals a change in the media landscape. This transition, generally referred to as convergence, is marked by grassroots media production and distribution, undermining the hierarchical structures of the traditional media industry and challenging notions of copyright and intellectual property. Similarly, "Shining" has spawned discussions about film trailers themselves and as part of Hollywood marketing strategies, as well as a reevaluation of the generic categorization of *The Shining* and the state of modern horror film.

But "Shining" also helped to shape a new genre of online video, serving as a prototype for thousands of other trailer parodies that emerged in the wake of the film's success, some of them reaching similar levels of popularity. While many of these films can be found with differing labels such as recut, remix, mash-up, spoof or mock trailer, I choose to refer to them as trailer parodies. Following Linda Hutcheon's definition of parody as "repetition with a difference" (32), these trailer parodies feed off the intertextual relations of the original source material and its repetition by recombining familiar elements with a critical and ironic distance: for example, anyone unfamiliar with *The Shining* will fail to enjoy the generic twist of "Shining." In a similar vein, by promoting a film which does not exist (at least not like this), trailer parodies draw attention to the strategies and formal conventions of film trailers themselves, thereby becoming "one of the most popular forms of fan subversion in the age of digital video" (Hilderbrand 52).

Combining these different aspects and layers of trailer parodies allows the hypothesis that videos of this genre serve as an audiovisual expression of current online film and video culture. This argument applies on two different levels. By recombining popular source materials, trailer parodies use their critical distance and intertextual potential to comment on and critique single films, the film industry, and its (generic) conventions, thereby acting as a manifestation of that discourse. At the same time, they offer themselves as vehicles for further discussion on the subject, as each video is potentially framed by several layers of contextualizing texts, allowing further comments, hyperlinking, and responding. While the first quality is mainly text-based, the latter is inscribed in the video's basic characteristic as an online video.

Online video genres

To analyze the genre of trailer parodies and its transformational aesthetics demands a broad approach to the concept of genre. Applying Jason Mittell's understanding of genre as a cultural category, the genre-defining elements cannot simply be reduced to textual components, but "exist only through the creation, circulation, and consumption of texts within cultural contexts" (11). It is therefore necessary to examine the inherent qualities of online video genres to understand how these videos are produced, distributed, and consumed, and how these factors shape the formal conventions and expressive potential of these trailer parodies. Online videos are still a very young form of media, but their emergence is arguably one of the most important and extensive developments in recent media evolution. The sheer volume of available videos exceeds that of all other types of audiovisual media: at the time of writing this chapter, more than 48 hours of material is being uploaded each minute to YouTube alone. The corresponding complexity of video material makes YouTube, and online video platforms in general, "a particularly unstable object of study, marked by dynamic change (both in terms of videos and organization), a diversity of content...and a similar quotidian frequency, or 'everydayness'" (Burgess and Green 6). In other words, online videos have become an integral component of our daily media consumption.

A major characteristic of online videos is their accessibility. This possibility to watch a streamed video wherever and whenever one likes has accelerated and changed media consumption and "has contributed to the culture of the clip...it fosters a new temporality of immediate gratification for the audiences" (Hilderbrand 49). But it would be wrong to presume that online videos are simple snacks of popular culture being consumed along the way. While this may be true in some cases, especially considering the brevity of popular videos, other videos offer far deeper levels of textual layering and cultural references.

It is important to note that not all online videos are consumed directly on the video platform's site, but can be embedded in blogs, other websites, and within social networks. The possible access points of an online video are as diverse as the motives behind watching, producing, and uploading them. As Henry Jenkins describes, not all these (cultural) practices originated with YouTube. Rather, YouTube and its likes serve as a vehicle for several pre-existing "communities of practice that supported the production of DIY media, already evolved video genres and built social networks through which such videos could flow" ("Before YouTube" 110). Within these dynamic communities, the videos are distributed and spread according to the personal and social value for the individual and/or the group by contributing and expressing elements of the corresponding self-perception and interests (Jenkins et al. 43). These spreadable videos are not necessarily produced by the community itself, but they offer themselves as facilitators for communal meaning production independent of origin, age or formal style, as those preferences vary within each given interest-based community.

The range of online video producers is heterogeneous. Platforms like YouTube operate simultaneously as a top-down distribution site for traditionally produced media, and as a publication and sharing platform for the bottom-up production processes of user-generated content and vernacular creativity. At the same time, new internet-based business models have evolved that commercially produce and distribute video content. Similarly, many former non-media-producing institutions began to use video as a communication means. To complicate things further, it is necessary to differentiate between the filmmaker and the uploader, as they might not be the same. Not only have the traditional hierarchal barriers between the media industry and the audience blurred, but the whole system of production, distribution, and consumption structures is being altered and reorganized, dynamically changing with every technological innovation, new software application or court ruling. As Jenkins puts it: "Rather than talking about media producers and consumers as occupying separate roles, we might now see them as participants who interact with one another according to a new set of rules that none of us fully understands" (*Convergence* 3). Neither do these participants hold an equal amount of influence or capabilities, nor do they all or always fulfill the same role within the process. Rather the spectrum of participation is dynamically evolving, heterarchial, and granular. While some participants produce media content, others publish them on their websites, work in advisory or curational positions, moderate discussions, and write wikis or program new software.

These decentralized, collaborative and often non-commercial production processes are part of what Axel Bruns calls "produsage," a concept that rethinks the terms "production" and "product" within network culture. One key aspect in his understanding of produsage is its continuing process and ongoing evolution, which results in (temporary) palimpsestic artifacts that are created through the artistic process, rather than delivered as finished products (231). This dynamic textual openness does not imply that the single works themselves are neither closed nor genuine. It rather implies that these audiovisual artifacts can serve as textual manifestations of and within their discursive creative and critical flow.

While flowing through the different interest-based communities, online videos are subject to complex and diverse processes of value creation, with each instance of circulation adding another layer of social and cultural commentary, shaping the way the text is perceived and understood. But the textual artifact itself also evolves as each text can potentially be remixed, sampled, commented on, remade, replied to, parodied, criticized, relived or turned into an auto-tune song. In all cases a fragment of the text and its potential meanings are reused within another formal framework, another context, referencing their intertextual predecessor with varying degrees.

Following Yochai Benkler's thoughts on the network information economy, the "flexibility with which cultural artifacts—meaning-carrying objects—can be rendered, preserved, and surrounded by different context and discussion makes it easy for anyone, anywhere, to make a self-conscious statement about culture" (293–94). In order to analyze an online video genre, it is therefore necessary not only to examine the text itself, but to consider the surrounding discourse of the videos and the processes of value creation as well. The questions of who produces and distributes them, where these videos can be found, and how they are consumed, are as important as understanding what they are referencing and what kind of comments, critiques, replies, and remixes they encourage.

The genre of trailer parodies

"Shining" itself was not the first trailer parody, but it has played a pivotal role in shaping and establishing the genre. The format of trailers and similar promotional texts had been appropriated in comedy videos, contest contributions, and fan videos in order to revisit and rework popular film and television texts, but none of the videos had enjoyed such a widespread popularity. In the wake of the success of "Shining," many of these videos began to surface for a broader audience, and Ryang's work inspired other filmmakers to use the newly available digital technology and video platforms to produce and distribute new works. The peak of the genre's popularity followed closely after the release of "Shining" in 2006, but it is still a stable genre, and new works are emerging constantly with some occasional mainstream (or so-called) viral hits.

Generally these videos are published on YouTube, occasionally on Vimeo, although the video is most likely to be accessed as spreadable content embedded in a blog, a mircoblog, or a journal entry. The communal interests are Hollywood movies, sometimes based within a broader focus on popular culture, in other cases with a distinct specialization in film. These film blogs are run by and cater for "film geeks." Chuck Tryon describes film geeks as "increasingly engaged with a wider film culture," implying an increased technical understanding and a detailed knowledge about films and a willingness to devise and apply personal and critical readings of the text, a development which has be fuelled by digital technologies and the rise of the DVD (36). It is the same context that informs the trailer parodies: "fake trailers, like the film blogs that link to and often discuss them, represent an emerging networked film culture in which film buffs produce, distribute, and discuss videos that rework and comment on Hollywood films" (172).

Unlike the still prevailing myth about user-generated content, most of the producers of (popular) trailer parodies, the film buffs, can hardly be described as amateurs. A lot of them, like Ryang, are professionals, or aspiring to be, who produce the videos for competitions, as side projects, or for their portfolio, often hoping for some internet fame to further their careers. Some of these creators have made a name for themselves by editing trailer parodies that will easily spread through the internet once released. A good example is Ivan Guerrero—aka whoiseyevan—on YouTube, who has reached a certain auteur status by producing "premakes," a self-coined term describing parodies that re-imagine a popular movie as being made several decades earlier. His videos, for example "Ghost Busters (1954)," reconstruct plot elements, iconic images, and characters from the title-giving movie by using source material and stylistic trailer conventions from a specific historic era, thereby creating a possibility of how a movie like *Ghostbusters* (Ivan Reitman, 1984) might have looked had it been produced in 1954. The premakes have an average of about half a million views, and offer a frame by frame breakdown for each film, commenting on his editorial choices within the parody. Other trailer parodies are made by film and media students as an experimental part of their curriculum, in the case of Robert McLoughlin's "Mrs Doubtfire—Recut" even linking to a questionnaire about genre indicators used in the parody for a study. But a growing number of videos have been produced or commissioned by internet-based companies and bloggers to engage people with content on their website.

These websites and film blogs offer places for discussion about the work, sometimes by locating a trailer parody within a broader critical discourse that already exists within the community. In this aspect, blogs act as a filter mechanism for the communal cultural knowledge and serve an interpretive community of film geeks. The comment section of each entry allows for a communal exchange and evaluation of the video and in some cases hypertextually connecting it with previous entries and discussions, not unlike the same feature on YouTube. But while the trailer parodies embedded in blogs are usually paratextually framed as a parody, YouTube's comment section shows that not every trailer parody is immediately recognized as such. "Shining," especially, offers a good example for such confusion, as the video is the first entry when searching "Shining + Trailer," but neither the title nor the film information offers any indication for it being a parody. As a result the comments vary from description of how and when the viewer understood it was a parody, to questions about its legitimacy as the official theatrical trailer, satirical recommendations of *The Shining* as a family movie, instances of trolling, and people insulting each other for not getting the humor of the video.

It is in fact the video's title that acts as the most important paratextual indicator for its transformative content. Usually "Recut" or "Remix" is added to the title of the original movie, sometimes including the generic twist of the parody, as in "Sleepless in Seattle: Recut as a horror movie" (Lyall-Wilson), or integrating the stylistic objectives of the transformation, as in "If David Lynch directed Dirty Dancing. ... " (Flick). Such a recontextualization can also be implied through an intertextual reference as in "10 Things I Hate About Commandments" (Dow)—*Ten Commandments* (Cecil B. DeMille, 1956) recut as a high school comedy—which mashes the original title with the popular teenager movie *10 Things I Hate About You* (Gil Junger, 1999), thereby using the comedy's generic delimitation to frame the parody. In a similar vein, mash-up trailer parodies often fuse the remixed movie titles using a portmanteau style like "Brokeback to the Future," (Chocolate Cake City) mashing *Brokeback Mountain* (Ang Lee, 2005) and the *Back to the Future* trilogy (Robert Zemeckis, 1985/1989/1990).

While the title is important for framing the videos and to make them easily recognizable, another major question is: what makes these parodies popular and allows them to spread throughout the internet? As the efficiency of a parody is based on the recognizability of the referenced material, trailer parodies ideally appropriate movies that carry a certain cultural value within the field of popular culture and especially for the interpretive community they are intended for. There are three major factors that facilitate such a condition: cult, nostalgia, and timeliness.

Familiarity with intertextual references from the latter category are fostered by the increased advertising material that is published by film studios in the wake of a major release in hope of creating a buzz surrounding the film to ensure its box office success. Trailer parodies using recent material, such as promotional clips or the theatrical trailers, become part of the "cultures of anticipation" that shape Hollywood's global popularity and economic success (Miller et al. 116). This connection to an already trending discussion increases the chances of a parody to be discovered and spread, but it also bears the danger to become obsolete once the buzz about the upcoming release has died down.

Trailer parodies with source material from cult media tend to be more timeless, as they refer to texts that have sustained a cultural value regardless of their age. The meaning and value of these texts are constantly updated and reconfirmed through different kinds of fan activities, such as discussions, fan fiction or transformative videos. Cult texts used within the genre of trailer parodies include science fiction franchises and comic adaptations, but also the works of certain directors, such as Quentin Tarantino or David Lynch, who enjoy a cult status within the community of film fans. Such trailer parodies move within the framework of interest-based communities, where their references are understood and valued. Similarly, trailer parodies that evoke the notion of nostalgia depend on a shared media socialization. In the case of the trailer parody genre, a substantial number of films reference popular movies from the 1980s and 1990s, or classical children's stories like *Mary Poppins* (Robert Stevenson, 1964).

By choosing particular sources to parody, these transformative trailers not only respond to an existing system of value attribution within popular culture, but they also help to reevaluate and shape it further. Their complex participation "in the intertextual sphere of relations defining the original text, [helps] the original to gain or maintain a toehold in mass cultural canons" (Klinger 233). As new meaning is added and spread, the original's value within popular culture is reinforced and updated, at the same time offering new access points for consumption. While the intentions of and strategies used in the parodies may vary, "as an ensemble they signal what is worthy of extended commentary" (233).

To facilitate such an extended commentary, texts need to allow alternative reading strategies, encourage intertextual connections, and offer narrative gaps for the audience to fill. This polysemic openness is described by John Fiske in the concept of the "producerly text." A producerly text "draws attention to its own textuality ... and it replaces the pleasures of identification and familiarity with more cognitive pleasures of participation and production" (95), a form of engagement that is clearly visible in the genre of trailer parodies.

Trailer parodies as a remix

Trailer parodies thrive on the constant interplay between the source text and its formal presentation in the new work. Through the recombination, the remixing of the material, elements from the source are transformed through an additional layer of meaning. Remixing has become a widely spread cultural practice and at the same time one of the central buzz words within the discourse of the emerging networked culture. Lawrence Lessig, probably the most outspoken supporter of remix culture, argues "that there's nothing essentially new in remix"; only the technology used in the production and distribution has changed, while the practice itself can be dated back to folk culture (28).

An understanding of remix as the systematic reworking of a source sees the video remix as an artistic artifact that recombines modular elements from pre-existing works according to an overlaying structure. This structure can take several forms: some remixes appropriate a sound bite; others construct their own narrative or use a more formal stylistic approach of rearranging their material. The main objective in any case is to create coherence, either in style or narration, to make the remix believable. But the formal structure of the remix is interdependent with the inherent textual meanings of the used material. While not all the possible connotations of the material need to be alluded to within a specific remix, the viewer has to be able to recognize the recombinatory aesthetic and to connect the different intertextual layers to read the remix. Edwards and Tryon refer to this emerging form of media literacy as "critical digital intertextuality":

> Rather than emphasizing ways of reading *against* the media and ana-lyzing the influences of media organizations, this form of media lit-eracy is reading through the media. Video mashup creators rely on the media savvy of a digitally and culturally literate audience. They use critical digital intertextuality to attract an audience because the mashing up of media texts is simultaneously an act of critical read-ing. (n. pag.)

The growing popularity of remix videos is a clear indication that this media literacy is constantly spreading and becoming more mainstream. This development has to be located within the larger context of the con-verging media landscape. This participatory media audience has been enabled by digitalization and the proliferation of broadband internet, but it was also encouraged by the media industry itself, which highly promoted and advertised technology and software to produce media content and share it. At the same time, texts have become more complex and producerly to engage the audience and have helped to establish a different readership more versed with intertextuality, self-referentiality, and storytelling. Similarly, the internet has pushed subcultural prac-tices of media engagement, namely fandom, to the surface, making fannish practices of cultural production and its aesthetics more visible and accessible to the public. This has led to a "serialization of the fan audience itself" (Hills 177), as fan activities become consumable goods within the media landscape and therefore help to spread fannish read-ing strategies and forms of cultural production.

The aesthetics of fan video production closely resemble those of the remix culture as they also "[center] on the selection, inflection, jux-taposition, and recirculation of ready-made images and discourses" (Jenkins, *Textual Poachers* 223–24). In both cases, the artistic value lies in the skilled recombination of material, but it is necessary to point out that most of the trailer parodies discussed here—although produced by film fans—differ from fan videos produced within a specific fandom. While the interest of fans, as Jenkins points out, is not strictly limited to one media product, as they "take pleasure in making intertextual connections across a broad range of media texts" (*Textual Poachers* 36), there is indeed a strong emphasis on a small selection of texts within each fan's work. Fannish engagement with a text tends to drill down, prolonging the immersion, resulting in very specific connotations of the material, which are often difficult to decode for outsiders. Fan videos produced within a specific fandom therefore rarely flow outside this community or enter the broader discourse surrounding Hollywood movies. Still, there are numerous examples of trailer parodies that originate in fandoms, as movie trailers prove to be an efficient template for appropriating and recontextualizing media texts.

The movie trailer as a template

Traditionally film trailers serve as advertisements for upcoming movie releases. By now, however, there are trailers for virtually any kind of media from television shows to computer games. Movie trailers are designed to give the audience an idea of the film in question with the aim to persuade people to go and see it in the cinema. As watching a movie is a very subjective experience, the enjoyment of the purchased product, in this case represented by the entry ticket, cannot be guaranteed. Therefore, trailers have to create an accurate impression of what is to be expected in the theater to avoid consumer disappointment and encourage word-of-mouth advertising. While most trailers use material from the film they are advertising, the formal structure to present it has changed during the years and is constantly adjusted to market conditions.

In classical Hollywood, trailers could best be described as depicting the film's discourse in an almost journalistic fashion. Classical trailers often use a voice-over narration and title cards, highlighting the production values and revealing almost no plot information. These trailers were designed to inform a regular cinema audience about upcoming releases, with no need to persuade them to visit the theater in the first place because moviegoing was a regular activity for most of the audience. But as the film industry faced the growing media competition of television and home entertainment, trailers needed to address a much more specific audience within the fragmented market space. As a consequence, they started to simulate the movie they were advertising in the hope of reaching the intended target audience. A new dominant trailer structure developed, which Vinzenz Hediger calls the "protagonist centered two-thirds trailer" (39). This three-act trailer introduces the movie's protagonist, lays out about two-thirds of its plot, and finishes with a cliffhanger to create tension and excitement about the story's ending. The extensive reveal of the film's narration posed a challenge regarding the brevity of a movie trailer and demanded a special editing technique to compress the relevant information. Most importantly, the sound track and the image have become detached and are treated as equally significant compository elements within the polyphonic montage. The structure of these trailers resembles a grid or a fork, with one narrative arc, mostly constructed from sound bites, thereby moving the narration to audio track, and several pockets or compartments with additional material. This additional imagery can either be analytical, consequential or illustrative of the events referred to in the main narration. Traditional editing techniques such as continuity editing and spatial convention are ignored in favor of a more compository style and associative openness. As a consequence, trailers are much faster paced and offer far more stimulus than the actual feature film. They are affectively closed, traditionally ending with the film's title and release date, but they remain cognitively open, leaving the viewer with unanswered questions and cognitive gaps in order to motivate a cinema visit.

As a trailer is usually the first introduction of the film text to its audience it also acts as an entryway paratext, which, as Jonathan Gray puts it, "sets up, begins, and frames many of the interactions we have with texts" (48). In this function, the trailer is largely responsible for the viewer's expectation of the feature and the kind of emotional and cognitive experience it will offer. One of the most important factors that will shape such an expectation is genre. Trailers rarely state their genre explicitly, but they use different kinds of genre indicators and intertextual references to allude to their generic classification. Musical cues are the most prominent indicator, as well as the film's general visual style, the trailer's rhetoric, the movie title, and stereotypical narrative structures, which can trigger generic assumptions. Equally, some actors and directors can clearly be associated with certain genres.

The viewer uses this intertextual knowledge and previous movie experience to fill the cognitive gaps and to construct an idea of the film advertised in the trailer. This reading strategy of using limited information to delineate a hypothesis about the whole film has become widely spread. Movie trailer consumption is an integral part of networked film culture, as the industry relies on these communities to create the aforementioned buzz, not only by supplying them with strategically released trailers, but by actually gearing the trailer design toward "the passionate end of the fan spectrum" (Johnston 152). The published trailers are then dissected and analyzed by the networked communities. Trailer literacy is prevalent within internet-based film culture, therefore making the trailer an easily recognizable form of media entertainment and a versatile structuring template for transformative works.

Transformational aesthetics of trailer parodies

By appropriating the trailer format as the structuring layer of their remix without actually advertising a movie, trailer parodies draw attention to its formal and stylistic conventions. But by adapting this template they also allow a new and critical reading of the appropriated material itself. Unlike other movie remixes, the compressed montage and narrative structure of the trailer calls for a mental recontextualization of a whole movie.

With "Shining," the humor arises not only by a familiar scene placed within a new context, but by imagining the whole movie *The Shining* under a new premise which clearly deviates from the original. This kind of transformational aesthetics can therefore be considered a genre parody, as it is the genre which is being transformed. This technique is quite common within the genre of trailer parodies, with the alluded genre being emotionally complementary to the original. In "Shining" the family terror and horror setting is changed into a family-friendly feel-good comedy. This transformation is achieved in most parts by trailer-specific genre indicators, such as the use of Peter Gabriel's "Solsbury Hill," a song well used in comedy trailers. But also the parody's rhetoric, the introduction of the main characters through the comedic invitation "Meet...," shifts its generic relocalization. "Sleepless in Seattle: Recut as a horror movie" does exactly the opposite, as the material used in the trailer is colored bluish and with this adds a cold and uncomfortable feeling, pairing it with dramatic music, choirs, and thundering sounds, evoking an audiovisual style associated with a thriller or horror film.

Interestingly, the narration in both examples remains almost unchanged. It is true that Jack is a struggling writer and Danny is a lonely child in a big empty house, but while things in *The Shining* take a turn for the worse, "Shining" offers a glimpse of hope, which is solely created from allusion drawn from the almost empty phrase "Sometimes, what we need the most, is just around the corner" and following musical choices, but never explicitly contradicting the original story. This form of believability also stays intact in "Sleepless in Seattle," where the original premise, a woman hears a man's voice on the radio and believes they are meant to be together, is reinterpreted by implying not the romantic notion of fate, but that of obsession and delusion, a plausible and valid argument. Similarly the basic storyline of *Mrs Doubtfire* (Chris Columbus, 1993) remains untouched in "Mrs Doubtfire—Recut": a man dresses up as a woman to work as a housekeeper for a family. The only information withheld in the parody is the fact that the man is the father who wants to spend time with his children, therefore making his actions uncanny and psychotic, enhancing the parody's generic recontextualization as a thriller or horror movie. These examples show that a successful trailer parody always depends on borrowing enough elements from the original so that the reinterpration remains plausible and remotely possible.

With mash-ups, the fusion of two or more distinct films, the transformational process operates in a similar way. Here the interplay between the referenced works is foregrounded and thrives on the works' harmonies and dissonances. In "Brokeback to the Future," *Brokeback Mountain* serves as a kind of directional lens to revisit *Back to the Future*, as the parody imitates the style of the former's trailer, cueing its iconic music and using similar title cards, while recombining material from the latter. Although there might exist theories that argue to differ, the relationship between Marty McFly and Doc Brown is generally seen as an intense but platonic friendship, bearing hardly any resemblance to the storyline of *Brokeback Mountain*. But with the opening shots of the trailer, showing images of Marty and Doc dressed as cowboys from the third installment of the trilogy within the stylistic framework of *Brokeback Mountain*, their relationship is almost automatically reinterpreted as a love story and all the following scenes are reevaluated according to this frame of reference.

Sometimes this examination of harmonies and dissonances can lead to a more critical evaluation, as is the case with Randy Szuch's "Avatar/Pocahontas Mashup." The video uses the soundtrack of the theatrical trailer for *Avatar* (James Cameron, 2009) and combines it with imagery from the Disney movie *Pocahontas* (Mike Gabriel and Eric Goldberg, 1995) in a synchronized mash-up, a very popular sub-genre of the trailer parody. This almost seamless comparison reveals that the plot of both films is based in the same American myth, and that despite all its technical innovations, *Avatar* relies on a very well-known legend and can best be understood as an updated retelling of the story.

To conclude, trailer parodies as an online video genre reflect cultural changes within the media landscape. They respond to the discourse surrounding film culture, relying on a new kind of media literacy to be understood, and fuel a dynamic exchange about popular culture. Trailer parodies use the techniques of the remix and act as audiovisual manifestations of cultural discourses. The movie trailers are an almost perfect template for such visual experiments because their formal structure relies on gaps and associations to be filled with new meaning, and which allow creative and personal interpretations of used material. This structure then allows a reevaluation of found material through appropriation by subverting and transforming it.

Works consulted

Benkler, Yochai. *The Wealth of Networks: How Social Production Transforms Markets and Freedom.* New Haven, CT: Yale University Press, 2006. Print.

Bruns, Axel. *Blogs, Wikipedia, Second Life, and Beyond: From Production to Produsage.* New York: Peter Lang, 2008. Print.

Burgess, Jean, and Joshua Green. *YouTube: Online Video and Participatory Culture.* Cambridge: Polity Press, 2009. Print.

Chocolate Cake City. "Brokeback to the Future." *Online Posting.* YouTube, 1 February 2006. Retrieved on 19 October 2011. www.youtube.com/watch?v=8uwuLxrv8jY.

Dow, Mike. "10 Things I Hate about Commandments." *Online Posting.* YouTube, 14 May 2006. Retrieved on 19 October 2011. www.youtube.com/watch?v=u1kqqMXWEFs.

Edwards, Richard, and Chuck Tyron. "Political Video Mashups as Allegories of Citizen Empowerment." *First Monday* 14.10 (2009): n. pag. Retrieved on 19 October 2011. http://firstmonday.org/htbin/cgiwrap/bin/ojs/index.php/fm/article/view/2617/2305

Fiske, John. *Television Culture.* London: Routledge, 1987. Print.

Flick, Greg. "If David Lynch Directed Dirty Dancing...." *Online Posting.* YouTube, 22 September 2008. Retrieved on 19 October 2011. www.youtube.com/watch?v=wjvuCOlkO4E.

Gray, Jonathan. *Show Sold Separately: Promos, Spoilers, and other Media Paratexts.* New York: New York University Press, 2010. Print.

Guerrero, Ivan. "'Premakes' Ghost Busters (1954)." *Online Posting.* YouTube, 19 July 2009. Retrieved on 19 October 2011. www.youtube.com/watch?v=kAboGO9MDsQ.

Hediger, Vinzenz. *Verführung zum Film: Der amerikanische Kinotrailer seit 1912.* Marburg: Schüren, 2001. Print.

Hilderbrand, Lucas. "YouTube: Where Cultural Memory and Copyright Converge." *Film Quarterly* 61.1 (2007): 48–57. Print.

Hills, Matt. *Fan Cultures.* London: Routledge, 2007. Print.

Hutcheon, Linda. *A Theory of Parody: The Teachings of Twentieth-Century Art Forms.* London: Methuen, 1985. Print.

Jenkins, Henry. *Textual Poachers: Television Fans and Participatory Culture*. London: Routledge, 1992. Print.

——. *Convergence Culture: Where Old and New Media Collide*. New York: New York University Press, 2006. Print.

——. "What Happened Before YouTube." *YouTube. Online Video and Participatory Culture*. By Jean Burgess and Joshua Green. Cambridge: Polity Press, 2009. 109–25. Print.

——, Xiaochang Li, Ana Domb Krauskopf, and Joshua Green. "If It Doesn't Spread It's Dead: Creating Value in a Spreadable Marketplace." Convergence Culture Consortium: March 2009. White Paper.

Johnston, Keith M. "'The Coolest Way to Watch Movie Trailers in the World': Trailers in the Digital Age." *Convergence: The International Journal of Research into New Media Technologies* 14.2 (2008): 145–60. Print.

Klinger, Barbara. *Beyond the Multiplex: Cinema, New Technologies, and the Home*. Berkeley, CA: University of California Press, 2006. Print.

Lessig, Lawrence. *Remix: Making Art and Commerce Thrive in the Hybrid Economy*. London: Bloomsbury, 2008. Print.

Lyall-Wilson, Demis. "Sleepless in Seattle: Recut as a Horror Movie." *Online Posting*. YouTube, 30 January 2006. Retrieved on 19 October 2011. www.youtube.com/watch?v=frUPnZMxr08.

Matt. "The Shining, Redux." *Online Posting*. The Tattered Coat, 28 September 2005. Retrieved on 19 October 2011. www.tatteredcoat.com/archives/2005/09/28/the-shining-redux/.

McLoughlin, Robert. "Mrs Doubtfire—Recut Trailer." *Online Posting*. YouTube, 28 January 2009. Retrieved on 19 October 2011. www.youtube.com/watch?v=N3bgipCebuI.

Miller, Toby, Nitin Govil, John McMurria, and Richard Maxwell. *Global Hollywood*. London: British Film Institute, 2001. Print.

Mittell, Jason. *Genre and Television: From Cop Shows to Cartoons in American Culture*. London: Routledge, 2004. Print.

Ryang, Robert. "Shining." *Online Posting*. YouTube, 27 February 2006. Retrieved on 19 October 2011. www.youtube.com/watch?v=sfout_rgPSA.

Szuch, Randy. "Avatar/Pocahontas Mashup." *Online Posting*. Vimeo, 11 February 2010. Retrieved on 19 October 2011. http://vimeo.com/9389738.

Tryon, Chuck. *Reinventing Cinema: Movies in the Age of Media Convergence*. New Brunswick, NJ: Rutgers University Press, 2009. Print.

12
Spoofin' Spidey—Rebooting the Bat: Immersive Story Worlds and the Narrative Complexities of Video Spoofs in the Era of the Superhero Blockbuster

Daniel Stein

Looking back at the *Batman* television series that had aired from 1966 to 1968 on ABC, Bob Kane wrote in his 1989 autobiography, *Batman and Me*:

> I've received many letters from comic book fans who didn't appreciate Batman being parodied in the TV series. ... My own opinion is that it was a marvelous spoof, ... but it certainly wasn't the definitive Batman. Since the seventies, those who have worked on the series have returned to my original conception of Batman as a lone, mysterious vigilante. (135)

Kane's words come across as the benevolent judgment of an author whose claim to being the creator of Batman had withstood decades of contestation and whose autobiography was published to coincide with the release of the equally contested first movie version of the caped crusader, Tim Burton's *Batman* (1989). Burton was featuring Kane as a production consultant, but he also disclaimed any sense of responsibility towards the professed interest of the comic fan community to ensure the film's fidelity to its comic book sources: "This is too big a budget movie to worry about what a fan of a comic would say" (qtd. in Uricchio and Pearson 184).

Yet notions of authorial intention and comic book fidelity never quite went away, as actor Christian Bale's statement about *Batman Begins*

(Christopher Nolan, 2005) reveals. Promoting this new release as a work that differed substantially from earlier filmic incarnations of Batman, Bale expressed a desire to tie the rebooted, darker and more mysterious, protagonist of *Batman Begins* to Kane's authorial vision, perhaps in order to emphasize the marked departure from the campy aesthetics for which the television series had come to be known and which director Joel Schumacher's two *Batman* movies (*Batman Forever*, 1995; *Batman & Robin*, 1997) had updated for a new generation of viewers. *Batman Begins*, Bale noted, "is what Bob Kane intended when he first created the character. ... I spoke with his wife, and she said that he was appalled when the (1960s) TV series spoofed what he had intended" (qtd. in Gordon et al. viii).[1] Kane's distinction between his "definitive" Batman and ABC's television series as a "marvelous spoof" and Bale's understanding of the series as a spoof that violated Kane's authorial intentions raise questions about narrative and discursive authority: who can authoritatively enter the fictional universe of specific superheroes and tell stories involving these iconic characters? Who determines which stories are legitimate continuations of a series and which are illegitimate, or at least non-definitive, spoofs? And what role have parodies and spoofs played in the recent extension of "the superhero comic book aesthetic" into "the wider cultural consciousness" (Ndalianis 4), including the trans-mediation of comic book superheroes into Hollywood cinema?[2]

John Cawelti has suggested that a proliferation of parodies indicates a genre's stage of final exhaustion:

> One can almost make out a life cycle characteristic of genres as they move from an initial period of articulation and discovery, through a phase of conscious self-awareness on the part of both creators and audiences, to a time when the generic patterns have become so well-known that people become tired of their predictability. It is at this point that parodic and satiric treatments proliferate and new genres gradually arise. (200)

Accordingly, the current boom of comic book blockbuster video spoofs posted on YouTube and other online sites would indicate the end of either the superhero comic book or the superhero blockbuster. If, however, we understand superhero parodies and spoofs in Linda Hutcheon's sense as "trans-contextualizations" (8) that cover a "range of intent ... from the ironic and playful to the scornful and ridiculing" and offer a mode of intertextual and intermedial engagement that can be described as "repetition with critical distance" (6), then their proliferation may also indicate something else: a substantive change from the kinds of fears and anxieties that shaped the transmediation of comic book superheroes into early blockbusters like Burton's *Batman* to the acceptance of films such as *The Dark Knight* (Christopher Nolan, 2008) and *Spider-Man* (Sam Raimi, 2002) as raw material for critical mocking and creative remaking. Instead of angry fan rejections of casting choices (Burton's decision to use Michael Keaton as Bruce Wayne) and vocal complaints about the protagonists' characterization (Batman and Robin's homoeroticism in Schumacher's films), we are now seeing the creative exploitation of blockbuster movies by an increasing number of productive viewers whose spoofs perform vital cultural work as alternative (mostly unauthorized) reboots that keep franchises topical and appeal to heterogeneous audience interests that the blockbuster format cannot accommodate.[3] The results of this cultural work are twofold: we are seeing more and more professional spoofs, and more often than not, individual spoofs are presented as installments in an overarching spoof series.[4]

   In order to test these hypotheses, I want to discuss two of the most successful Hollywood superhero franchises, *Batman* (Warner/DC Comics) and *Spider-Man* (Columbia/Marvel Entertainment), in terms of their status as comic book transmediations and as evidence of a trend that may be described as the serialization of the Hollywood blockbuster.[5] This trend has sparked a substantial number of video spoofs as much as it has been supported by such spoofs, which keep audiences engaged between movies and allow them to write themselves into expanding movie metaverses. These parodies and spoofs range from amateurish productions to elaborate mini-films and animated cartoons, and they show that the distinction between amateur productions and professional productions is increasingly hard to make on a purely aesthetic level. They also suggest a growing self-consciousness and self-awareness among producers of professional, semi-professional, and amateur materials about the kind of convergence culture in which they operate and in which their productions are received.[6] My primary sources will be a *Batman* spoof produced by the *Key of Awesome* comedy group, the MTV Movie Awards Special Presentation of *Spider-Man* (Joel Gallen, 2002; available on YouTube), and the animated cartoon spoof *Spider-Man 3: How It Should Have Ended*.[7] In various ways, these productions are motivated by the "narrative complexities" (Jason Mittell) and "immersive story worlds" (Sam Ford) that have come to shape not only US American quality television but superhero comics as well (especially the more adult-oriented graphic novels). What is more, they incorporate and also comment on these characteristics and thereby illustrate the degree to which fan practices—or self-described fan practices by an increasingly diffuse allotment of cultural producers with professional tools—have moved into the heart of American media culture as a pervasive mode of engagement with serially organized popular narratives.

Hollywood comic book superhero movies have come to occupy a central place within the "modern blockbuster era," whose beginnings can be dated with the release of the first *Superman* film in 1978 (Richard Donner) (Gordon et al. viii).[8] This process has been driven by the re-orientation of Marvel and DC Comics from comic book publishers to intellectual property developers and licensing corporations, and it has resulted in successful franchises like the *X-Men* (a trilogy and two prequels; Bryan Singer et al.), *Spider-Man* (Sam Raimi's trilogy and Marc Webb's 2012 reboot), and *Batman* (seven films since 1989). Even though these franchises do not constitute a serial narrative in the same way in which television narratives unfold in weekly progression across multiple seasons, I would argue that a film like *The Dark Knight* is more than just a sequel to *Batman Begins* but can indeed be watched as one episode in an unfolding filmic *Batman* metatext made up of successive reboots by different directors.[9] As Luca Somigli has argued, the very basis of superhero film adaptations is the serial nature of the superhero itself, and the fact that such films have to incorporate different elements of previous articulations—including various remakes and reboots—of particular characters and plots makes every movie adaptation "always already a remake" (286). This goes double for superhero video spoofs, which are always already remakes of an existing media text as well as remakes twice removed: they remake (that is, spoof) remakes (that is, superhero blockbusters) of comic books which are themselves composed out of a long series of remakes so that every new episode is essentially a remake of existing stories. In that sense, superhero video spoofs should not be viewed as derivative exploitations of an original source text but must rather be regarded as an integral part of a larger process—the serialization of popular entertainment in today's transmedia environment—that can be usefully discussed in terms of the "narrative complexities" and "immersive story worlds" it both displays and produces.

Mittell has suggested that many contemporary American television series adhere to a "distinct narrational mode" (29) that follows an "operational aesthetic" (a term introduced by Neil Harris), a metareflexive viewing according to which audiences "care about the story world while simultaneously appreciating its construction" (35). He elaborates:

"This operational aesthetic is on display within online fan forum dis-sections of the techniques that complex comedies and dramas use to guide, manipulate, deceive, and misdirect viewers, suggesting the key pleasure of unraveling the operations of narrative mechanics." This dif-fers from the bombastic aesthetics of Hollywood blockbusters in that it presents "narrative spectacles" that are "akin to special effects" but have viewers "marveling at the craft required to pull off such narrative pyro-technics," asking not only "what will happen" but also "how did he do that?" Narratively complex television favors long and intricate story arcs, complicated character constellations, "in-jokes and self-aware ref-erences," and "parodic media references." Moreover, it "convert[s] many viewers to amateur narratologists, [who] not[e] usage and violations of convention, chronicl[e] chronologies, and highlight...both inconsist-encies and continuities across episodes and even series" (34, 35, 38).

These observations mesh well with the concept of "immersive story worlds" that Ford proposes in his analysis of popular narratives. Immersive story worlds are defined first and foremost by serial story-telling. Since no single person is ultimately capable of mastering, say, 70 years' worth of multiple monthly Batman comics (plus movie seri-als, live action television, animated cartoon series, video games, and Hollywood movies), such narratives offer a rich space for interaction among the producers of a text, the text itself, and its recipients. A second element of immersive story worlds is that they usually extend beyond the control of a single author. Both *Batman* and *Spider-Man* were cre-ated by teams of artists and writers from the very outset, and they have since then been continued by generations of creative teams. A third characteristic is long-term continuity. At least since the 1970s superhero comics have thrived on the premise that previous stories have a bearing on the stories of the present, that the stories of the present will have a bearing on future stories, and that the stories in different series are interconnected because they take place in a single overarching fictional universe.[10] Ford's fourth and fifth characteristics, character backlog and deep history, follow from the principle of long-term continuity. Serial characters and plot lines tend to grow more and more complex over time as each new installment adds new facets to an increasing back-log of information. Among the practices that follow from the extensive story archives produced by long-running series are the policing of con-tinuity, the checking of character consistency, the indexing of charac-ter constellations, the documentation of chronologies, and so on.

So how do the notions of "narrative complexity" and "immersive story worlds" play out in recent video spoofs of superhero blockbusters?

My first example is a spoof of Nolan's *The Dark Knight* titled "The Dark Knight Is Confused" by the *Key of Awesome*.[11] Rather than pick up where the movie left off and continue the narrative, it casts a metareflexive glance on Nolan's blockbuster and issues its comical critique of the movie's weaknesses in just two minutes and forty seconds.[12] Revisiting the final scene of the film, it uses Commissioner Gordon's words to his son as its starting point and narrative impulse:

Son: "Batman! – Why is he running, Dad?"
Gordon: "Because we have to chase him."
Son: "Why?"
Gordon: "Because he can take it. Because he is not a hero. He is a silent guardian, a watchful protector, the dark knight."
Son: "I don't get it."
Gordon: "Neither do I, son, but it sounds cool."

This is clearly a critique of the cliché ending of the blockbuster. It mocks the re-branding of Batman as the dark knight of Frank Miller's comics, and it faults the privileging of franchise logic over plausible plot resolution by insinuating that creating a satisfying dramatic ending was less important than setting the stage for a potential sequel. The dialogue redeploys the commissioner's son as a stand-in for the producers and the viewers of the spoof. He sees through the film's overblown rhetoric and compels viewers to retract their willing suspension of disbelief and get ready for the dose of comic disbelief that the spoof will dish out in the ensuing performance. Thus, while one may argue that Nolan's *The Dark Knight* might have failed in handling the narrative complexities following from its complicated relationship with the deep comic book history of the source material and its earlier translations into film, one could also argue that it was successful in converting viewers into producers who cast themselves in the role of Mittell's amateur narratologists.

Furthermore, the producers of the spoof translate their puzzlement about the faulty plot into their depiction of the characters from the movie. The opening dialogue is followed by a jump cut to actor Mark Douglas, who, dressed up as Batman, is riding a motorcycle towards the viewer and raps: "As I ride on my bike at the end of *Dark Knight* / There's a few plot points that just don't feel right / Like, why the hell did I agree to take the rap / Harvey Dent killed those people / Who gives a crap?"; and in the sappy chorus: "This movie of my life just doesn't hold together"; "Is it too much to ask that it all makes sense?" Here and later on, Batman, Alfred, and the Joker are transmediated from the authorized diegesis of the film (Douglas plays all of them) into the diegesis of the unauthorized music video. What we are seeing here is a type of engagement with the film that in some ways resembles the performing (role-paying and costume-wearing) fans that Kurt Lancaster describes in his analysis of *Babylon 5* audiences. It is, however, also different because the spoof uses these popular fan practices as raw material for the creation of a serial popular narrative.[13] Moreover, the cast of the *Key of Awesome* consists of professional actors who spoof a different media text every week (including parodies of Lady Gaga, Kanye West, Justin Bieber, Katy Perry, Ke$ha, Eminem, and so on), produce behind-the-scenes videos in which they answer fan comments ("Gaga vs Batman, or Taylor Swift? Behind the Awesome"), and deconstruct, rather than reenact or extend, their source material. Thus, they participate in the "commercial development of performative spaces for audiences" that Henry Jenkins allocates in the "new interactive culture" in which "participatory impulse[s are transformed] into a new marketing strategy" (Foreword xix), yet they do so not as fan producers prodding the culture industry towards creating new forms of entertainment but as commercial players who occupy a middle ground between the owners of the Batman franchise and their own fan following.[14]

The heightened metareflexivity that Mittell diagnoses in narratively complex television shows is particularly obvious in "The Dark Knight Is Confused," which ranks *The Dark Knight* within the serial history of the franchise in a language we know from fan discourses and online commentaries: it "beats the crap out of *Batman Forever*," "at least they got rid of Joel Schumacher," and so on. More remarkable, however, are the metamedial references that appear in the final third of the spoof, when the Joker brings the DVD of *The Dark Knight* so that he, Batman, and Alfred can watch it in order to untangle the convoluted plotting of the film. "Rewatchability" is the catch phrase here, according to which narrative complexity is rewarding because it offers the pleasure of decoding complicated story arcs, understanding obscure intra-serial allusions, and catching cross-references to competing series (cf. Mittell 31). In "The Dark Knight Is Confused," however, Batman, Alfred, and the Joker appear as clever narratologists exasperated by movie's lack of narrative complexity.

The depiction of characters as amateur narratologists leads to the type of in-jokes that Mittell lists as integral elements of narrative complexity. For instance, Batman cannot figure out the plot of his own movie and needs his arch enemy, the Joker, to make sense of it, and butler Alfred almost reveals the secret identity principle that *Batman* and other superheroes have inherited from their comic book origins. It takes a good amount of suspended disbelief to accept the fact that Bruce Wayne cannot be spotted under his bat mask. Therefore, when Alfred turns to the Joker, asking, "Joker, are you busy? Let's call a truce, I need you to help explain the plot to ... Batman" (that is, Bruce), he is pretty much stating the obvious: that Batman is Bruce Wayne in his civilian life and that Gotham's best-guarded secret makes sense only when it is read as an effect of deep character backlog and long-term continuity (Burton had angered fans when he allowed Vicky Vale, played by Kim Basinger, to learn the secret). Another in-joke depends on the viewer's ability to decode the logic of serial storytelling. The Joker's final question, "Did I ever tell you how I got these scars?" winks at the obsessive return of superhero comics to the origin stories of central characters. These origins stories function as foundational myths that hold expanding narrative universes and increasingly complex story arcs together. But, as Batman's disgruntled answer, "Yes, several versions!" indicates, they also produce redundancy. Even rebooted versions of the narrative tend to reiterate the basic elements of origin stories, and for those who are familiar with the deep history and character backlog of the series, they might become so tedious that unauthorized versions hold greater attraction because they are not bound by the sanctity of the franchise: "I was **working** at an **exotic pet store**, and the **owner** bet me **five bucks** I wouldn't **French kiss** a **pms-ing ocelot**," is *MAD Magazine*'s version of how the Joker got his scars (Devlin and Richmond 177).

"The Dark Knight Is Confused" is a particularly evocative superhero blockbuster spoof, and it can be usefully contextualized with the professionally produced MTV Movie Awards Special Presentation of *Spider-Man* starring Jack Black and Sarah Michelle Gellar.[15] This is a "semi-authorized" media text because it splices together original footage with new material and thus depends on the approval of Columbia Pictures and Marvel Entertainment, the copyright and trademark owners of *Spider-Man*, without being completely restricted by the narrative universe of the film. The spoof places the notion of an immersive story world at its center. Black and Gellar actually immerse themselves in the diegesis of Sam Raimi's film; like fans who dress up as their favorite superheroes and restage scenes from comic books and movies, they enter the world of the film in new scenes that director Joel Gallen intersplices with original footage in a seamless continuum of moving images. The spoof's focalizer is Peter Parker, who appears as the stereotypical comic book fanboy. Instead of completing his transformation from skinny high school geek into the muscular and heroic Spider-Man, teen idol Tobey Maguire is substituted with a substantially older and substantially chubbier Jack Black, which creates humorous discrepancy between spoof and movie and foregrounds the illusory nature of fanboy fantasies.

One of the more notorious stereotypes about comic book fans is that they have no sex life. Thus, it is not surprising that the MTV Special Presentation spoofs the sexual subtext of the movie's romantic love plot: Peter's infatuation with Mary Jane Watson, the girl from next door who only in time comes to see Peter's superheroic nature. While movies like *Spider-Man* tend to project a sanitized image of heterosexual love that stays above the waistline, Black and Gellar's semi-authorized performance has more leeway when it comes to the depiction of sexuality. When Peter ogles Mary Jane through the bedroom window, he represents a male gaze that both acknowledges and parodies the pubescent perspective of a major segment of the blockbuster's target audience: male teenagers. This gaze literally climaxes in Peter's discovery of his web-shooting powers and thereby remodels the movie's initiation plot into a masturbatory fantasy. Obviously, this Spider-Man will not comply with the "coming-of-age" narrative from "adolescent 'abjection' to adult 'agency'" that Martin Flanagan finds in Raimi's film (137). He will not follow the conventional "teen trajectory" and will not become the responsible citizen-hero celebrated by the official byline of the movie, "with great power comes great responsibility." Not only does he stuff a pair of socks into his pants in order to "transform" himself from an "ordinary average guy" into what he believes is an omnipotent superhero, but when he is called upon to save a baby from a burning house, he shows no interest in heroism: "I'll pass." This Spider-Man uses his superpowers to seek sexual gratification, which is made explicit in the scene in which his spider sense does not warn him of oncoming danger but signals the appearance of his prime sexual fantasy: Mary Jane in a see-through top, looking for a "man-tastic" co-host for the MTV Movie Awards: "I'm getting a tingling sensation in my arachnads," he states with a horny grin.

It is important to recognize that the spoof is simultaneously critical and affirmative. It appeals to an older and sexually more knowledgeable MTV demographic, thereby extending the movie's recipients from the blockbuster's target audience to a group of viewers who may feel intellectually superior to Raimi's narrative but will nonetheless indulge in it by watching the parodic remake. As such, it performs the "reassessment and acclimatization" function typical of modern parody (Hutcheon 2), and it does so by enlisting its viewers in the act of decoding the repressed sexuality of Raimi's movie. Earlier in the spoof, Peter sketches various "gay" versions of his superhero costume, ranging from a sailor's outfit to S&M leather attire to the final Spider-Man costume, which is "just the right amount of gay." Here, the spoof taps into a discourse that has a long history in American comics: the homoerotic subtext and troubled heterosexuality of superheroes, both of which have inspired countless examples of superhero slash fiction and have added to the narrative complexities of these series. Batman's potential homosexuality was famously alleged by psychologist Fredric Wertham, who argued in *Seduction of the Innocent* (1954) that Bruce Wayne's love for his youthful ward Robin was of a sexual nature.[16] Often denied by industry professionals, this homoerotic subtext was supported by the nipple suits and crotch/butt shots of George Clooney and Chris O'Donnell in Schumacher's *Batman & Robin*. In many of the spoofs I have surveyed for this chapter, however, it is Spider-Man who is associated with notions of homosexuality and homoeroticism. One example is the second segment of the two-volume spoof "Superlunch" (Tarik Alherimi, 2009; available on YouTube), where Spider-Man confesses to Superman and Batman that he cannot satisfy Mary Jane sexually ("when I'm about to, you know, my spider-sense goes crazy, and I can't") and is confronted with Batman's conclusion, "You're gay." Apparently, Nolan's attempts to reboot Batman as a dark knight successfully downplayed the homoeroticism of Schumacher's films, while Raimi's melodramatic depiction of Peter Parker as a teen heartthrob triggered them.

While most of the English-language spoofs on YouTube are rather tame in terms of their depiction of Spider-Man's homosexuality, an Argentinean fan trailer, which was posted in January 2008 and has received almost five million clicks, is much more explicit. Its title is already a pun on Peter's alleged homosexuality; instead of "El hombre araña" (Spider-Man), it reads "El hombre que araña" (the man who fondles/caresses). Using digitally altered scenes from the original movie, the spoof launches a series of explicit homosexual references: Mary Jane asks Peter repeatedly when he will finally have sex with her ("Cuando me vas a garchar?" "Chúpame la concha!"), but he declines ("Ay, ni loca!"); Peter comes out to Aunt May ("Abuela, soy putazo!"); Spider-Man poses for a series of naked butt shots for Eddie Brock, the photographer of the *Daily Bugle*; the voice-over's double entendre portrays Peter as "!un superhéroe que sí se rompe el culo por la justicia!": a superhero who will bust his ass (but maybe not just for justice?). These kinds of homoerotic fictions by unauthorized producers are, of course, not new. Indeed, they stand in a tradition of queer rewritings of serial narratives such as *Star Trek*

and many others. Yet the cultural work they perform within the transmedia shift of superhero narratives from comic book stories to blockbuster movies is new. They make movie superheroes like Batman and
Spider-Man palatable for a highly diverse audience, sections of which
will hold contradictory views of the characters, and they do so not by
inventing entirely new scenarios but by tapping into narrative possibilities already prefigured—or repressed—in the superhero movies.

In terms of Mittell's "parodic media references," spoofs generally
have a field day. They are by nature parodic, their whole purpose being
to establish humorous references to the media text they remake and
remodel. Frequently, they follow from the spoof producers' narratological expertise and their decision to depict superheroes as amateur
narratologists. The animated web video "Spider-Man 3: How It Should
Have Ended" (HISHE), for instance, delivers a running metareflexive
commentary on the structural weaknesses and formulaic storytelling
of the *Spider-Man* film.[17] It begins with a cartoon version of the opening shots of the movie, Spider-Man swinging through the New York
skyline and addressing his audience through voice-over: "Hey there,
it's me, Peter Parker, your friendly neighborhood, you know [that is,
Spider-Man]. I've come a long way after being bit by a spider. Before,
nothing went right for me. Now, people really like me. I keep the city
safe, I'm the top of my class, and I'm even in love with the girl of my
dreams," he chatters away, only to be interrupted by a little boy who
wears a Spider-Man t-shirt and pleads, "Spider-Man, will you stop narrating, please?" This is essentially a comical take on what Margaret
Rose has called parody's "shock destruction of expectations" (23) since
Parker's lines are reproduced verbatim and because the young boy is
based on the group of kids who appear in the movie. But the boy in the
spoof differs from the kids from *Spider-Man 3* (Sam Raimi, 2007) in that
he acts as a knowledgeable fan who does not succumb to the interpel-
lation of screen images but reflects critically on them from an outside
perspective. He also expresses frustration with the redundancy of the
initial voice-over. "You're narrating; it's kind of unnecessary," the boy
notes, and to Spider-Man's question, "How are people gonna know what
I've been up to all this time?" (that is, between movies), he responds:
"We're not idiots."[18]

The MTV Special Presentation is even more versed in the practice
of parodic-media referencing. It remakes Tobey Maguire and Kirsten
Dunst's upside-down kiss by turning the romantic love scene into a
mash-up fan fiction in which a goofball Spider-Man woos Mary Jane
by impersonating Yoda from George Lucas' *Star Wars* (supported by a

snippet from John Williams' title melody). Another parodic media reference appears when Mary Jane, upon seeing Peter, exclaims: "the creep from *Pleasantville* is back." This is not just a reference to Gary Ross' 1998 film, in which Maguire plays the male lead, but also an implicit reflection on the spoof's mocking of teen fantasies on television. While *Pleasantville* involves two teenagers who are sucked into their television set, where they become part of a 1950s-style television show, the *Spider-Man* spoof immerses its actors in a comic book fantasy (that is, the storyworld of the movie). By combining new material with original footage—and thus by becoming actively involved in the remaking of the movie—the fan (here: Black) gets to play his favorite superhero, and he even gets the girl—and not just any girl, but Wonder Woman from the 1970s television show (ABC/CBS, 1975–9), into whom Mary Jane turns by spinning around. In that sense, it is not just the male adolescent viewer of *Spider-Man* who is transformed into a superhero, but also the female object of his fantasies. The spoof thus represents an intercompany crossover story—Marvel's Spider-Man falls for DC Comics' Wonder Woman—but goes one step further. It enacts an additional transmedia narrative in the sense that the movie *Spider-Man* (and actor Jack Black) encounters the television series *Buffy the Vampire Slayer* (1997–2003, WB/UPN) through the person of Sarah Michelle Gellar, whose roles include hosting MTV Movie Awards, playing a spoof version of Mary Jane as a stand-in for Kirsten Dunst, and transforming into Wonder Woman as a stand-in for Lynda Carter.

To conclude: parodies and spoofs play a substantial role in the current transmediation of comic book superheroes into serialized Hollywood blockbusters. They contribute to the continued relevance of superhero narratives by offering a double perspective—the "dual drives of conservative and revolutionary forces" Hutcheon defines as a crucial element of parodies (26)—that matches the twin dynamics of both film remakes and popular seriality: "reliability (repetition) and novelty (innovation)" (Verevis 4). As viewers become more and more skilled at decoding the narrative complexities of contemporary American television series, they tend to approach superhero blockbusters with an increasingly critical eye and comedic sensibility. Parody may be "a method of inscribing continuity while permitting critical distance" and a form of engagement with authorized texts that can "function as a conservative force in both retaining and mocking other aesthetic forms," but it also possesses "transformative power in creating new syntheses" (Hutcheon 20). In that sense, deconstructing the faulty plot of *The Dark Knight* or mocking the redundancy of the *Spider-Man 3* opening simultaneously raises awareness of superhero stories and conventions but also offers a transformative space for the potentially cathartic expression of comic disbelief. This expression certainly works to contain feelings of dissatisfaction and discontent with the bombastic aesthetics of blockbusters, and it implicitly authorizes the transmediation of comic book superhero narratives into Hollywood film. In doing so, however, it also creates new syntheses in the form of creatively convincing and commercially viable remakes of these narratives that counterbalance the narrative weaknesses of serialized superhero franchises and tap into their productive potential to unfold their very own transformative power.

Notes

1. Kane had passed away in 1998.
2. These and related questions are also the subject of a larger research project conducted by Frank Kelleter and myself. The project examines the generic development of American superhero comics and is part of the Research Unit on "Popular Seriality: Aesthetics and Practice" at the University of Göttingen (funded by the German Research Foundation). I use "transmediation" to foreground the transposition of material from one medium to another but also in reference to Jenkins' conception of "transmedia storytelling" as "stories that unfold across multiple media platforms" and as "a more integrated approach to franchise development than models based on urtexts and ancillary products" (*Convergence* 334). Not much scholarship on the role of parodies and spoofs in American comics exists, even though they are "one of the medium's most common forms" (Pustz 139; see also Groensteen). On the spoof as a film genre, see Gehring.
3. My usage of "cultural work" follows Jane Tompkins' classical analysis of nineteenth-century American fiction, in which she writes: "Rather than asking, 'what does this text mean?' or, 'how does it work?,' I ask, 'what kind of work is this novel trying to do?'" (38). The idea is to turn to the functions of blockbuster video spoofs in the transmediation of comic book material to the big screen and to think about the larger effects of these transmediations on the evolution of (American) popular culture.
4. This cultural work is supported by decisions of American courts "to protect 'transformative' unauthorized uses against copyright owners' allegations of infringement" (Tushnet 61). Parodies and spoofs are transformative because they "add new material that reflects critically on the original" and urge viewers to reconsider their understanding of the parodied and spoofed source (67). If "the legal concept of transformative use denies the author the authority to control all interpretations of his text" (70), it allows previously unauthorized authors to present their productions beyond the legal grasp of multimedia corporations.
5. My understanding of "serialization" does not differ substantially from the term "sequelization" that Jess-Cooke and Verevis propose in their *Second Takes* essay collection (4), but it places my analysis within the wider context of comics superheroes as a phenomenon of popular seriality.

6. Jenkins defines "convergence" as "an ongoing process or series of intersections between different media systems" and as "a situation in which multiple media systems coexist and where media content flows fluidly across them" (*Convergence* 322).

7. This focus seeks to reduce the source material to a manageable corpus and is not meant to suggest that the same kind of analysis could not be conducted with other examples (Superman, the X-Men, Wonder Woman, and so on). A more extensive analysis of superhero spoofs would have to consider the male bias in the superhero genre (mostly male creators, mostly male characters) and address questions of gender in spoofs of franchises based on female superheroines.

8. Sequels were released in 1980, 1983, and 1987. These films are rarely discussed in connection with the current superhero blockbuster boom despite Bryan Singer's commercially successful *Superman Returns* (2006). Transmediations of comic book content began early: the Fleischer Studios produced the first Superman animated cartoon in 1941; around the same time, audiences could watch movie serials such as *Adventures of Captain Marvel* (dir. John English and William Witney, 1941) and *Batman and Robin* (dir. Lamber Hillyer, 1943). A more extensive analysis of blockbuster serialization would have to account for George Lucas' *Star Wars* franchise, the *Stark Trek* movies, and many other film series.

9. These blockbusters cannot compete with the tightly woven plot structures, complex character constellations, and intra-serial references that characterize long-running contemporary quality television series such as the *Sopranos* or *The Wire*, but Meehan had a point when she wrote in 1991 that the $30 million production costs for Burton's *Batman* were "the root costs of a film series" (54).

10. Most earlier superhero comics, Eco noted in his analysis of *Superman*, "develop in a kind of oneiric climate—of which the reader is not aware at all—where what has happened before and what has happened after [each particular story] appear extremely hazy" (153).

11. According to their website, the *Key of Awesome* is a weekly program of film and music spoofs produced by Mark Douglas, Jake Chudnow, and Rusty Ward and hosted by *barely.digital.com.*

12. All of the spoofs discussed in this chapter are relatively short, ranging from about two to seven minutes.

13. The *Key of Awesome* has produced a whole series of Batman spoofs, including "Pimp My Automobile," which is modeled on the MTV show *Pimp My Ride* and shows how Batman's "piece of crap Hyundai" is transformed into the batmobile; "Batman Gets Pwnd," "Batman: Pwnd at E3," and "Batman vs. Wolverine," which show a protagonist-turned-fan who is outmatched by the complexities of contemporary computer gaming; and "Batman vs. Mr Freeze," "Batman vs. the Joker in New York," "Batman vs. Poison Ivy," "Man-Bat vs. Lady Cat," in which Batman works for the New Yorker *Red Flag Tours* agency (all clips are available on www.barelydigital.com). On fan practices, media fandoms, and fan studies, see Hills; Jenkins, *Fans*; Gray et al.

14. The music video format of "The Dark Knight is Confused" follows in the footsteps of "Weird Al" Yancovic, who popularized music video spoofs in the 1990s. It also parodies the practice of selling movies through theme songs

and soundtracks, for instance Prince's *Batman* album and his "Batdance" music video for Burton's movie. "The Dark Knight is Confused" features Batman as lead rapper/singer, guitarist, and DJ.

15. Black and Gellar starred in a second movie spoof presented at the 2002 MTV Movie Awards, "Lord of the Piercing" (dir. Joel Gallen).
16. On the homoerotic subtext of *Batman* and its reception, see Brooker, chapter 2.
17. The members of HISHE are Daniel Baxter, Tommy Watson, and Tina Alexander. In my nomenclature, their "parody animation" is an unauthorized text because it uses little original material and does not depend on the legal sanctioning of Columbia/Marvel.
18. The spoof ends with a parodic depiction of the final showdown between Spider-Man and villain Eddie Brock/Venom which further deconstructs the conventions of serialized superhero blockbusters: "This is my third movie. *Spider-Man Tres*, amigo. You think they're gonna kill me off?"

Works consulted

Batman. Prod. William Dozier. Perf. Adam West and Burt Ward. 120 Episodes. 20th Century Fox Television. ABC, 12 January 1966–14 March 1968.

Batman. Dir. Tim Burton. Perf. Michael Keaton, Jack Nicholson, and Kim Basinger. Warner Bros., 1989.

Batman Begins. Dir. Christopher Nolan. Perf. Christian Bale, Michael Kane, Liam Neeson, Katie Holmes, and Morgan Freeman. Warner Bros., 2005.

Batman: The Dark Knight. Dir. Christopher Nolan. Perf. Christian Bale, Michael Kane, Aaron Eckhart, Heath Ledger, Maggie Gyllenhaal, Morgan Freeman. Warner Bros, 2008.

Batman Forever. Dir. Joel Schumacher. Perf. Val Kilmer, Chris O'Donnell, Tommy Lee Jones, Jim Carrey, and Nicole Kidman. Warner Bros., 1995.

Batman & Robin. Dir. Joel Schumacher. Perf. George Clooney, Chris O'Donnell, Arnold Schwarzenegger, Alicia Silverstone, and Uma Thurman. Warner Bros., 1997.

Brooker, Will. *Batman Unmasked: Analysing a Cultural Icon.* London: Continuum, 2000. Print.

Cawelti, John. "*Chinatown* and Generic Transformation in Recent American Films." *Film Genre Reader.* Ed. Barry Keith Grant. Austin, TX: University of Texas Press, 1986. 183–201. Print.

Devlin, Desmond, and Tom Richmond. "The Dork Knight." *MAD* #485 (Nov. 2008). *MAD About Super Heroes Volume 2.* Ed. John Ficarra. New York: *MAD* Books, 2010. 174–9. Print.

Eco, Umberto. "The Myth of Superman." 1964. *Arguing Comics: Literary Masters on a Popular Medium.* Ed. Jeet Heer and Kent Worcester. Jackson, MS: University Press of Mississippi, 2004. 146–64. Print.

Flanagan, Martin. "Teen Trajectories in *Spider-Man* and *Ghost World.*" Gordon, Jancovich, and McAllister 137–59. Print.

Ford, Sam. "Immersive Story Worlds (Part One)." *Confessions of an Aca/Fan: The Official Weblog of Henry Jenkins.* 2 May 2007. Retrieved on 24 October 2011. www.henryjenkins.org/2007/05/immersive_story_worlds.html.

——. "Immersive Story Worlds (Part Two)." *Confessions of an Aca/Fan: The Official Weblog of Henry Jenkins*. 3 May 2007. Retrieved on 24 October 2011. www.henryjenkins.org/2007/05/immersive_story_worlds_part_tw.html.

Gehring, Wes D. *Parody as Film Genre: "Never Give a Saga an Even Break."* Westport, CT: Greenwood Press, 1999. Print.

Gordon, Ian, Mark Jancovich, and Matthew P. McAllister, eds. *Film and Comic Books*. Jackson, MS: University Press of Mississippi, 2007. Print.

——. Introduction. *Film and Comic Books*. Gordon, Jancovich, and McAllister vii–xvii. Print.

Gray, Jonathan, Cornel Sandvoss, and C. Lee Harrington, eds. *Fandom: Identities and Communities in a Mediated World*. New York: New York University Press, 2007. Print.

Groensteen, Thierry. *Parodies: La Bande Dessinée au Second Degré*. Paris: Skira Flammarion, 2010. Print.

Hills, Matt. *Fan Cultures*. New York: Routledge, 2002. Print.

"El hombre que araña." *Online Posting*. tu-tv, 31 October 2007. Retrieved on 24 October 2011. http://tu.tv/videos/el-hombre-que-arana_4.

Hutcheon, Linda. *A Theory of Parody: The Teachings of Twentieth-Century Art Forms*. New York: Methuen, 1985. Print.

Jenkins, Henry. *Convergence Culture: Where Old and New Media Collide*. New York: New York University Press, 2006. Print.

——. *Fans, Bloggers, and Gamers: Exploring Participatory Culture*. New York: New York University Press, 2006. Print.

——. Foreword. *Interacting with* Babylon 5*: Fan Performances in a Media Universe*. By Kurt Lancaster. Austin, TX: University of Texas Press, 2001. xv–xxi. Print.

Jess-Cooke, Carolyn, and Constantine Verevis, eds. *Second Takes: Critical Approaches to the Film Sequel*. Albany, NY: State University of New York Press, 2010. Print.

Kane, Bob, with Tom Andrae. *Batman and Me*. Forestville, CA: Eclipse, 1989. Print.

The Key of Awesome. "Batman Parody: The Dark Knight Is Confused—Key of Awesome #8." *barelydigital.com*. Barely Digital, 7 December 2009. Retrieved on 24 October 2011. www.barelydigital.com/awesome/episode/KA_20091207/batman-parody-the-dark-knight-is-confused-key-of-awesome-8.

Lancaster, Kurt. *Interacting with* Babylon 5*: Fan Performances in a Media Universe*. Austin, TX: University of Texas Press, 2001. Print.

Meehan, Eileen R. "'Holy Commodity Fetish, Batman!' The Political Economy of a Commercial Intertext." Pearson and Uricchio 47–65. Print.

Mittell, Jason. "Narrative Complexity in Contemporary American Television." *The Velvet Light Trap* 58 (Fall 2006): 29–40. Print.

"An MTV Special Presentation: *Spider-Man*." Dir. Joel Gallen. Perf. Jack Black and Sarah Michelle Gellar. 1 June 2002.

Ndalianis, Angela. "The Comic Book Superheroes: An Introduction." *The Contemporary Comic Book Super Hero*. Ed. Angela Ndalianis. New York: Routledge, 2009. 3–15. Print.

Pearson, Roberta E., and William Uricchio, eds. *The Many Lives of the Batman: Critical Approaches to a Superhero and His Media*. New York: Routledge, 1991. Print.

Pustz, Matthew. *Comic Book Culture: Fanboys and True Believers.* Jackson, MS: University Press of Mississippi, 1999. Print.

Rose, Margaret A. *Parody/Meta-Fiction.* London: Croom Helm, 1979. Print.

Somigli, Luca. "The Superhero with a Thousand Faces: Visual Narratives on Film and Paper." *Play It Again, Sam: Retakes on Remakes.* Ed. Andrew Horton and Stuart Y. McDougal. Berkeley, CA: University of California Press, 1998. 279–94. Print.

Spider-Man. Dir. Sam Raimi. Perf. Tobey Maguire, Kirsten Dunst, William Dafoe, and James Franco. Sony/Columbia, 2002.

Spider-Man 3. Dir. Sam Raimi. Perf. Tobey Maguire, Kirsten Dunst, James Franco, and Topher Grace. Sony/Columbia, 2007.

"Spider-Man 3: How It Should Have Ended (HISHE)." Dir. Daniel Baxter. www. howitshouldhaveended.com. 9 August 2007. Retrieved on 28 October 2011. www.youtube.com/watch?v=HoNgMVFQNBI.

Superlunch. Dir. Tarik Alherimi. Perf. Alec Rayme, Reid Collums, and Marel Medina. 2009.

Tompkins, Jane. *Sensational Designs: The Cultural Work of American Fiction 1790–1860.* 1985. New York: Oxford University Press, 1986. Print.

Tushnet, Rebecca. "Copyright Law, Fan Practices, and the Rights of the Author." Gray, Sandvoss, and Harrington 60–71. Print.

Uricchio, William, and Roberta E. Pearson. "'I'm Not Fooled By That Cheap Disguise." Pearson and Uricchio 182–213. Print.

Verevis, Constantine. *Film Remakes.* Edinburgh: Edinburgh University Press, 2006. Print.

Wertham, Fredric. *Seduction of the Innocent.* New York: Holt, 1954. Print.

Index